Lecture Notes in Computer Science 2186

Edited by G. Goos, J. Hartmanis, and J. van Leeuwen

Springer

Berlin
Heidelberg
New York
Barcelona
Hong Kong
London
Milan
Paris
Tokyo

Jan Bosch (Ed.)

Generative and Component-Based Software Engineering

Third International Conference, GCSE 2001
Erfurt, Germany, September 10-13, 2001
Proceedings

Springer

Series Editors

Gerhard Goos, Karlsruhe University, Germany
Juris Hartmanis, Cornell University, NY, USA
Jan van Leeuwen, Utrecht University, The Netherlands

Volume Editor

Jan Bosch
University of Groningen, Faculty of Mathematics and Natural Sciences
Department of Mathematics and Computing Science
P.O. Box 800, 9700 AV Groningen, The Netherlands
E-mail: J.Bosch@cs.rug.nl

Cataloging-in-Publication Data applied for

Die Deutsche Bibliothek - CIP-Einheitsaufnahme

Generative and component based software engineering : third international
conference ; proceedings / GCSE 2001, Erfurt, Germany, September 9 - 13,
2001. Jan Bosch (ed.). - Berlin ; Heidelberg ; New York ; Barcelona ; Hong
Kong ; London ; Milan ; Paris ; Tokyo : Springer, 2001
    (Lecture notes in computer science ; Vol. 2186)
    ISBN 3-540-42546-2

CR Subject Classification (1998): D.2, K.6, J.1

ISSN 0302-9743
ISBN 3-540-42546-2 Springer-Verlag Berlin Heidelberg New York

Springer-Verlag Berlin Heidelberg New York
a member of BertelsmannSpringer Science+Business Media GmbH

http://www.springer.de

© Springer-Verlag Berlin Heidelberg 2001

Typesetting: Camera-ready by author, data conversion by Markus Richter, Heidelberg
Printed on acid-free paper   SPIN: 10840559   06/3142   5 4 3 2 1 0

Preface

The size, complexity, and integration level of software systems is increasing constantly. Companies in all domains identify that software defines the competitive edge of their products. These developments require us to constantly search for new approaches to increase the productivity and quality of our software development and to decrease the cost of software maintenance. Generative and component-based technologies hold considerable promise with respect to achieving these goals. GCSE 2001 constituted another important step forward and provided a platform for academic and industrial researchers to exchange ideas.

These proceedings represent the third conference on generative and component-based software engineering. The conference originated as a special track on generative programming from the Smalltalk and Java in Industry and Education Conference (STJA), organized by the working group "Generative and Component-Based Software Engineering" of the "Gesellschaft für Informatik" FG 2.1.9 "Object-Oriented Software Engineering." However, the conference has evolved substantially since then, with its own, independent stature, invited speakers, and, most importantly, a stable and growing community.

This year's conference attracted 43 submissions from all over the world, indicating the broad, international interest in the research field. Based on careful review by the program committee, 14 papers were selected for presentation. I would like to thank the members of the program committee, all renowned experts, for their dedication in preparing thorough reviews of the submissions.

In association with the main conference, there will be two workshops, i.e. the GCSE Young Researchers Workshop 2001 (YRW) and a workshop on Product Line Engineering – The early steps: Planning, Managing, and Modeling. I thank the organizers of YRW, i.e. Kai Boellert, Detlef Streitferdt, Dirk Heuzeroth, Katharina Mehner, and Stefan Hanenberg, for their initiative to bring young researchers together and to provide them with feedback from senior members of our community. I am also grateful to Klaus Schmid and Birgit Geppert for their initiative to organize the product line engineering workshop. Software product lines provide a quickly developing and succesful approach to intra-organizational component-based software development that deserves much attention.

We are also indebted to this year's keynote speakers, Ted Biggerstaff and Oscar Nierstrasz. I am honoured that they accepted the invitation and thank them for their contribution to GCSE 2001. Finally, I wish to thank all those who worked hard to make this third conference happen, especially the authors and the Netobjectday organizers.

I hope you will enjoy reading the GCSE 2001 contributions!

July 2001   Jan Bosch

Organization

GCSE 2001 was co-located with the Net.ObjectDays 2001 conference and held in Erfurt, Germany, September 10-13.

Executive Committee

Program Chair:	Jan Bosch (University of Groningen, The Netherlands)
Publicity Chairs	
Europe:	Ulrich Eisenecker (University of Applied Sciences Kaiserslautern, Zweibrüecken, Germany)
The Americas:	Greg Butler (Concordia University, Montreal, Canada)
Asia/Pacific:	Stan Jarzabek (National University of Singapore, Singapore)

Program Committee

Don Batory (University of Texas, USA)
Greg Butler (Concordia University, Montreal, Canada)
Jim Coplien (Bell Labs, USA)
Krzysztof Czarnecki (DaimlerChrysler AG, Germany)
Ulrich Eisenecker (University of Applied Sciences Kaiserslautern, Zweibrücken, Germany)
Bogdan Franczyk (Intershop Research, Germany)
Cristina Gacek (University of Newcastle upon Tyne, United Kingdom)
Harald Gall (Technical University of Vienna, Austria)
Görel Hedin (Lund University, Sweden)
Stan Jarzabek (National University of Singapore, Singapore)
Peter Knauber (Fraunhofer Institute for Experimental Software Engineering, Germany)
Kai Koskimies (Tampere University of Technology, Finland)
Mira Mezini (Technical University Darmstadt)
Gail Murphy (University of British Columbia, Canada)
Henk Obbink (Philips Research, The Netherlands)
Clemens Szyperski (Microsoft Research, USA)
Todd Veldhuizen (Indiana University, USA)
Kurt Wallnau (Software Engineering Institute, USA)

Table of Contents

Components and Architecture

A Characterization of Generator and Component Reuse Technologies

Ted J. Biggerstaff

tbiggerstaff@austin.rr.com

Abstract. This paper characterizes various categories of reuse technologies in terms of their underlying architectures, the kinds of problems that they handle well, and the kinds of problems that they do not handle well. In the end, it describes their operational envelopes and niches. The emphasis is on generative reuse technologies.

1   Introduction

As an organizing framework for the niches, I will characterize them along two important dimensions of scaling: 1) how well they scale up in terms of raw size and thereby programming leverage, which I will call *vertical scaling*, and 2) how well they scale up in terms of feature variation, which I will call *horizontal scaling*. These two dimensions are typically opposed to each other.

In the course of this analysis for each technology niche, I will describe the key elements of the technology (e.g., the nature of the component building blocks or specification languages) and the kinds of operations typical of the technology (e.g., inlining or expression transformations). While I make no effort to cover all or even much of the specific research in these areas, I will identify some illustrative examples. Finally, I will summarize the strengths and weaknesses of the technologies in each niche. (See also 3.)

2   Concrete Components

The simplest form of reuse is the reuse of *concrete components*, which are components that 1) are written in conventional programming languages, 2) are largely internally immutable, and 3) represent a *one-size-fits-all* style of reuse. They include such categories as functions, Object Oriented classes, generic functions and classes, frameworks, and COM-like middleware components. They often exhibit serious reuse flaws such as inadequate performance, missing functionality, inadequately populated libraries, etc.

They succeed well in a few sub-niches. The first successful sub-niche is very large-scale components that just happen to fit the programmer's needs or are designed to a standard that predestines a good fit. Such components trade customized fit and wide scale reusability for high programming leverage. They cannot be used in a lot of applications but when they can be used, they significantly reduce the programming effort. The second successful sub-niche is smaller-scale components (e.g., as UI components) that can achieve high customization via compositionally induced variation and yet still exhibit adequate performance in spite of the compositionally induced computational overhead. While performance is a typical problem of concrete component reuse, it is often avoided in this sub-niche because of the nature of the domain. For example in the UI, relatively poor performance is adequate because the computational overhead of the one-size-fits-all componentry is masked by other factors such as human response times. Further, domains in this sub-niche are often defined by standards (e.g., the Windows UI) for which design tools and aids are easy to build (e.g., UI tools). This sub-niche trades performance degradation (which may be masked) for high levels of customization and substantial programming leverage within the domain of the sub-niche. The proportion of the application falling outside the sub-niche domain receives little or no reuse benefit. The third successful sub-niche is where standards have been so narrowly defined that one-size-fits-all components are satisfactory. The weakness of this sub-niche is the *shelf life* of the componentry since their reusability declines as the standards on which they are based are undermined by change. Communications protocols are a good example of this sub-niche.

A serious weakness of concrete component reuse is caused by the restrictions of conventional programming languages (CPLs). CPLs force early specificity of designs (e.g., a component's control structure may be subtly dependent on the structure of a set of databases). This forcing of early specificity reduces the opportunities for reuse. Other weaknesses are wrought by the method's dependence on human involvement in the reuse and adaptation process.

3   Composition-Based Generators

A fundamental difficulty of concrete components is the tension between optimality of component fit and the need to scale the components up in size to achieve higher levels of programming productivity. To address this difficulty, technologies have been developed to custom tailor the fit by **generating** custom components from compositions of more primitive building blocks that capture features orthogonal to the programming constructs (e.g., orthogonal to OO classes).

Representative of this approach is GenVoca [1]. GenVoca, for example, provides components from which frameworks of several related classes can be constructed layer by layer (e.g., a *collection* framework with the classes *container*, *element*, and *cursor*). Each layer represents a feature that will customize the classes and methods of the framework to incorporate that feature. Thus, one layer might define how the collection is shared (e.g., via semaphores), another might define its physical design (e.g., doubly linked lists), another might define whether the collection is persistent or transient and so forth. This allows a fair bit of customization of the detailed framework design while the higher levels of the application (i.e., the algorithms that use the collection) can remain generic.

This strategy works well in niches where the part of the application behind the interfaces varies over such features while the central application core is generic with respect to the features. For example, different operating systems, middleware, and databases often induce such interface-isolated variation within application classes. The feature-induced variations in the generated components are largely a local phenomenon that does not induce too much global variation in the application as a whole nor too much interdependence among distinct features.

Such reuse strategies are fundamentally based on substitution and inlining paradigms that refine components and expressions by local substitutions with local effects. Their shortcomings are that global dependencies and global reorganizations are either not very effective or tend to reduce the optimality of fit introduced by using feature-based layers. If the architectures vary more broadly or globally than such features can deal with, other approaches are required.

Recent work [2, 10] attempts to extend the method to allow greater levels of application customization by further factoring the layers into yet smaller components called *roles*. Roles can be variously composed to effect greater parameterization of the classes and methods comprising the layers. Fundamentally, role-induced variations manifest themselves as 1) inheritance structure variations and 2) mixin-like variations and extensions of the classes and methods comprising the layers.

The main weakness of composition-based generators is the lingering problem of global inter-component dependencies and relationships, a problem that is amplified by the fact that the specification languages are largely abstractions of conventional programming languages (CPLs). That is, the control and data structures of CPLs predominate in the specifications. While these structures may be ideal for computation, they are often ill suited for specification. Specifications are easiest to compose, transform and manipulate when they have few or no dependencies on state information, on computational orderings, and on other CPL structures that are oriented to Von Neumann machines. Unfortunately, the abstracted CPL component specifications of this niche induce global dependencies that require globally aware manipulation of the programs, a task that is fundamentally hard to do. These global dependencies often require the structure of the generated application to be manipulated in ways (e.g., merging iteration structures of separate **components**) that are determined by the particular combination and structure of the inlined components. Such dependencies often require highly customized application reorganizations (or re-weavings) that occur after the composition step is completed. Such manipulations are not easily accomplished on program language-based components that are assembled by simple composition and inlining strategies (even on those PL components that are somewhat abstracted).

4   Pattern-Directed Generators

Pattern-directed (PD) generators [8] allow greater degrees of customization (horizontal scaling) than composition-based generators because they use domain specific language (DSL) components that are less rigidly constrained than the CPL-based components. For example, a DSL may have domain operators with **implicit** iteration structures that can be combined and optimized in an infinity of problem specific ways late in the generation process. In contrast, CPLs are biased toward explicit expression of iterations, which limits the level of feasible customization and forces the component builder to make early and overly specific design choices. In short, CPLs necessitate early binding of detailed design structures whereas DSLs allow late binding.

PD generators divide the world into domains each of which has its own mini-language (e.g., the relational algebra) in which components can be defined. The mini-languages are typically prescriptive (i.e., operational) rather than declarative. The generation paradigm is based on rules that map from program parts written in one or more mini-domain language into lower level mini-languages recursively until the whole program has been translated into the lowest level mini-domain of some conventional programming language (e.g., C, C++, or Java). Between translation stages, optimizations may be applied that reorganize the program for performance.

These techniques achieve significantly greater degrees of custom component fit for the target application (i.e., horizontal scaling) while simultaneously allowing scaling up the size of the components. However, the cost is (sometimes) reduced target program performance because while the rules that reorganize and optimize the program at each stage can, in theory, find the optimal reorganization, the search space is often very large. So in practice, target program performance is sometimes compromised. Nevertheless, there are many application domains for which the performance degradation is not onerous or may be an acceptable tradeoff for the vastly increased programming leverage. The CAPE system [8] for generating communications protocols, which is based on DRACO, is an example of a domain where the tradeoff is acceptable.

5 Reorganizing Generators

Reorganizing generators extend the pattern-directed generator paradigm by attacking the program reorganization problem so that the optimizing reorganizations can be accomplished without significant search spaces. [4, 5] The trick is the introduction of *tag-directed* (TD) transformations that are triggered based on tags attached to the program components. The tags **anticipate** optimizations that are likely to succeed once the program is finally translated into a form closer to a conventional programming language. They allow optimization planning to occur in the problem domain and execution of the optimizations to occur in the programming domain. They reorganize the target program for high performance execution and do so without engendering the large search spaces that pure pattern-directed generators often do.

I have built a system in LISP called the Anticipatory Optimization Generator (AOG) to explore this approach. Fundamentally, AOG allows the separation of the highly generic, highly reusable elements of an application from the application specific, not so reusable elements. AOG provides methods to weave these generic and application specific elements together into a high performance form of the application program. This approach recognizes that an application program is an integration of information from many sources. Some information is highly general and (in principle) applicable to many specific application programs that fall into the same product line of software (e.g., payroll programs). For example, the formula

```
Pay(Employee, PayPeriod) = Salary(Employee) *
            HoursWorked (Employee, PayPeriod)
```

represents a conceptual domain relationship among the concepts Pay, Employee, Salary, HoursWorked, and PayPeriod. Further, one can define specializations of this conceptual relationship that account for various kinds of pay, various kinds of employees (e.g., salaried versus hourly), and various kinds of pay periods (e.g., regular, overtime, and holiday). Such relationships are highly reusable but, of course, they are not yet code. That is, they are not **directly** reusable constructs. In general, they cannot be cast directly into acceptable code by simple substitution paradigms (e.g., inlining) because if we incorporate information about the specific databases, for example, we will find that this simple relationship gets changed and woven into programming structures that obscure its clean simple structure. For example, several of the data fields may (or may not) come from the same database (e.g., employee identification, salary, record of hours worked for various pay periods). However, for those data fields that do come from the same database and potentially, the same record in that database, the generated code should be organized to minimize accesses to those fields that are in the same record of a database (e.g., access to the employee identification and the employee address, which might be required if the check is to be mailed, or access to employee identification and the employee's bank identification, which might be required if the check is to be direct deposited). Such accesses are likely to be independently (and redundantly) specified in the component specifications and therefore, they will likely be generated in separated areas of the target code. Such redundancies must be identified and removed in the application code. Similarly, sequential dependencies (e.g., the requirement to first get an employee id in order to get the address of that employee) will have to be reflected properly in the control structure of the resulting code. Neither requirement is easy to accomplish with simple composition, inlining, and simplification technologies.

AOG addresses such problems by introducing a new generator control structure that organizes transformations into phases and adds a new kind of transformation (i.e., a *tag-directed* transformation) that is particularly well suited to the task of reweaving components to assure global relationships and constraints like those imposed by specific graphics, database, UI or web structures.

Because AOG does so much program reorganization, thereby creating redundant and abstruse program structures, simplification is a big part of many optimization steps. AOG uses a partial evaluator to perform straightforward simplifications (e.g., arithmetic and logical reductions). It uses a Prolog-like inference engine to execute those simplifications that require some inference (e.g., generating the simplest form of loops derived when a single loop is split into special case and non-special case forms of the loop).

The AOG reusable library contains different kinds of reusable components:

- Pattern-Directed Transformations
  - o Object-Oriented Pattern-Directed (OOPD) Transforms
  - o Operator Definitions
  - o ADT Methods
- Tag-Directed Transformations
- Dynamic Deferred Transformations
- Type Inference Rules

All PD transformations have the same conceptual and internal form:

XformName, PhaseName, TypeName:
        Pattern $\Rightarrow$ *RewrittenExpression, Pre, Post*

The transform's name is *XformName* and it is stored as part of the *TypeName* object structure. It is enabled only during the *PhaseName* phase. *Pattern* is used to match an AST subtree and upon success the subtree is replaced by *RewrittenExpression*. *Pre* is the name of a routine that checks enabling conditions and performs some bookkeeping chores (e.g., creating translator variables). *Post* performs various computational chores during the rewrite. *Pre* and *Post* are optional.

The various kinds of PD transforms are expressed in slightly different external forms to allow AOG to do some of the specification work for the programmer where defaults such as *PhaseName* are known. For example, the definition of the graphics convolution operator $\oplus$ (sum of products of pixels and weights) might look like a *component* named Bconv where the default *PhaseName* is known and the default storage location (i.e., *TypeName*) is determined by the specific operator $\oplus$. Bconv would be expressed as:

```
(DefComponent Bconv (⊕ ParameterListPattern)
        (Σp,q ...sum of products expression...))
```

On the other hand, a trivial but concrete example of an OOPD would be

```
(⇒ FoldZeroXform SomePhaseName dsnumber `(+ ?x 0) `?x)
```

This transform is named FoldZeroXform, is stored in the type structure of dsnumber, is enabled only in phase SomePhaseName, and rewrites an expression like "(+ 27 0)" to "27". In the pattern, the pattern variable "?x" will match anything in the first position of expressions of the form "(+ __ 0).

AOG uses the various PD transformations to refine abstract DSLs to more specific DSLs and eventually to CPLs. However, it organizes the PD transforms by phases where each phase will perform a small step of the overall refinement. For example, the PD transforms of one phase introduce loops implied by the operators such as $\oplus$ and then move and merge those loops to minimize redundant looping.

On the other hand, TD transforms are used to accomplish various kinds of optimizations such as *architectural shaping*, which alters the structure of the computation to exploit domain knowledge of the hardware, middleware, or data. For example, the *SplitLoopOnCases* transformation shapes a loop that is doing a graphics image convolution operation so that the loop can exploit the parallelism of the Intel MMX instruction set. It recognizes the case where the body of the loop is a case-based if-then-else statement that depends on the loop indexes and splits the single loop into a series of loops each of which handles a single case. The *SplitLoopOnCases* optimization produces code that allows the pixel data to flow on the computer's data bus in chunks uninterrupted by conditional branches. This speeds up the overall convolution. For example, it would split a loop like

```
for(i=0, j=0; i<m && j<n; i++, j++)
        if(i==0 || j==0 || i==(m-1) || j==(n-1))
            ...then case...;
```

```
          ...else case...;
```

into loops like

```
for(j=0; j<n; j++)...then case with i=0...;
for(j=0; j<n; j++)...then case with i=(m-1)...;
for(i=0; i<m; i++)...then case with j=0...;
for(i=0; i<m; i++)...then case with j=(n-1)...;
for(i=1, j=1; i<(m-1) && j<(n-1); i++, j++)
          ...else case...;
```

These new forms of the loop are dealing with separate sections of the image separately. The first four special case loops are operating on the edge pixels in the image (i.e., top, bottom, left and right) and the else-case loop is operating on the non-edge pixels in the image. Subsequent TD transformations will shape the else-case loop body into forms that can be directly translated to MMX instructions. The resulting code of the then-cases will often simplify significantly under partial evaluation because of the constants that are substituted for i and j (e.g., 0 for i).

Architectural shaping transformations attempt to exploit as much retained domain specific information as they can. In this case, the tag that triggered the *SplitLoopOnCases* transformation contains the knowledge that the loop will be performing a computationally intense convolution operation and that such operations lend themselves to the parallelism of the MMX instructions. This knowledge allows a very focused and purposeful restructuring of the code.

Dynamic deferred transformations are part of specialized machinery for moving generated code to contexts that do not yet exist when the code is generated. *Type inference rules* are specialized transforms that infer the types of expressions for use in finding applicable transformations to apply.

For a contrasting approach, the reader may want to explore Aspect Oriented Programming. [6, 7] This approach has similar reorganization or reweaving objectives but differing implementation machinery.

Reorganizing generators, like PD Generators, are well suited for translating domain specific languages (DSLs) and because the DSLs can be quite abstract, they can generate a lot of functionality for a small amount of specification (high vertical scaling). In addition, they achieve a more optimal fit (high horizontal scaling) within the application than with composition-based systems because, like PD generators, they are composing DSL abstractions rather than the more concrete CPL abstractions. Each DSL abstraction refines in combinatorially many ways at each DSL level based on the particular DSL abstractions with which it is composed. Moreover, reorganizing generators solve a problem that has long plagued PD generators -- that of achieving context specific optimizations without a generator search space explosion. Those combinatorially many choices at each DSL level that provide the desirable horizontal scaling also tend to foster the generation of complex and convoluted code, which may have unacceptable performance. Attempting to solve this performance problem using global soups of transformations, as PD generators do, often leads to a search space explosion and for many domains is not feasible. The trick of using tags to retain key domain knowledge and use that knowledge to guide the process of optimization vastly reduces the search space and leads to a focused and purposeful optimization process with very little search involved.

6 Inference-Based Generators

These generators lean toward more declarative specifications that require general inference engines to re-structure the pieces into prescriptive code. [9] The downside is that domain engineering is more challenging than in previous cases and therefore, only a few highly specialized domains have been developed. Nevertheless, such generators can create the most highly customized (i.e., horizontally scaled) target programs with target program performance that can be superior to hand-tailored code.

7 Conclusion

Table 1. Characterization of Reuse Catagories

Niche	Key Elements	Key Operations
Concrete Reuse	Programming Language Basis	Hand Assembly
Composition-Based Generators	Abstracted Programming Languages	Inlining & Simplification
Pattern-Directed (PD) Generators	Domain Specific Languages (DSLs)	Pattern-Directed (PD) Transformations & Weak Inference Methods
Reorganizing Generators	Tagged DSLs	PD and Tag-Directed Transformations & Domain Specific Inference Methods
Inference-Based Generators	Formal Specification Languages	Heavy Dependence on Fully General Inference Methods

Table 1 summarizes the essence of these niches. As we proceed up the niche list, we find that the technologies have an increasing ability to do more of the programming work (vertical scaling) and an increasing ability to produce more customized solutions (horizontal scaling). The price for this scaling is that successive technologies require a greater up front investment in domain analysis and reuse library creation. For a detailed look into some representative generator systems, see 6.

References

1. Batory, Don, Singhal, Vivek, Sirkin, Marty, and Thomas, Jeff, "Scalable Software Libraries," *Symposium on the Foundations of Software Engineering*. Los Angeles, CA, December, 1993.

2. Batory, Don, and Martin, Jean-Philippe, "An Algebraic Foundation for Program Automation," *Personal Communication*, 2001.

3. Biggerstaff, Ted J., "A Perspective of Generative Reuse," Annals of Software Engineering, 5, 1998, pp. 169-226.

4. Biggerstaff, Ted J., "Fixing Some Transformation Problems," *Automated Software Engineering Conference*, Cocoa Beach, Florida (1999).

5. Biggerstaff, Ted J., "A New Control Structure for Transformation-Based Generators," In *Software Reuse: Advances in Software Reusability*, Vienna, Austria (Springer Lecture Notes in Computer Science, June, 2000).

6. Czarnecki, Krzysztof and Eisenecker, Ulrich, *Generative Programming*, Addison-Wesley, 2000.

7. Kiczales, Gregor, Lamping, John, Mendhekar, Anurag, Maede, Chris, Lopes, Cristina, Loingtier, Jean-Marc and Irwin, John: Aspect Oriented Programming. Tech. Report SPL97-08 P9710042, Xerox PARC (1997)

8. Neighbors, James M., "Draco: A Method for Engineering Reusable Software Systems." In Ted J. Biggerstaff and Alan Perlis (Eds.), *Software Reusability*, Addison-Wesley/ACM Press, 1989, pp. 295-319. (See also http://www.bayfronttechnologies.com/ for more information on DRACO and CAPE.)

9. Smith, Douglas R., "KIDS-A Knowledge-Based Software Development System," in *Automating Software Design*, M. Lowry & R. McCartney, Eds., AAAI/MIT Press, 1991, pp.483-514.

10. VanHilst, M. and D. Notkin, "Using C++ Templates to Implement Role-Based Designs", *JSSST International Symposium on Object Technologies and Systems (ISOTAS'96), 1996.*

A Standard Problem for Evaluating Product-Line Methodologies

Roberto E. Lopez-Herrejon and Don Batory

Department of Computer Sciences
The University of Texas
Austin, Texas 78712
{rlopez,batory}@cs.utexas.edu

Abstract. We propose a standard problem to evaluate product-line methodologies. It relies on common knowledge from Computer Science, so that domain-knowledge can be easily acquired, and it is complex enough to expose the fundamental concepts of product-line methodologies. As a reference point, we present a solution to this problem using the GenVoca design methodology. We explain a series of modeling, implementation, and benchmarking issues that we encountered, so that others can understand and compare our solution with theirs.

1 Introduction

A *product-line* is a family of related software applications. A *product-line architecture* is a design for a product-line that identifies the underlying building blocks or *components* of family members, and enables the synthesis of any particular member by composing these components. Different family members (product-line applications) are represented by different combination of components. The motivation for product-line architectures is one of economics and practicality: it is too expensive to build all possible family members; it is much cheaper to build components and to assemble desired family members from them.

Many methodologies have been invented to create product-line architectures (e.g., [2, 3, 7, 9, 11, 12, 13, 14, 17, 20]). Unfortunately, the state-of-the-art is immature. We are unaware of any attempts to evaluate different methodologies on a common set of problems. If this were done, we would understand better the strengths and weaknesses of different methodologies. We would know when to use a particular methodology, and when not to. Further, we would know if different methodologies relied on the same concepts. For example, different OO design approaches rely on a common conceptual foundation of classes, interfaces, and state machines, but offer different ways of producing a design expressed in terms of these concepts. For product-line methodologies, we generally do not know even this. Different methodologies have rather different meanings for the terms "architecture", "component", and "composition" so that it is not at all obvious what, if anything, is in common. It is not evident that the same concepts are shared among product-line methodologies, let alone knowing what these concepts are. From a practical standpoint, the choice of which methodology to use in a situation is dictated by convenience (at best) or by random selection (at worst) rather than by scientific fact. This is unacceptable.

For this area to mature, it is essential that we compare and evaluate proposed methodologies. The scientific principles that underlie this area must be identified and the contributions and novelties of different methodologies be exposed in a way that all can appreciate and recognize. The immaturity of this area is not unique and has occurred in other areas of Computer Science. In such cases, a standard problem has been proposed and different authors have applied their methodologies to solve it (e.g., [1]). Doing so exposes important details that would otherwise be overlooked or misunderstood. Such studies allow researchers to more accurately assess the strengths, benefits, commonalities, and variabilities of different methodologies. We believe this approach would be beneficial for product-lines.

In this paper, we propose a standard problem for evaluating product-line methodologies. We believe a standard problem should have the following characteristics:

- It draws on common knowledge from Computer Science, so that the often difficult requirement of becoming a domain expert or acquiring domain-expertise is minimized.

- It is not a trivial design problem; it is complex enough to expose the key concepts of product-lines and their implementation.

These characteristics should enable others to see the similarities and differences among approaches both at a superficial level and more importantly, at a deeper conceptual level.

To carry this idea forward, we present as reference point a solution to this problem using the GenVoca design methodology. We outline a set of design, implementation, and benchmarking issues that we had to resolve before we settled on our final design. Doing so exposed a variety of concerns and insights that we believe others would benefit hearing. Our designs, code, and benchmarks are available at a web site (http://www.cs.utexas.edu/users/dsb/GPL.html) for others to access.

2 A Standard Problem: The Graph Product Line

The *Graph Product-Line (GPL)* is a family of classical graph applications that was inspired by early work on software extensibility [16, 19]. GPL is typical of product-lines in that applications are distinguished by the set of features that they implement, where no two applications have the same set of features.[1] Further, applications are modeled as sentences of a grammar. Figure 1a[2] shows this grammar, where tokens are names of features. Figure 1b shows a GUI that implements this grammar and allows GPL products to be specified declaratively as a series of radio-button and check-box selections.

---

1. A *feature* is a functionality or implementation characteristic that is important to clients [15].
2. For simplicity, the grammar does not preclude the repetition of algorithms, whereas the GUI does.

(a)
```
GPL := Gtp Wgt Src Alg⁺;

Gtp := Directed | Undirected;

Wgt := Weighted | Unweighted;

Src := DFS | BFS | None;

Alg := Number | Connected | StronglyConnected
     | Cycle | MST Prim | MST Kruskal | Shortest;
```

(b)

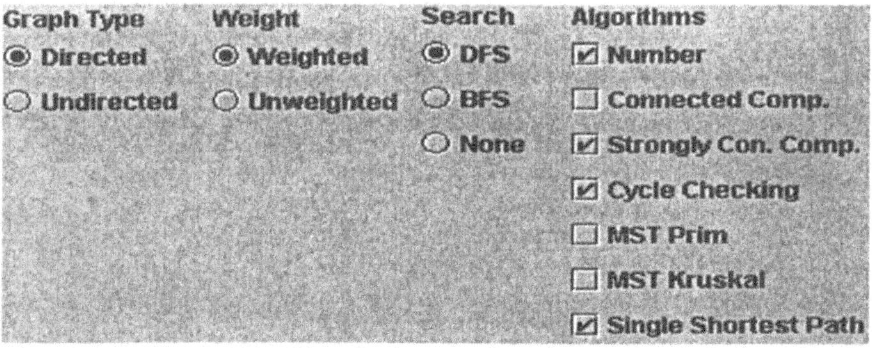

Graph Type	Weight	Search	Algorithms
◉ Directed	◉ Weighted	◉ DFS	☑ Number
○ Undirected	○ Unweighted	○ BFS	☐ Connected Comp.
		○ None	☑ Strongly Con. Comp.
			☑ Cycle Checking
			☐ MST Prim
			☐ MST Kruskal
			☑ Single Shortest Path

Figure 1. GPL Grammar and Specification GUI

The semantics of GPL features, and the domain itself, are uncomplicated. A graph is either Directed or Undirected. Edges can be Weighted with non-negative numbers or Unweighted. Every graph application requires at most one search algorithm: breadth-first search (BFS) or depth-first search (DFS); and one or more of the following algorithms [10]:

- **Vertex Numbering** (Number): Assigns a unique number to each vertex as a result of a graph traversal.

- **Connected Components** (Connected): Computes the *connected components* of an undirected graph, which are equivalence classes under the reachable-from relation. For every pair of vertices x and y in an equivalence class, there is a path from x to y.

- **Strongly Connected Components** (StronglyConnected): Computes the *strongly connected components* of a directed graph, which are equivalence classes under the reachable-from relation. A vertex y is reachable form vertex x if there is a path from x to y.

- **Cycle Checking** (Cycle): Determines if there are cycles in a graph. A cycle in directed graphs must have at least 2 edges, while in undirected graphs it must have at least 3 edges.

- **Minimum Spanning Tree** (MST Prim, MST Kruskal): Computes a *Minimum Spanning Tree (MST)*, which contains all the vertices in the graph such that the sum of the weights of the edges in the tree is minimal. We include both algorithms because they present distinct and interesting performance and design issues.

- **Single-Source Shortest Path** (Shortest): Computes the shortest path from a source vertex to all other vertices.

A fundamental characteristic of product-lines is that not all features are compatible. That is, the selection of one feature may disable (or enable) the selection of others. GPL is no exception. The set of constraints that govern the GPL features are summarized in Table 1.

Algorithm	Required Graph Type	Required Weight	Required Search
Vertex Numbering	Directed, Undirected	Weighted, Unweighted	BFS, DFS
Connected Components	Undirected	Weighted, Unweighted	BFS, DFS
Strongly Connected Components	Directed	Weighted, Unweighted	DFS
Cycle Checking	Directed, Undirected	Weighted, Unweighted	DFS
Minimum Spanning Tree	Undirected	Weighted	None
Single-Source Shortest Path	Directed	Weighted	None

Table 1. Feature Constraints

A GPL application implements a valid combination of features. As examples, one GPL application implements vertex numbering and connected components using depth-first search on an undirected graph. Another implements minimum spanning trees on weighted, undirected graphs. Thus, from a client's viewpoint, to specify a particular graph application with the desired set of features is straightforward. And so too is the implementation of the GUI (Figure 1b) and constraints of Table 1.

We chose Java as our implementation language. Besides its simplicity over C++ and availability of GUI libraries, we made use of Java containers, iterators, and sort methods, to avoid reimplementing these low-level routines by hand. We recommend others to follow our lead to make comparisons easier.

3 GenVoca

GenVoca is a model of product-lines that is based on step-wise extension [3-6][3]. Among its key ideas is programs are values. Consider the following constants that represent programs with individual features:

```
f           // program that implements feature f
g           // program that implements feature g
```

An *extension* is a function that takes a program as input and produces an extended (or feature-augmented) program as output:

```
i(x)        // adds feature i to program x
j(x)        // adds feature j to program x
```

It follows that a multi-featured application is an *equation*, and that different equations define a set of related applications, i.e., a *product-line*, such as:

```
a₁ = i(f)       // application a₁ has features i and f
a₂ = j(g)       // application a₂ has features j and g
a₃ = i(j(f))    // application a₃ has features i, j, and f
```

Thus one can determine features of an application by inspecting its equation.

3.1 GPL

A GenVoca model of GPL is the set of constants and functions defined in Table 2. There are three extensions that are not visible to the GUI: Transpose, Benchmark, and Prog. Transpose performs graph transposition and is used (only) by the StronglyConnected algorithm. It made sense to separate the StronglyConnected algorithm from Transpose, as they dealt with separate concerns. (This means that an implementation constraint in using the StronglyConnected extension is that the Transpose extension must also be included, and vice versa). Benchmark contains functions to read a graph from a file and elementary timing functions for profiling. Prog creates the objects required to represent a graph, and calls the algorithms of the family member on this graph.

Extensions can not be composed in arbitrary orders. The legal compositions of extensions in Table 2 are defined by simple constraints called *design rules* [3] whose details we omit from this paper, but do include with our source code. Our GUI specification tool translates a sentence in the grammar of Figure 1 (in addition to checking for illegal combinations of features) into an equation. Because features are in 1-to-1 corre-

---

3. A *refinement* adds implementation detail, but does not add methods to a class or change the semantics of existing methods. In contrast, *extensions* not only add implementation detail but also can add methods to a class and change the semantics of existing methods. Inheritance is a common way to extend classes statically in OO programming languages.

spondence with extensions, this translation is straightforward. For example, a GPL application app that implements vertex numbering and connected components using depth-first search on an undirected graph is the equation:

```
app = Prog( Benchmark( Number( Connected( DFS( Undirected )))))
```

Directed	directed graph	Cycle(x)	cycle checking
Undirected	undirected graph	MSTPrim(x)	MST Prim algorithm
Weighted(x)	weighted graph	MSTKruskal(x)	MST Kruskal algorithm
DFS(x)	depth-first search	Shortest(x)	single source shortest path
BFS(x)	breadth-first search	Transpose(x)	graph transposition
Number(x)	vertex numbering	Benchmark(x)	benchmark program
Connected(x)	connected components	Prog(x)	main program
StronglyConnected(x)	strongly connected components		

Table 2. A GenVoca Model of GPL

3.2 Mixin-Layers

There are many ways in which to implement extensions. We use mixin-layers [18]. To illustrate, recall the Directed program implements a directed graph. This program is defined by multiple classes, say Graph, Vertex, and Edge. (The exact set of classes is an interesting design problem which we discuss in Section 4). A mixin-layer that represents the Directed program is the class Directed with inner classes Graph, Vertex, and Edge:

```
class Directed {
   class Graph  {...}
   class Vertex {...}
   class Edge   {...}
}
```

An extension is implemented as a mixin, i.e., a class whose superclass is specified by a parameter. The depth-first search extension is implemented as a mixin DFS that encapsulates extensions (mixins) of the Graph and Vertex classes. That is, DFS grafts new methods and variables onto the Graph and Vertex classes to implement depth first search algorithms:

```
class DFS<x> extends x {
    class Graph  extends x.Graph  {...}
    class Vertex extends x.Vertex {...}
}
```

The above describes the general way in which GenVoca-GPL model constants and functions are implemented. When we write the composition A = DFS(Directed) in our model, we translate this to the equivalent template expression:

```
class A extends DFS<Directed>;
```

In general, there is a simple mapping of model equations to template/mixin expressions. Of course, Java does not support mixins or mixin-layers, but extended Java languages do. We used the *Jakarta Tool Suite (JTS)* to implement mixin-layers [4].

4 Graph Implementation

Designing programs that implement graph algorithms is an interesting problem. Every implementation will define a representation of graphs, vertices, edges, and *adjacency* — i.e., what vertices are adjacent (via an edge) to a given vertex. Further, there must be some way to represent annotations of edges (e.g., weights, names). We did not arrive at our final design immediately; we went through a series of designs that incrementally improved the clarity of our code, which we document in the following sections. In the process, we learned a simple rule to follow in order to simplify extension-based designs.

4.1 Adjacency Lists Representation (G)

The first representation we tried was based on a "legacy" C++ design [18, 5] that had been written years earlier and that implemented few of the extensions listed in Table 2. It consisted of 2 classes:

- Graph: consists of a list of Vertex objects.
- Vertex: contains a list of its adjacent Vertex objects.

That is, edges were implicit: their existence could be inferred from an adjacency list. Figure 2 illustrates this representation for a weighted graph. The advantage of this representation was its simplicity. It worked reasonably well for most extensions that we had to implement. However, it failed on edge annotations (e.g., weights). Because edges were implicitly encoded in the design, we had to maintain a weights list that was "parallel" to the adjacency list. While this did indeed work, our layered designs were obviously not clean or elegant — e.g., for operations like graph transposition which needed to read edge weights, and Kruskal's algorithm which needed to manipulate edges directly. Because of these reasons, this lead us to our second design.

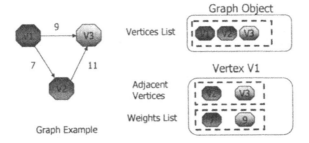

Figure 2. Adjacency Lists Representation Example

4.2 Neighbor List Representation (GN)

The second representation consisted of three classes:

- `Graph`: contains a list of `Vertex` objects.

- `Vertex`: contains a list of `Neighbor` objects.

- `Neighbor`: contains a reference to a `Vertex` object, the other end of an edge.

Edge annotations were encoded as a extensions — i.e., extra fields — of the `Neighbor` class. Figure 3 illustrates this representation. By pushing the neighbor `Vertex` object and edge annotations into a `Neighbor` object, we reduced the number of list accesses required to obtain these annotations. While this did lead to a simplification of the coding of some mixin-layers, it did not simplify the complexity of the Kruskal algorithm. Since this mixin-layer was unnecessarily difficult to write (and read!), we knew there was still something wrong. This lead to our final design.

4.3 Edge-Neighbor Representation (GEN)

Textbook descriptions of algorithms are almost always simple. The reason is that certain implementation details have been abstracted away — but this is, in fact, the strength of layers and extensions. We wanted to demonstrate that we could (almost literally) copy algorithms directly out of text books into mixin-layer code. The benefits of doing so are (a) faster and more reliable implementations and (b) easier transference of proofs of algorithm correctness into proofs of program correctness. We realized that the only way this was possible was to recognize that there are a standard set of "conceptual" objects that are referenced by all graph algorithms: Graphs, Vertices, Edges, and Neighbors (i.e., adjacencies). Algorithms in graph textbooks define the fundamental extensions of graphs, and these extensions modify Graph objects, Vertex objects, Edge objects, and Neighbor objects. Thus, the simplest way to express such extensions is to reify all of these "conceptual" objects as physical objects and give them their own distinct classes.

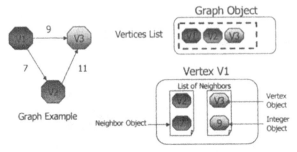

Figure 3. Neighbor Lists Representation Example

The problems of our previous designs surfaced because we tried to make "short-cuts" to avoid the explicit representation of certain conceptual objects (e.g., Edge, Neighbor). Our justification for doing so was because we felt the resulting programs would be more efficient. That is, we were performing "optimizations" in our earlier designs that folded multiple conceptual objects into a single physical object. In fact, such *premature optimizations* caused us nothing but headaches as we tried to augment our design to handle new extensions and to produce easy to read and maintain code. (We think that this may be a common mistake in most software designs, not just ours). So our "final" design made explicit all classes of objects that could be explicitly extended by graph algorithms. Namely, we had four classes:

- `Graph`: contains a list of `Vertex` objects, and a list of `Edge` objects.

- `Vertex`: contains a list of `Neighbor` objects.

- `Neighbor`: contains a reference to a neighbor `Vertex` object (the vertex in the other end of the edge), and a reference to the corresponding `Edge` object.

- `Edge`: extends the `Neighbor` class and contains the start `Vertex` of an `Edge`.

Edge annotations are now expressed as extensions of `Edge` class, and were expressed by the addition of extra fields in the `Edge` class. This representation is illustrated in Figure 4.

Equating conceptual objects with physical objects may simplify source code, but the question remains: were our original designs more efficient? Is "premature design optimization" essential for performance? These questions are addressed next.

5 Profiling Results

We performed a series of benchmarks to quantify the trade-offs between our three designs. Several implementations of the designs were tried, using different containers, and different strategies to access and copy the edge annotations. This section shows the results for our most fine-tuned implementations. The benchmarks were run on a Windows 2000 platform using a 700Mhz processor with 196MB RAM.

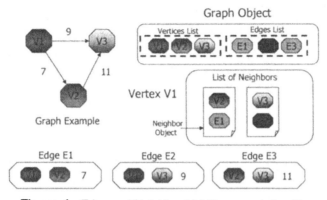

Figure 4. Edge and Neighbor List Representation Example

The first program used the vertex number algorithm on undirected graphs using depth first search. This program measured the performance of graph creation and traversal. A randomly generated graph with 1000 vertices was used as test case. Figure 5 shows the benchmark results.

Figure 5a indicates that design **G** (our first) performs better than the other two; 6%-22% better that **GN** (our second), and 75%-120% better than **GEN** (our third). This is not surprising: **GN** and **GEN** have object creation overhead that is absent in **G** — Neighbor objects are created in **GN**, and Neighbor and Edge objects are created in **GEN**. While this is an obvious difference, the overall speed of the benchmark was dictated by the time reading the graph from disk. Figure 5b shows this total execution time, where the difference between the **G** application and the **GN** application is about 5% and **G** with **GEN** is about 9%.

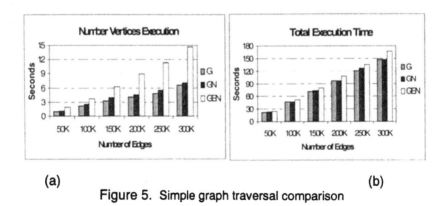

(a)   (b)

Figure 5. Simple graph traversal comparison

The second program benchmarked the impact of copying a graph with edge annotations. StronglyConnected utilizes such an operation, transpose, that creates a new copy of a graph but with the direction of the edges reversed. A randomly generated graph with 500 vertices was used as test case. In general, there was no significant difference (see Figure 6a). The **G** design performed 2% better than **GN** and 6% better than **GEN**. Although cost of graph creation is different among designs (as indicated by Figure 5a), the differences are swamped by the large computation times of the StronglyConnected algorithm. In particular, only 15% of the total execution time in Figure 6b was spent in reading the graph in from disk.

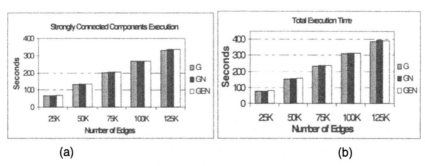

(a)   (b)

Figure 6. Strongly Connected Components

The third program benchmarked the impact of algorithms that use edges explicitly, like Kruskal's algorithm. A randomly generated graph with 500 vertices was used as a test case. As expected, the **GEN** representation outperformed the other two simply because it does not have to compute and create the edges from the adjacency or neighbor lists. It performed between 43% and 98% faster than representation **G**, and between 59% and 120% faster than representation **GN** (see Figure 7a). The difference between **G** and **GN** is due to the fact that in the latter, to get the weights for each edge, an extra access to the weights lists is required; and that the creation of the output graph is more expensive because it has to create Neighbor objects as well. Of the total execution time (Figure 7b), approximately 60% was spent reading a graph of 25K edges from disk, and less than 5% when the graph had 125K edges.

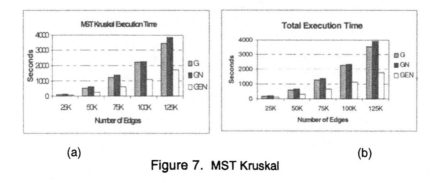

(a)   (b)

Figure 7. MST Kruskal

Overall, we found that the performance of algorithms that did not use weighted edges (e.g., numbering, cycle-checking, connected components, strongly-connected components) had slightly better performance with the **G** design. For those algorithms that used weighted edges (e.g., MST Prim, MST Kruskal, shortest path), the **GEN** design was better. Because an application is specified by the same equation for all three models, we could exploit our performance observations in a "smarter" generator that would decide which design/implementation would be best for a particular family member — i.e., one equation might be realized by a **G** design, another by a **GEN** design (see [6]).

Focussing exclusively on performance may be appropriate for most applications. But a more balanced viewpoint needs to consider program complexity (which indirectly measures the ease of maintenance, understandability, and extensibility). The main issue for us was the impact that the representation of edges had on program complexity. By in large, all layers had visually simple representations. But the Kruskal layer seemed more complicated than it needed to be. The reason was that in both the **G** and **GN** designs, the Kruskal layer had an explicit Edge class that was private to that layer, and used by no other layer[4]. (The Kruskal algorithm demanded the existence of explicit edge objects). The fact that all layers might benefit from making Edge explicit drove us to the **GEN** design, which we considered visually and conceptually more elegant than our earlier designs. As it turns out, our instincts on "visual simplicity" were not altogether accurate. To see why, we use two metrics for program complexity: *lines of code* (**LOC**) and *number of symbols* (**NSYMB**).[5] Table 3 shows these statistics for the Kruskal layer. Making edges explicit did indeed simplify this layer's encoding. However, other parts of our design grew a bit larger (mostly because we had to make the Neighbor and Edge classes and their extensions explicit). Table 4 shows these same statistics, across all layers, for all three designs. Overall, the statistical complexity of all three designs was virtually identical. So the drive for "visual simplicity" among layers in the end did improve our designs, but surprisingly did not impact their size statistics.

There is a benefit to the **GEN** design that is not indicated by the above tables. If we chose to enlarge the **G** and **GN** product-line with more algorithms that directly manipulate edges, then it is likely a local copy of the Edge class would be introduced into these layers. And doing so would result in replicated code, possibly leading to problems with program maintenance. By making the Edge class global to all extensions as in the **GEN** design, we would expect little or no code replication — precisely what we want in a product-line design.

Finally, we wanted to see if explicit layering (which mixin-layers produce) affects the overall performance. We created equations for each design that contained the most layers (10), and manually-inlined the resulting chain of mixin-layers into an unlayered package called *Flat*. There are two equations that have 10 layers, namely:

---

4. The local version of Edge in the Kruskal layer is indicated in Table 4 as 7 lines of 52 tokens.
5. We used other metrics [8], but found they provided no further insights.

		LOC			NSYMB	
	G	**GN**	**GEN**	**G**	**GN**	**GEN**
Kruskal	87	90	69	927	928	695

Table 3. Kruskal Algorithm Statistics

Class Name		LOC			NSYMB	
	G	**GN**	**GEN**	**G**	**GN**	**GEN**
Graph	372	387	380	3554	3600	3492
Vertex	209	202	198	1832	1758	1631
Neighbor	0	30	16	0	229	49
Edge	7	7	26	52	52	304
Total	**588**	**626**	**620**	**5438**	**5639**	**5476**

Table 4. Lines of Code (LOC) and Number of Symbols (NSYMB)

- *Directed, Weighted, DFS, StronglyConnected, Number, Transpose, Shortest, Cycle, Benchmark, Prog:* in this case the difference between the layered version and the flattened one oscillates between 0% and 2% in **G**, -1% and 1% for **GN**, and -1% and 1% for **GEN**. A randomly generated graph with 500 vertices was used as test case. These results are shown in Figure 8a.

- *Undirected, Weighted, DFS, Connected, Number, Cycle, MST-Kruskal, MST-Prim, Benchmark, Prog:* for this application the difference between the layered version and the flattened one varies between 0% and 3% in **G**, 0% and 5% in **GN**, and between -1% and 1% in **GEN**. A randomly generated graph with 300 was used as test case. The results are shown in Figure 8b.

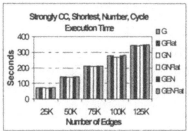
(a)

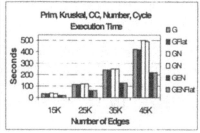
(b)

Figure 8. Effect of Class Layering

The small difference between the layered version and its corresponding flattened one is due to the fact that few methods override their parent method. When overriding does occur, it involves fewer than 3 layers. Again, this result is specific to GPL and may not hold for other domains.

6 Conclusions

GPL is a simple and illustrative problem for product-line designs. Different applications of the GPL product-line are defined by unique sets of features, and not all combinations of features are permitted. The state of the art in product-lines is immature, and the need to understand the commonalities and differences among product-line design methodologies is important. We want to know how methodologies differ, what are their relative strengths and weaknesses, and most importantly what are the scientific principles that underlie these models. We do not know answers to these questions. But it is our belief that by proposing and then solving a standard set of problems, the answers to these questions will, in time, be revealed.

We believe GPL is a good candidate for a standard problem. It has the advantages of *simplicity* — it is an exercise in design and implementation that can be discussed in a relatively compact paper — and *understandability* — domain expertise is easily acquired because it is a fundamental topic in Computer Science. Further, it provides an interesting set of challenges that should clearly expose the key concepts of product-line methodologies.

In this paper, we presented a product-line model and implementation of GPL using the GenVoca methodology and the Jakarta Tool Suite (JTS). We showed how GenVoca layers correspond to features, and how compositions of features are expressed by equations implemented as inheritance lattices. We presented a sequence of designs that progressively simplified layer implementations. We benchmarked these implementations to understand performance trade-offs. As expected, different designs do have different execution efficiencies, but it is clear that a "smart" generator (which had all three designs available) could decide which representation would be best for a particular application. As an additional result, we showed that there is a very small impact of class layering in overall application performance.

We hope that others apply their methodology to GPL and publish their designs and findings. We believe that our work would benefit by a close inspection of others, and the same would hold for other methodologies as well. Our code can be downloaded from http://www.cs.utexas.edu/users/dsb/GPL.html.

Acknowledgements. We would like to thank Vijaya Ramachandran for her valuable help with the subtle details of the theory of graph algorithms. We also thank Jay Misra for clarifying the distinction between refinements and extensions.

7 References

[1]   J-R Abrial, E. Boerger, and H. Langmaack, *Formal Methods for Industrial Applications: Specifying and Programming the Steam Boiler Control*, Lecture Notes in Computer Science, Vol. 1165, Springer-Verlag, 1996.

[2]   P. America, et. al. "CoPAM: A Component-Oriented Platform Architecting Method Family for Product Family Engineering", *Software Product Lines: Experience and Research Directions*, Kluwer Academic Publishers, 2000.

[3]   D. Batory and B. Geraci. Composition Validation and Subjectivity in GenVoca Generators. *IEEE Transactions on Software Engineering*, February 1997.

[4]   D.Batory, B.Lofaso, and Y.Smaragdakis. "JTS: Tools for implementing Domain-Specific Languages", *Int. Conf. on Software Reuse*, Victoria, Canada, June 1998.

[5]   D. Batory, R. Cardone, and Y.Smaragdakis. "Object-Oriented Frameworks and Product Lines", *1st Software Product-Line Conference*, Denver, Colorado, August 2000.

[6]   D. Batory, G. Chen, E. Robertson, and T. Wang, "Design Wizards and Visual Programming Environments for GenVoca Generators", *IEEE Transactions on Software Engineering*, May 2000, 441-452.

[7]   J. Bosch, "Evolution and Composition of Reusable Assets in Product-Line Architectures: A Case Study", *Software Architecture*, Kluwer Academic Publishers, 1999.

[8]   S.R. Chidamber and C.F. Kemerer, "Towards a Metrics Suite for Object Oriented Design", *OOPSLA 1991*.

[9]   S. Cohen and L. Northrop, "Object-Oriented Technology and Domain Analysis", *Int. Conf. on Software Reuse*, Victoria, Canada, June 1998.

[10]   T.H. Cormen, C.E. Leiserson, and R.L.Rivest. *Introduction to Algorithms*, MIT Press, 1990.

[11]   K. Czarnecki and U.W. Eisenecker, "Components and Generative Programming", *SIGSOFT 1999*, LNCS 1687, Springer-Verlag, 1999.

[12]   K. Czarnecki and U.W. Eisenecker, *Generative Programming: Methods, Tools, and Applications*, Addison-Wesley, 2000.

[13]   J-M. DeBaud and K. Schmid, "A Systematic Approach to Derive the Scope of Software Product Lines", *Int. Conference on Software Engineering 1999*.

[14]   H. Gomaa et al., "A Prototype Domain Modeling Environment for Reusable Software Architectures", *Int. Conf. on Software Reuse*, Rio de Janeiro, November 1994, 74-83.

[15]   M. Griss, "Implementing Product-Line Features by Composing Component Aspects", *First International Software Product-Line Conference*, Denver, Colorado., August 2000.

[16]   I. Holland. "Specifying Reusable Components Using Contracts", *ECOOP 1992*.

[17]   D.L. Parnas, "On the Design and Development of Program Families", *IEEE Transactions on Software Engineering*, March 1976.

[18]   Y. Smaragdakis and D. Batory, "Implementing Layered Designs with Mixin Layers", *ECOOP 1998*.

[19]   M. VanHilst and D. Notkin, "Using C++ Templates to Implement Role-Based Designs", *JSSST International Symposium on Object Technologies for Advanced Software*, Springer-Verlag, 1996, 22-37.

[20]   D.M. Weiss and C.T.R. Lai, *Software Product-Line Engineering*, Addison-Wesley, 1999.

Components, Interfaces and Information Models within a Platform Architecture[1]

Jan Gerben Wijnstra

Philips Research Laboratories
Prof. Holstlaan 4, 5656 AA Eindhoven, The Netherlands
JanGerben.Wijnstra@philips.com

Abstract. In this paper we describe our experiences with the development of a platform in the medical imaging domain. Three important ingredients of this platform are components, interfaces and information models. We will explain the requirements for the platform, why these three ingredients have been chosen, and our experiences when using this approach.

Keywords: component, interface, information model, diversity, platform, product family, product population

1. Introduction

Products in the medical imaging market are becoming more complex and more diverse, must support easy extension with new features (feature propagation across products), should have similar appearance to its users, and have to be of high quality. A short time-to-market and limited development costs are also important factors. These requirements should be met by a product family that covers a large part of the market. The development of a product family and its individual members (i.e. single products) can be supported by a shared family architecture.

Similarities can even exist between various product families. These similarities can be exploited in a similar way as they would be within a single product family. Such a group of related product families is sometimes referred to as a product population [2]. A shared architecture can also be defined for such a product population. Based on this architecture, we can define and provide assets that can be reused across the product families belonging to the product population.

In this paper we describe our approach for components, interfaces and information models within a platform for a product population. This approach is applied to a project, which aims at the delivery of common components across a number of different product families. These product families share the characteristic of acquiring and processing digital images of the inside of a human body. The platform can also be directly used for products; the 'indirection' via a product family is not required. Section 2 introduces the requirements and set-up of the platform. In section 3, we elaborate on the ingredients of the platform, i.e. components, interfaces and information models. Section 4 describes the approach of using these ingredients to build a platform. Finally, section 5 presents result of practical experiences with the approach, followed by concluding remarks in section 6.

---

[1] This work has been partially funded by the European ITEA project ESAPS.

2. Product Population Platform

In the previous section, we introduced the arguments for a platform approach to support the development of products in the medical imaging domain. The platform has to support a number of properties. The most important ones are:

- *open systems*
  The platform is intended for various systems within the hospital. These systems must be interconnectable and must be able to incorporate new functionality.
- *forward/backward compatible*
  It is desirable that older and newer products made with the platform can work together. Also within a product, it must be possible to combine functions of different versions.
- *independent life-cycles*
  The platform contains different groups of coherent functionality. Each of these groups should have an independent life-cycle, so that it can be updated without affecting the rest of the platform.
- *configurability, extendibility*
  The composability/configurability of individual specific products from specific parts of the platform is very important. It should also be easy to extend products with new functionality.
- *complexity management*
  When defining a platform that must be applicable for several product families and will evolve over time, it is important that the complexity is manageable.
- *outsourcing and third-party software*
  In the light of the growing size and complexity of the software, we want to be able to buy-in certain parts or to outsource well-defined functionality.
- *portability (technology independence)*
  The platform is used for different products that may have different operating systems or component technology. The platform must be usable in these contexts.

To support these properties, the product population platform will consist of a number of components. These components have clearly defined interfaces. Information models are defined for some of these interfaces, describing the semantics of the data that is exchanged over these interfaces (components, interfaces and information models are explained in section 3). Specific products can reuse the components, taking the interfaces and information models into account.

The term 'platform' has different meanings, depending on the context in which it is used. For example, when looking at operating systems or middleware such as COM, the platform is a piece of infrastructure functionality on top of which you can build your own product. Another way in which the term platform is used is for a collection of frameworks to which specific functionality can be added via plug-ins (see [4]). In the context of this paper, we define a platform to be a set of generally reusable components. The users of this platform are free to decide which components to use. This is illustrated in Fig. 1. Here, two product families and one product are depicted based on the platform. Each of them is composed from product-specific components and components that are selected from the platform.

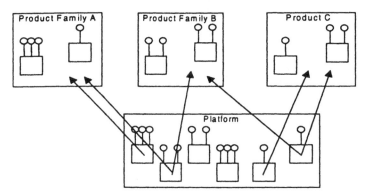

Fig. 1. Platform Set-up

3. Components, Interfaces and Information Models

The three main construction elements for the platform are components, interfaces and information models. They will be discussed in this section.

In our platform, components are units containing re-usable functionality with explicit interfaces that offer:

- a quick delivery of existing functionality through stable interfaces,
- composability of products from components by product groups,
- independent life-cycles of components and products, allowing incremental updates,
- easy distribution/installation of updated/new functionality,
- an opportunity to (re-)use third-party and legacy software,
- improved control over outsourcing,
- integration of heterogeneous technologies (operating system, programming language).

In addition to the components, interfaces are essential for our approach. Important characteristics of these interfaces are:

- access points to clearly defined functionality for use by other components,
- contracts between component creators and component users,
- components must implement interfaces in their entirety (no optional methods),
- components usually implement a set of logically-related interfaces,
- the same interface may be implemented by multiple components,
- the interfaces should be stable, the implementation can be flexible.

Interfaces are closely related to components. This relation is illustrated in Fig. 2. A component has two types of interfaces, namely:

- *provided* interface; the component guarantees that it will implement the functionality associated with the interface
- *required* interface; the component accesses functionality through this interface and relies on the functionality to be implemented *outside* the component

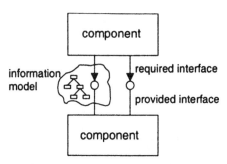

Fig. 2. Components, Interfaces and Information Models

The interfaces and components are smaller parts that are defined in the context of the overall platform architecture. In addition to these interfaces and components, there are concepts that are relevant at several places in the architecture. An example of such a concept in the medical domain is a medical image. The concept of an image is relevant when displaying an image on the screen, when printing an image on film, or when storing an image on a CD. The image concept is a complex structure, and includes for example the pixel matrix and attributes that refer to the acquisition of the image. Concepts like this are included in a so-called 'information model'. An information model captures relevant concepts from the domain, and is independent of the underlying technology. A number of information models have been defined. It is possible for one information model to build upon another (extending it).

As an example, Fig. 3 shows part of the imaging information model, which is based on the DICOM (Digital Imaging and Communications in Medicine) standard. Each of the objects in the structure has a number of attributes. There may be attributes that are specific for specific product families. It can also be the case that specific objects are added for individual product families.

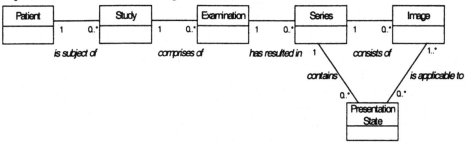

Fig. 3. Information Model Example

The concepts in an information model play a role at several places in the architecture, between various components. For example, an application component makes a request to a print service to print an image. One way of realising this functionality is to let the print service provide a number of methods, each with a number of parameters, so that the application component can pass all the individual attributes that belong to the image and the attributes that control the printing of the image. However, instead of this possibility, the request is passed via one method call as a structure of data objects as defined in the information model. As a consequence, there are fewer and simpler interface methods, and the semantics are moved to the information model.

Fig. 2 illustrates how an information model is related to an interface. An information model defines the structure and semantics of the data objects that are exchanged between components via a certain type of interface. Such an interface enables data objects that adhere to the related information model to be passed. Two interacting components both must know the information model in order to deal with the data that is exchanged.

Changes can occur within an information model, as the concepts within the domain may evolve. This means that several versions of an information model can exist. A certain component therefore provides a combination of an interface together with a particular version of the related information model. Since these two elements together actually determine the functionality that is provided by the component, they form the complete interface provided by the component.

Each of the product families supports the basic set of concepts that are defined for a particular information model. However, there may also be extensions that are specific for a product family. This means that when data is transferred from one system to another, the receiving system will at least understand the basic set. The receiving system may or may not ignore additional elements or not, depending on the information models used by the sending and receiving systems.

The main benefits of using information models within the definitions of component interfaces are as follows:

*   *reuse within several interfaces*
    An information model captures concepts that play a system-wide role in the interaction between components. For example, an image can be printed, stored, or displayed, requiring interaction with different components. These concepts can easily be reused in different contexts by defining them as data objects that can be passed via interfaces. Interfaces might also be reusable for several information models. This is likely when one information model is an extension of another information model.

*   *stable methods in interfaces*
    Since the syntactic part (the methods and their attributes) of the interfaces become smaller, they will remain more stable than traditional interfaces. This means that fewer new interfaces will be introduced during evolution of the system than when applying the 'COM-rule', that is, when an interface needs to be modified, a new interface has to be introduced.

*   *handling concepts as separate entities*
    As in object-orientation, we intuitively deal with concepts in the real world as objects in an information model. These objects can be exchanged as entities over interfaces, and can be passed from component to component. This is different to the situation where an object's attributes have to be put in the parameters of a method call, one by one. This would lead to complex method descriptions, particularly when concerning object structures consisting of several hierarchical levels. It is even possible that when a data object is passed through a number of components, the intermediate components do not know the complete semantics of the data object, but simply pass the data object to the next component. This

allows the introduction of generic services that can handle data objects with slightly different structures and semantics, e.g. a service that queues and handles print requests.

- *data objects can be stored (persistent)*
  Since the data that is passed between components is in the form of data objects, it can easily be stored. For example, the request to print an image with all its data can be handled by a print service, and can later on be passed to a printer that is free. The same object structure can also be used to store these objects. Also for the exchange of information between interconnected system, the data objects are used.

- *support for forward and backward compatibility*
  Since the methods of the interfaces remain stable, each component can receive data objects belonging to an older or newer version of the information model. If the version of the information model used by the requesting component is older, the receiving component knows how to deal with the data. If the version is newer, some new attributes in the data may have to be skipped, as the receiving component will not understand what they mean. This mechanism should of course be used with care, since although the methods of the provided and required interfaces are compatible, the combination of different versions of an information model may lead to undesired behaviour.

- *enabling declarative way-of-working*
  The components in a product population platform have to be used together with components from specific products. This means that a stable level of interaction must be chosen for these component interfaces. By applying data objects, a declarative way-of-working is enabled in which the functionality is requested in terms of end-results (more *what*) and not in a sequence of steps (less *how*). So, the request to perform some action is captured in a data structure and is passed to the performer of that action. This kind of interaction is more stable than interaction based on interfaces that have methods for each individual step.

- *data driven tools*
  The use of information models increases the value of tooling that is based on data structures. As mentioned earlier, the data objects can easily be stored in a database. Another example is the generation of test data, based on an information model that defines the allowed structures and values for the data objects.

This information models approach follows the trend of separating syntax and semantics, which can also be seen in XML. The information models are not applied for all interfaces. Usually those interfaces that deal with relevant system-wide concepts have related information models. There are specific interfaces for local interaction between components, since the advantages mentioned above mostly apply to the interfaces related to relevant system-wide concepts.

In addition to the advantages of the information model approach, there are also some drawbacks. One of these drawbacks is that it becomes more difficult to see what an interface is used for, since the methods of the interface are more generic. It also requires a different way of working than in the situation in which 'normal' interfaces are used.

4. Approach

In this section, we give a general description of our platform approach (section 4.1), the main architectural styles (section 4.2), the way diversity is supported by the platform (section 4.3), and look in more detail at how the components, interfaces and information models are defined (section 4.4).

4.1 Platform Definition

As mentioned earlier, the first aim of the shared approach is to arrive at an architecture that is shared across the various medical imaging systems. Such a shared architecture is essential to be able to define shared components, interfaces and information models. All parties involved, both the platform group and the product groups, contribute to an architecture group that defines the shared platform architecture. The next steps are as follows:

- To define shared interfaces and information models, enabling the exchange and sharing of medical (imaging) data;
- To develop and deliver a set of medical imaging software components, that adhere to the agreed interfaces and information models, and that can be used within the various products.

A prerequisite for this approach is that the information models and interfaces are explicitly defined and managed. To achieve this, there are two working groups, one for the information models and one for the interfaces, each containing members from the various platform and product groups. The focus is on the standardisation of functionality that already existed in multiple systems. As a rule of thumb, a component is part of the platform when it is required by at least two products.

The platform group defines and realises reusable components for the platform. These components can be built quite independently of each other. They will be released when they are finished, and will be integrated into the platform in a next step. The product groups take a version of the platform and build their products on top of it. Any product may use its own selection of reusable assets.

The product groups also use components that they have built for their own purpose. If these components comply with the interfaces of the shared architecture and are useful to other product groups, they may also be integrated into the shared platform. Note that this integration step will often need a redesign, both of the component itself and of those component interfaces that are not yet available. The reason for this is that the functionality that the component provides may have to be slightly adapted to make it reusable within other products.

4.2 Platform Architecture

The shared platform architecture defines a number of layers. The layers are (from bottom to top): base layer (containing infrastructure functionality), service layer (medical service components) and application layer (medical application components). The application components provide integrated functionality that forms an application. Applications are integrated to form products. The functionality of the application components is realised by using the functionality of the underlying service components. Each service component can thus be reused for several applications.

As shown in Fig. 4 below, the information models play an important role in the interaction between application and service components. These information models form a stable factor, allowing exchange of services and applications. Furthermore, the data objects that are exchanged between application and services can be made persistent by storing them in repositories. Since each of these repositories supports the same interfaces and information models, these repositories can be exchanged. When a product family wants to incorporate platform services and applications, it has to provide its own implemented functionality, e.g. a specific repository implementation, via the defined interfaces and information models so that platform applications and services can be reused. The use of data objects also supports the co-operation of services and applications on distributed systems.

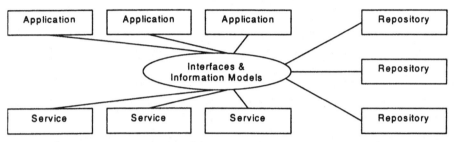

Fig. 4. Applications and Services

4.3 Dealing with Diversity

The product population platform is used in the context of different medical imaging products, each with its own architecture. Each of these products provides its own functionality and requires specific functionality from the platform. These products will each evolve over time, as will the platform. This means that the platform must have an excellent level of support for diversity and evolvability.

The architecture of the platform contains three main concepts that support the diversity needed across products and product families, as explained below:

- configuration data per component
- required interface concept
- information model concept

Each component within the platform has a required interface for configuration data. During start-up configuration data is read from the configuration database and is used to initialise each of the components. We will not elaborate further on this mechanism.

The required interfaces form explicit points of variability in the platform architecture. They allow the exchange of components that have the same provided interfaces, but have been implemented differently due to specific requirements. A simple example is the Logging interface. This is a provided interface of the Logging component within the platform, which is responsible for storing the logging data. The Logging interface is also a required interface for all other platform components. A specific product family is however not obliged to use the logging implementation provided by the platform. If there are specific logging implementation requirements, the product family can implement a specialised logging component that adheres to the Logging interface. This is illustrated in Fig. 5. All platform components perform logging through the Logging required interface, so none of the other components need to be changed.

Platform components should make as few assumptions as possible about their (execution) environment. As a design rule required interfaces should be defined for each function that may require variability in one or more products.

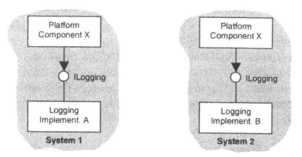

Fig. 5. Different Implementations for One Required Interface

The third variability mechanism is the use of abstract, general interfaces in combination with information models. In order to keep the interfaces simple and stable, most of the semantics are passed on as structured data objects that adhere to a specific information model, resulting in a declarative style. This allows a single implementation of the generic component that can support requirements from different products (see Fig. 6). If the differences in requirements cannot be met by one single implementation, however, the declarative style facilitates a completely different implementation, since the individual steps to arrive at the result are not defined in the interface.

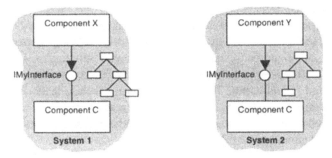

Fig. 6. One Implementation Supporting Different Requests

4.4 Defining Components, Interfaces and Information Models

The interfaces and their related information models play an important role in the development of the platform. We could say that instead of a component-centric architecture description we have an interface-centric architecture description. In a component-centric approach, the focus lies on describing the various components and not on how these components interact with each other. In an interface-centric approach, the focus lies on the interaction patterns between the components, thus putting the focus on interfaces. The following steps can be identified when defining interfaces and components for the platform:

- Determine which functionality must be provided, which kinds of components play a role in the solution, and which roles they play in collaborations. This is based on the domain knowledge.
- Based on the interactions between these kinds of components, define the interfaces and the information models for the information exchanged. These interfaces determine which roles components can play. The interfaces have to enable a declarative way of working.
- Using the interface specification, and taking the functional requirements into account, define the various components. Such a component definition heavily relies on these interface specifications, i.e. they can be seen as compositions of interface specifications. The functionality is then realised inside these components.

5. Experiences

In the previous sections, we described the approach for using components, interfaces and information models. Some of the experiences with this approach have taught us that:

- Clear separation of platform internal and external interfaces (and components) is important;
- When moving from a component-oriented approach to a more interface-oriented approach, do not forget good definitions of components;
- Prototyping of interfaces and components is an important means to validate the design choices at an early stage;
- Starting on a small scale gives the opportunity to fine-tune the process and to gain experience for next developments;
- It is important to involve all parties (platform and product groups) in the relevant decisions about the interfaces, information models and components;
- The declarative approach supported by the data objects makes it easier to build systems from components that are developed by different teams;
- The design should not become too generic; this leads to unnecessary implementation complexity and increased integration effort;
- The chosen interfaces and information models support the required diversity in the specific components.

6. Concluding Remarks

In this paper we have described our approach and experiences with components, interfaces and information models in the development of a product population platform for medical imaging products. Interfaces, information models and components support the required platform variability in the following ways:

- By paying explicit attention to interfaces, they will be usually more stable. The explicit handling of required interfaces means that each interface can be implemented by different components, each with their own behaviour. This enables diversity.

- The interfaces are expected to remain stable. The variation, both at a particular moment in time and over time, is enabled by the information models. An information model can have a generic part that applies to all products, in addition to product-family-specific extensions.
- By having separate components in the platform, it is possible to select the relevant components from the platform, add your own components, and build a product. This would not be possible if the platform was not componentised.

References

[1] Len Bass, Paul Clements, Rick Kazman, *Software Architecture in Practice*, Addison Wesley, Reading, Mass., 1998.
[2] Rob van Ommering, *Beyond Product Families: Building a Product Population?*, Proceedings of the IW-SAPF-3, Las Palmas de Gran Canaria, March 2000.
[3] Clemens Szyperski, *Component Software – Beyond Object-Oriented Programming*, Addison Wesley, Reading, Mass., 1997.
[4] Jan Gerben Wijnstra, *Supporting Diversity with Component Frameworks as Architectural Elements*, Proceedings of the ICSE 2000, Limerick, June 2000.

XVCL Approach to Separating Concerns in Product Family Assets

Hongyu Zhang, Stan Jarzabek and Soe Myat Swe

Department of Computer Science, School of Computing,
National University of Singapore
Lower Kent Ridge Road, Singapore 117543
{zhanghy, stan, soemyats}@comp.nus.edu.sg

Abstract. In this paper, we describe an XML-based language, called XVCL, for managing variants in component-based product families. Using XVCL, we can organize product family assets and instrument them to accommodate variants. A tool that interprets XVCL and provides semi-automatic support for asset customization is also introduced. In our projects, we applied XVCL to manage variants in UML domain models and in generic architectures for product families. We have achieved simple forms of separation of concerns (in both models and architectures) and we are investigating advanced forms in current work. We plan to compare XVCL to other emerging techniques that lead to separating of concerns in software models, documents, architectures and code.

1 Introduction

Advanced separation of concerns is now emerging as a new area in software engineering field. Advanced separation of concerns suggests that concerns in different dimensions are useful for different reasons for different stakeholder, thus it is necessary for developers to be able to identify, encapsulate and integrate any kinds or dimensions of concerns simultaneously.

Much work described in the literature focuses on the separation and composition of the concerns [11, 7]. In this paper, we describe our initial experiments with an XML-based language and tool for separating concerns and managing variants within concerns. We try to apply our approach to a wide range of product family assets including domain models, documentation, generic architecture and code. We have achieved simple forms of separation of concerns and we are investigating advanced forms in current work.

Variants are raised from the needs of product family [9]. A product family (or product line) is a set of products that share a common set of requirements, but also differ in certain ways. The variants within concerns are imposed, as we have to handle the variabilties among different product family members.

Like concerns, variants may cross cut each other: the impact of variants may scatter across many modules and may be also tangled with the impact of other variants. As the number of variants increases, the explosion of possible variant combinations and complex inter-dependencies among variants may further complicate the maintenance and evolution of the systems.

We designed an XML-based Variant Configuration Language (XVCL) [12], to handle variants in a product family. With XVCL, we can organize and manage a wide range of software assets such as domain models (e.g., in UML), software documents, product family architectures, code and test cases. We use the term x-frame to refer to the software asset in a product family instrumented for flexibility and reuse with XVCL commands. The XVCL processor is a simple yet powerful tool that can customize and compose the x-frames, to produce a specific system, member of a product family. Our XVCL is inspired by the frame technology from Netron Inc. [1]. The XVCL processor is an XML implementation of the industry-proven Frame Processor.

In our approach, concerns are encapsulated in groups of x-frames. An x-frame is instrumented with XVCL commands that show how to incorporate variants within concerns. Given specific variants, custom components/systems can be generated from the x-frame hierarchy on demand. Although the XVCL was originally designed for addressing variants within concerns, the basic concept can be extended to compose multiple concerns as well.

In the remaining part of the paper, we will illustrate our approach using examples from our domain engineering project on Computer Aided Dispatch (CAD) domain.

2 Related Work

As early as in 1970's, Parnas [9] proposed modularization, information hiding and separation of concerns principles for handling variants in a product family. Marco processors, PCL [10], application generators [2], Frame Technology [1], Object-Oriented framework [5], template and meta-programming techniques [3] – they all offer mechanisms to handle variants in product family.

Recent work focuses on advanced separation of concerns. A number of approaches have been proposed to address crosscutting concerns and concern compositions. In aspect-oriented programming [7], each computational aspect is programmed separately and rules are defined for waving aspects with the base code. In multi-dimensional separation of concerns and hyperspace approach [11], hyperslices encapsulate concerns in dimensions other than the dominant one and can be composed to form the complete system.

Our approach, in general, falls into the category of "generative programming" [3]. In our approach, concerns are encapsulated in groups of x-frames. A specific system, member of a product family, can be generated from the x-frame hierarchy on demand. Unlike AOP, we explicitly mark the points where code (or other reusable contents) related to variants (or aspects) can be inserted.

3 The CAD Domain Overview

We shall use the domain of Computer Aided Dispatch (CAD) to illustrate our approach. CAD systems are mission-critical systems that are used by police, fire &

rescue, health service, port operations and others. Figure 1 depicts a basic operational scenario and roles of a CAD system for Police.

Fig. 1. A basic operational scenario in CAD system for Police

Once a Caller reports an incident, the Call Taker captures the details of the incident and the Caller, and creates a task for this incident. The Dispatcher then selects suitable Resources (e.g. Police Units) and dispatches them to execute the task. The Resources carry out the task instructions and report to the Task Manager. The Task Manager actively monitors the situation and at the end - closes the task.

3.1 The Initial CAD System

We adopt an use-case driven, architecture centric approach to develop the initial (default) CAD system. The problem and solution space are decomposed along the class boundaries, which are identified from the use case analysis and design. A three-tiered architecture style guides the realization of the use cases.

Figure 2 gives a component view of the initial CAD system. Some of the concerns are separated and localized. User Interface concerns are encapsulated in the UI classes (e.g., the CallTakerUI class contains the code related to *Call Taker UI*). Concerns related to business process (workflow) are encapsulated in the control classes (e.g., the CreateTaskProcess class localized the implementation of the *Create Task* business process). Concerns related to entities are encapsulated in entity classes (e.g., Task class contains the implementation that provides the *Task data* service). Data Access class only provides the data access service.

The initial CAD system is modeled in UML, implemented in Java, and deployed on a CORBA-compliant component platform.

3.2 Variants in CAD Product Family

At the basic operational level, all CAD systems are similar - basically, they support the dispatch of units to handle incidents. However, considered the product family situation, there are also differences across CAD systems. The specific context of the operation (such as police or fire & rescue) results in many variations on the basic operational scheme. Here are some of the variant requirements in the CAD domain:

1. *Call Taker and Dispatcher roles* (referred to as CT-DISP variant). In some CAD systems, Call Taker and Dispatcher roles are separated (played by two different people), while in other CAD systems the Call Taker and Dispatcher roles are merged (played by one person). This "Call Taker and Dispatcher roles" variant has impact on system functionalities. For example, in the former case, the Call Taker needs to inform Dispatcher of the newly created task, but in the latter case, once the Call Taker creates a task, she/he can straightway dispatch resources (e.g., Police Units) for this new task.

2. *Validation* of caller and task information differs across CAD systems. In some CAD systems, a basic validation check (i.e., checking the completeness of the Caller and Task info) is sufficient; in other CAD systems, validation includes duplicate task checking, VIP place checking, etc.; in yet other CAD systems, no validation is required at all.

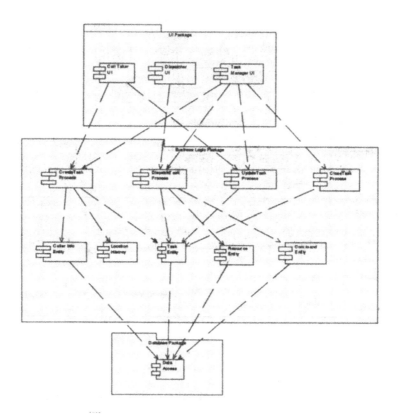

Fig. 2. The component view of the initial CAD system

Feature diagrams [6] are often used to represent the common and variant requirements in a domain. Figure 3 shows an excerpt from the CAD feature diagram. We use extensions described in [3]. The legend in Figure 3 explains notations. Mandatory requirements appear in all the instances of a parent concept. Variant requirements only appear in some of the instances of the parent concept being described. Variant requirements are further qualified as optional, alternative and or-requirements. An alternative describes one-of-many requirements. For example, the "Call Taker and Dispatcher roles" requirement described above has two alternative variants: "Separated" and "Merged". An or-requirement describes any-of-many requirements. For example, the optional "Validation" requirement has two or-variants: "Basic Validation" and "Advanced Validation", which means that the "Validation" requirement can be "Basic Validation", "Advanced Validation", or both or neither of them.

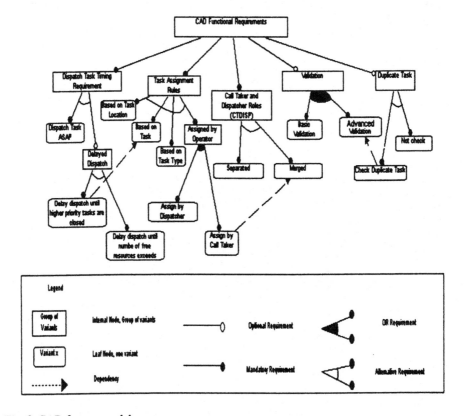

Fig. 3. CAD feature model

4 XVCL: An XML-based Variant Configuration Language

XVCL [12] is a simple markup language based on XML conventions. We use XVCL to organize domain assets and to instrument domain defaults with variants. Table 1 lists some of the major XVCL commands. We use the term *x-frame* to refer to domain defaults instrumented with variants marked as XVCL commands. An x-frame can be processed by the XVCL processor.

XVCL Command	Description
<X-FRAME name="*name*"> </X-FRAME>	Denotes an x-frame.
<X-PACKAGE name="*name*"> </X-PACKAGE>	Denotes a group of related x-frames.
<COPY x-frame="*x-frame*"> *customization commands* </COPY>	Includes a copy of the specified *x-frame* after applying *customization commands* to the *x-frame*
<INSERT-BEFORE name="*breakpoint*"> </INSERT-BEFORE> <INSERT name="*breakpoint*"> </INSERT> <INSERT-AFTER name= "*breakpoint*"> </INSERT-AFTER>	Allows insertions of fragments of information at the *breakpoint*. The inserted content can be placed before, after the breakpoint, or replace the existing content at the breakpoint.
<BREAK name="*breakpoint*"> </BREAK>	Specifies a *breakpoint* in an x-frame body, where customizations may occur.
<SET name="*varname*" value="*varvalue*"> </SET>	Declares an XVCL variable *varame* with value *varvalue*.
<VAR name="*varname*"/>	Denotes an XVCL variable *varname*.
<SELECT option="*variable*"> <OPTION value="*value*"> </OPTION> <OTHERWISE> </OTHERWISE> </SELECT>	Selects one of many customization options based on the *value* of the *variable*.

Table 1. A list of XVCL commands as XML tags

Our XVCL is inspired by the frame technology from Netron Inc. [1]. Frame method and tool have an excellent record in industrial applications. A quantitative study has shown that Frame technology can lead to reduction in time-to-market (70%) and project costs (84%) [1]. Frame technology is tightly coupled with COBOL. Our XVCL supports all major frame commands and provides extensions for distributed component-based systems written in Java. Being based on XML, XVCL is an open, extendable and easy to use language.

XVCL helps us organize product family assets and instrument them for flexibility, to achieve systematic and effective reuse. We applied XVCL to manage variants in software assets such as UML domain models and product family architecture. In domain models, an x-frame contains fragments of use case, activity diagram or object collaboration models. In product family architecture, an x-frame may contain a component (or part of it such as method, class, declarations of data structures) or a connector (defined, for example, in IDL).

We organize x-frames into a hierarchy that shows how to build complex x-frames out of simpler ones. Like in aspect-oriented programming [7], we also attempt to isolate different computational concerns (both functional and non-functional) into separate x-frames to achieve separation of concerns. For example, data x-frames only contain the implementation of the entity concerns. Workflow (Business Process) x-frames only contain the code related to flexible workflow concerns. Logging x-frames only contain the code related to the Logging concern. Different views of a domain model are also localized in separate UML x-frames. The composition of x-frames also achieves composition of multiple concerns.

In the rest of the paper, we will show how we apply XVCL in handling variants within concerns, using examples from the CAD domain engineering project.

5 Applying XVCL in Handling Variants in CAD Domain

5.1 Handling Variants within Concerns

To handle variants in CAD product family, we instrument each class in the initial CAD system (as shown in Figure 2) with XVCL commands. Figure 4 shows the x-frame for the *CreateTaskProcess* class in Figure 2. The *CreateTaskProcess* x-frame only pertains to the concern of *Create Task* business process.

```
<x-frame name="CreateTaskProcess">
    <set name="ERRMSG" value="Error in Creating the Task!"/>

    <copy package="Common" x-frame = "Header"/>
    package BusinessLogic;

    public class CreateTaskProcess {
        private Task      aTask;
        private String    szErrMsg = <var name="ERRMSG"/>;
            ...
        public CreateTaskProcess() {
            ...                   // Class Initialization code
            return;
        }
        <copy package = "CreateTaskFrames" x-frame = "GetCallerInfo"/>

        <copy package = "CreateTaskFrames" x-frame =  "GetTaskInfo"/>

        <break name ="Validation"/>

        <copy package = "CreateTaskFrames" x-frame =  "SaveTask"/>

        <break name="CT-DISP">
                <copy package = "CreateTaskFrames" x-frame = "InformDispatcher"/>
        </break>
    }
</x-frame>
```

Fig. 4. The *CreateTaskProcess* x-frame

```
<x-frame name="GetCallerInfo">
    public String GetCallerInfo(String szPhoneNumber) {
        Caller aCaller = new Caller(szPhoneNumber);      // Create a Caller Object
        String sCallerInfo = aCaller.name + aCaller.ID + aCaller.address;     // Prepare the Caller Info
        return sCallerInfo;
    }
</x-frame>
```

Fig. 5. The *GetCallerInfo* x-frame

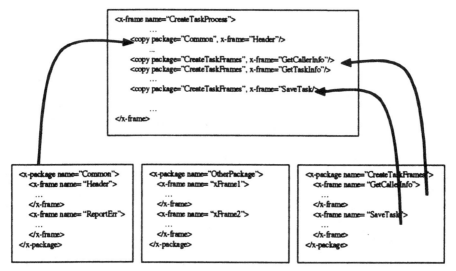

Fig. 6. The composition of the *CreateTaskProcess* x-frame

The *CreateTaskProcess* x-frame is composed of many x-frames, such as *Header* (contains reusable program header for program description, version info, copyright, etc.), *GetCallerInfo* (for the *Get Caller Info* function, as shown in Figure 5), *SaveTask* (for the generic *Save Task* function), etc. The composition of x-frames is achieved by the <copy> commands, which indicate the composition points. When the XVCL processor encounters the <copy> command, it will import the specified x-frame from the corresponding x-package, customize it and include it into the composite x-frame. In this example, all x-frames that are related to *Create Task* are stored in the *CreateTaskFrames* x-package. x-frames that can be reused by all other x-frames are stored in the *Common* x-package. Figure 6 illustrates the composition of the *CreateTaskProcess* x-frame.

A <break> command indicates the variation point where additional customization may occur to cater for unexpected variants. In Figure 4, the <break name="VALIDATION"> command indicates the variation point brought up by the variant requirement *VALIDATION*. The <break name="CT-DISP"> command indicates the variation point brought up by the variant requirement *CT-DISP*.

XVCL variables, such as "ERRMSG", provide another means to inject variability. XVCL variables are defined with default values, which can be modified during program customization to fit the specific requirement.

5.2 Specification Frame (SPC)

In our approach, the impact of the variants is encapsulated in a special kind of x-frames called *Specification Frames* (SPC). A SPC localizes the changes required for one variant. Figure 7 shows the x-frame for the VALIDATION variant.

```
<SPC name="VARIANT_VALIDATION ">
    <copy x-frame="CreateTaskProcess"    package="BusinessLogic">
      <insert name="VALIDATION">
        public boolean Validation(Task aTask) {
            ...              // Code about BasicValidation
            return ValidationResult;
        }
      </insert>
    </copy>
</SPC>
```

Fig. 7. A SPC for the VALIDATION variant

The <copy> command indicates the x-frame that this variant has impact on. In Figure 7, the VALIDATION affects the *CreateTaskProcess* x-frame.

The code specified in the <insert> section can be <insert>ed into/after/before the breakpoint defined in the x-frames specified by the <copy> command. For example, in Figure 7, the VALIDATION variant is specified as "Basic Validation". Code that meets the "Basic Validation" requirement can be <insert>ed into the "VALIDATION" breakpoint defined in the *CreatTaskProcess* x-frame during program customization.

Figure 8 gives an example of the x-frame that encapsulates the impact of the CT-DISP variant. The CT-DISP variant has impact on two x-frames: the *CreateTaskProcess* x-frame and the *CallTakerUI* x-frame. Code or x-frames that meets the requirement of "Merged Call Taker and Dispatcher Roles" can be <insert>ed into the breakpoints defined in these x-frames.

```
<SPC name="VARIANT_CTDISP">
    <copy x-frame="CreateTaskProcess"    package="BusinessLogic">
      <insert name="CT-DISP">
        <copy package = "CreateTaskFrames" x-frame = "DispatchTask"/>
      </insert>
    </copy>

    <copy x-frame="CallTakerUI"    package="UI" >
      <insert name="CT-DISP">
        public void AddDispatchButton(TaskInfo taskinfo) {
            ...         // Code about adding a button for dispatching task
            return;
        }
      </insert>
    </copy>
</SPC>
```

Fig. 8. A SPC for the CT-DISP variant

5.3 Composition

Once x-frames for classes and variants are separately identified and encapsulated, the XVCL processor can help us automate the composition process (including both customization and assembly). XVCL processor is a tool that can interpret the XVCL. During program composition, the XVCL processor reads x-frames specified in the <copy> commands, customizes them according to the instructions, and generates the executable source code. Figure 9 illustrates the composition process.

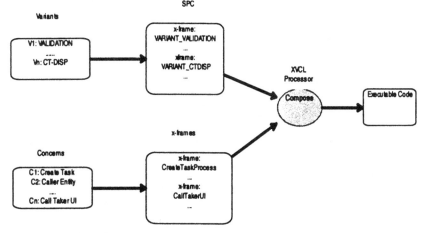

Fig. 9. The composition of the SPCs and the x-frames

Figure 10 shows the generated *CreateTaskProcess* class, which meets the specific requirements ("Basic Validation" and "Merged Call Taker & Dispatcher Roles") for a specific system, a member of CAD product family.

```
/*
 * Title:        CreateTaskProcess.Java
 * Description:  This is the control class for creating a task business process
 * Version:      v1.0
 */
    package BusinessLogic;

    public class CreateTaskProcess {
        private Task   aTask;
        private String szErrMsg = "Error in Creating the Task!";
            ...
        public CreateTaskProcess() {
            ...              // Class Initialization code
            return;
        }
        public String GetCallerInfo(String szPhoneNumber) {
            Caller  aCaller = new Caller(szPhoneNumber);          // Create a Caller Object
            String  sCallerInfo = aCaller.name + aCaller.ID + aCaller.address;  // Prepare the Caller Info
            return sCallerInfo;
        }
        public int GetTaskInfo(int nTaskID) {
            ...              // Code for getting task info
            return 0;
        }
        public boolean Validation(Task aTask) {
            ...              // Code about BasicValidation
            return ValidationResult;
        }
        public int SaveTask(Task aTask ) {
```

```
        ...              // Code about saving a task
     return 0;
   }
   public int DispatchTask(Task aTask ) {
        ...              // Code about dispatching a task
     return 0;
   }
 }
```

Fig. 10. The generated *CreateTaskProcess* class

5.4 Handling Variants in CAD Domain Model

We construct the CAD domain model by using UML and its extension mechanisms. Each UML diagram represents one view of a domain model. To handle variants in the domain model, we first convert UML diagrams into equivalent textual representation. Then we instrument the XML document with XVCL commands to accommodate variants within concerns. We can then perform the same kind of composition on textual UML diagram as we have done on the Java code. Finally, we convert the generated text back to the UML diagrams.

To achieve this, we use an XMI (XML Metadata Interchange) tool Unisys Rose/XMI to convert the UML diagrams to equivalent textual representation in XML. XMI [8] is a new OMG standard that combines UML and XML. XMI supports round-trip transformation of UML models from a tool (e.g. Rational Rose) to an XML file and back without loss of information.

To conserve the space, here we do not show the example of x-frames for handling variants in CAD domain model. We refer the reader to [4] for more details.

5.5 Variant Dependencies

Variants may be dependent on each other. For example, in the CAD domain, the "*Check Duplicate Task*" variant in Figure 3 is dependent on the "*Advanced Validation*". If the "*Advanced Validation*" requirement doesn't exist, it's not necessary to consider the "*Check Duplicate Task*" variant at all. We modeled some of the variant dependencies as dashed arrows in Figure 3.

As the volume of information in a domain model grows, the number of possible variant combinations explodes. Suppose we have m variants in requirement r_1 and n variants in requirement r_2. The total number of possible variant combinations is m x n. However, the total number of combinations is less if requirement r_1 and requirement r_2 are dependent.

Variant dependencies reduce the number of possible variant combinations. It is important to identify the variant dependencies so that the logical complexity of the system can be reduced. In our project, we only scratched the surface of this difficult problem. We are still experimenting with various types of variant dependencies.

6 Conclusions

We described an XML-based language, called XVCL, and a tool to manage variants in product family assets. With XVCL, we can organize product family assets (such as domain models, documents, test cases, product family architecture and its implementation), and instrument them to accommodate variants. In our projects, we applied XVCL to manage variants in the UML domain models and in the generic architecture for CAD product family. We have achieved simple forms of separation of concerns and our goal is to address advanced separation of concerns.

Acknowledgments

The XML-based tool for domain asset customization was inspired by Bassett's frames. This work was supported by research grant NSTB/172/4/5-9V1 funded under the Singapore-Ontario Joint Research Programme by the Singapore National Science and Technology Board and Canadian Ministry of Energy, Science and Technology, and by NUS Research Grant R-252-000-066.

Reference

1. Bassett, P. *Framing Software Reuse - Lessons from Real World*, Yourdon Press, Prentice Hall, 1997
2. Batory, D., Lofaso, B. and Smaragdakis, Y. JST: Tools for Implementing Domain-Specific Languages. *Proc. 5th Int. Conf. on Software Reuse*, Victoria, BC, Canada, 1998
3. Czarnecki, K. and Eisenecker, U. *Generative Programming: Methods, Tools, and Applications*, Addison-Wesley, Reading, 2000
4. Jarzabek, S. and Zhang, H.Y. XML-based Method and Tool for Handling Variant Requirements in Domain Models, To appear, *Int. Symposium on Requirements Engineering (RE'01)*, Toronto, Canada, August 2001
5. Johnson, R. and Foote, B. 1988. Designing reusable classes, *Journal of Object-Oriented Programming*, 1, 2, pp. 22-35.
6. Kang, K. et al. "Feature-Oriented Domain Analysis (FODA) Feasibility Study", Technical Report, CMU/SEI-90-TR-21, Software Engineering Institute, Carnegie Mellon University, Pittsburgh, Nov. 1990
7. Kiczales, G. et al. Aspect-Oriented Programming, *Proc. European Conference on Object-Oriented Programming (ECOOP)*, Finland, June 1997
8. OMG, XML Metadata Interchange (XMI) 1.1 RTF, OMG Document ad/99-10-02, 25 October 1999
9. Parnas, D. On the Design and Development of Program Families, *IEEE Trans. on Software Eng.*, March 1976
10. Sommerville, I. and Dean, G. PCL: A language for modeling evolving system architectures, *Software Engineering Journal*, 1996, pp. 111-121.
11. Tarr, P., Ossher, H., Harrison, W. and Sutton, S. N Degrees of Separation: Multi-Dimensional Separation of Concerns, *Int. Conference on Software Engineering, ICSE'99*, Los Angeles, 1999, pp. 107-119
12. Wong, T.W., Jarzabek, S., Soe, M.S., Shen, R. and Zhang, H.Y. XML Implementation of Frame Processor, *Symposium on Software Reusability, SSR'01*, Toronto, Canada, May 2001

AspectJ Paradigm Model: A Basis for Multi-Paradigm Design for AspectJ*

Valentino Vranić

Department of Computer Science and Engineering
Faculty of Electrical Engineering and Information Technology
Slovak University of Technology, Ilkovičova 3, 812 19 Bratislava, Slovakia
vranic@elf.stuba.sk
http://www.dcs.elf.stuba.sk/~vranic

Abstract Multi-paradigm design is a metaparadigm: it enables to select the appropriate paradigm among those supported by a programming language for a feature being modeled in a process called transformational analysis. A paradigm model is a basis for multi-paradigm design. Feature modeling appears to be appropriate to represent a paradigm model. Such a model is proposed here for AspectJ language upon the confrontation of multi-paradigm design and feature modeling. Subsequently, the new transformational analysis is discussed.

1 Introduction

In this paper the AspectJ paradigm model, a basis for multi-paradigm design for AspectJ programming language (version 0.8), is proposed. AspectJ is an aspect-oriented extension to Java [6]. Multi-paradigm design for AspectJ is based on Coplien's multi-paradigm design [3] (originally applied to C++ and therefore known as multi-paradigm design *for C++*) to a different solution domain. It employs feature modeling [5] for the task Coplien's multi-paradigm design used scope, commonality, variability, and relationship analysis [4].

Scope, commonality, variability, and relationship analysis, which is basically a scope, commonality, and variability analysis [1] enhanced with the analysis of relationships between domains [4], is used to describe the paradigms (mechanisms of a programming language) provided by the solution domain (i.e., programming language), as commonality-variability pairings [4, 3]. This way of describing paradigms is compact, but not expressive enough to meet the requirements of the transformational analysis, a process of aligning problem domain structures with available paradigms.

Moreover, the paradigms are often connected, but multi-paradigm design provides no means to express how. The application of feature modeling instead of scope, commonality, variability, and relationship analysis could help solve the problems mentioned here, as will be shown in this paper.

---

* This work was partially supported by Slovak Science Grant Agency, grant No. G1/7611/20.

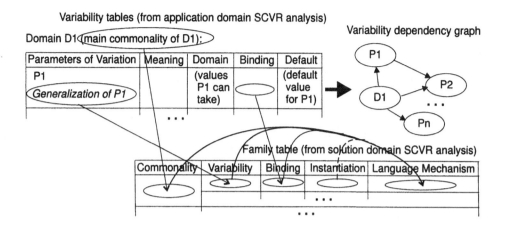

Figure 1. Transformational analysis in MPD.

Before presenting the actual AspectJ paradigm model, a critical survey of the issues regarding the multi-paradigm design for C++ (Sect. 2) and a basic information on feature modeling notation is provided (Sect. 3). Also, the relationship between feature modeling and techniques used in multi-paradigm design is analyzed (Sect. 4). AspectJ paradigm model is then presented (Sect. 5) and the impact of incorporating feature modeling into MPD on transformational analysis discussed (Sect. 6). Conclusions and further research directions close the paper (Sect. 7).

2 Multi-paradigm design for C++

Multi-paradigm design (MPD) for C++ [3] is based on the notion of small-scale paradigm [8], that can simplistically be perceived as a language mechanism (e.g., inheritance), as opposed to the (more common) notion of large-scale (programming) paradigm [2] (e.g., object-oriented programming; see [7] for a comparison of programming paradigms).

Figure 1 gives an overview of MPD. Scope, commonality, variability, and relationship (SCVR) analysis is performed on both domains, application and solution, with results summarized in variability (one for each domain) and family tables, respectively. The variability tables are incapable of capturing dependencies between the parameters of variation (that are also considered to be domains), so this is enabled by a simple graphical representation called *variability dependency graphs*. Each row of the family table represents a 4-tuple *(Commonality, Variability, Binding, Instantiation)* that determines the language mechanism.

The transformational analysis is actually a process of matching the application domain structures with the solution domain ones. First, the main commonality of the application domain, as identified by a developer, is matched with a commonality in the family table. This yields a set of rows in which the individual parameters of variation are resolved. Since parameters of variation (e.g., working set management) are too specific to be matched with general variabilities (e.g., algorithm) in the family table, each parameter of variation must be generalized before matching. This seem as a too big step to make at once.

The generalization problem and the fact that the matching is performed between variability table *3*-tuples and family table *4*-tuples (variability table has no instantiation column), are eclipsed by another problem: some C++ language mechanisms are missing from the paradigm model proposed. For example, classes and methods (procedures) are not even mentioned. On the other hand, inheritance is embraced in the model. Maybe Coplien considered classes and methods too trivial to mention, but this has not been stated explicitly.

Moreover, C++ mechanisms listed in the family table and negative variability table[1] are inconsistent with those described in the text [3]. Yet another problem with the paradigm model in MPD is that it does not capture the dependencies between paradigms. This is an important information, since there are paradigms that make no sense without other paradigms (e.g., inheritance without classes in C++).

3 Feature Modeling

Feature modeling is a conceptual modeling technique used in domain engineering. The version of the feature modeling whose notation is described here comes from [5].

Feature diagrams are a key part of a feature model. A feature diagram is basically a directed tree with the edge decorations. The root represents a concept, and the rest of the nodes represents features. Edges connect a node with its features. There are two types of edges used to distinguish between *mandatory* features, ended by a filled circle, and *optional* features, ended by an empty circle. A concept instance *must* have all the mandatory features and *can* have the optional features.

The edge decorations are drawn as arcs connecting the subsets of the edges originating in the same node. They are used to define a partitioning of the subnodes of the node the edges originate from into *alternative* and *or-features*. A concept instance has exactly one feature from the set of alternative features. It can have any subset or all of the features from the set of or-features.

The nodes connected directly to the concept node are being denoted as its *direct features*; all other features are its *indirect features*, i.e. *subfeatures*. The indirect features can be included in the concept instance only if their parent node is included.

An example of a feature diagram with different types of features is presented in Fig. 2. Features f_1, f_2, f_3, and f_4 are direct features of the concept c, while other features are its indirect features. Features f_1 and f_2 are mandatory alternative features. Feature f_3 is an optional feature. Features f_5, f_6 and f_7 are mandatory or-features; they are also subfeatures of f_3.

---

[1] A table that summarizes language mechanisms corresponding to exceptions to variability.

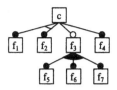

Figure 2. A feature diagram.

4 Applying Feature Modeling to Multi-Paradigm Design

Feature modeling is not unlike SCVR analysis. SCVR analysis, the heart of MPD, is based on the notions of commonality and variability (hence the name), and the notions of *common* and *variable* features is not unknown to feature modeling.

A common feature of a concept is a feature present in all concept instances, i.e. there must be a path of (pure) mandatory features leading from the concept to the feature. All other features are variable, i.e. any optional, alternative or or-feature is variable. The features to which variable features are attached are called *variation points*.

The scope in SCVR analysis, defined as a set of entities, is nothing but the concept in an *exemplar* representation.[2] The SCVR commonalities (assumptions held uniformly across the scope) and variabilities (assumptions true for only some elements in the scope) map straightforwardly to common and variable features of feature modeling, respectively.

The feature modeling enables to represent SCVR analysis commonalities and variabilities hierarchically and thus to express relationships among variabilities. For a solution domain SCVR analysis this means enabling to express how the paradigms it provides are related.

The most important results of SCVR analysis are provided in variability and family tables and variability dependency graphs.

4.1 Variability and Family Tables

Table 1 aligns the terms of feature modeling with its variability and family table counterparts (the columns). Only a fraction of the information provided usually by a feature model covers most of the needs of variability and family tables.

The parameters of variation are sometimes considered as subdomains (especially in variability dependency graphs). This is consistent with the feature modeling; the feature can be viewed as a concept.

Binding mode in feature modeling corresponds to binding time in MPD. The difference is that the set of binding times used in MPD is richer than the one used in feature modeling. This is due to a fact that the binding times in MPD are the actual binding times of a solution domain, like compile time, run

---

[2] The exemplar view of a concept is the one in which a concept is defined by a set of its instances [5].

Table 1. Feature modeling and MPD variability and family tables.

Feature modeling	Variability tables	Family tables
concept	commonality domain	language mechanism
common feature		commonality
variable feature		variability
variation point	parameter of variation	
alternative features	domain (of values)	
binding mode	binding	binding
semantic description, rationale	meaning	
default dependency rules	default (value)	
additional information		instantiation

time, etc. Feature modeling provides more abstract binding times, namely static, changeable, and dynamic binding. Each MPD binding time falls into one of these categories: source time and compile time bindings are static binding, link (load) time binding is a changeable binding, and run time binding is a dynamic binding.

The binding time applies only to variable features. It should be understood only as an auxiliary information to the transformational analysis. There is no notion of a unique binding time for a whole concept, as it is the case with a paradigm in MPD. Binding time should be indicated where it belongs—at variable features.

The feature modeling provides no counterpart for the family table column "instantiation", which indicates whether a language mechanism provides instantiation. This information should be provided as an attribute among the rest of the information associated with a feature model.

Possible values for instantiation in MPD are: *yes, no, not available (n/a)*, and *optional*. It seems that *no* and *n/a* values are redundant: if a language mechanism does not provide instantiation, it can be only because the instantiation is not available for that mechanism. The *yes* value indicates that a mechanism is used only with instantiation, while *optional* means that it can be used both with instantiation and without it (a class doesn't have to be instantiated to make a use of the static fields and methods). Furthermore, the *optional* value does not make sense in the application domain—the instantiation is either needed or not.

4.2 Variability Dependency Graphs

In variability dependency graphs, the nodes represent domains and the directed edges represent the "depends on (a parameter of variation)" relationship; domain corresponds to a concept or feature (considered as a concept).

Parts of variability dependency diagrams can be derived from the feature diagrams. Commonality domain depends on its parameters of variation, or—in the feature modeling terminology—concept depends on its variation points. But, generally speaking, while the relationships between domains in variability dependency graphs have a particular semantics, this cannot be said for the relationships in feature diagrams. Moreover, the feature diagrams are trees, not general graphs. All this suggests that variability dependency graphs should be kept as a separate notation. For each domain from the variability dependency graphs there should be a corresponding concept or feature in the feature model.

5 AspectJ Paradigms

AspectJ is an interesting programming language to explore in the sense of MPD because it supports two large-scale paradigms: object-oriented programing and aspect-oriented programming. However, large-scale view is not sufficient to make a full use of the programming language in the design. We must turn to a finer granularity and find out what small-scale paradigms, i.e. language mechanisms, AspectJ provides (referred to as *paradigms* in the following text). As was discussed in the previous sections, feature modeling will be employed to describe these paradigms.

Figure 3 shows a feature diagram of AspectJ. The paradigms in the feature diagram are indicated by a capitalization of the initial letter (e.g., Class). Binding time is indicated at variable features; if not, source time binding is assumed. Sometimes binding time of a feature depends on other features, as indicated in the diagram. In the text, the names of paradigms are typeset in the **boldface style**. The root of the feature diagram is AspectJ as a solution domain. It provides the paradigms that *can* be used, which is indicated by modeling the topmost paradigms as optional features.

The paradigm model establishes a paradigm hierarchy. Each paradigm is presented in a separate diagram as an alternative to the one big overall diagram. Wherever a root node of a paradigm tree is present, it is as if a whole tree was included there.

6 Transformational Analysis

Transformational analysis—aligning application domain structures with the solution domain ones—is the key part of MPD. The basic idea of how the transformational analysis is to be performed when these structures are represented by feature models is presented by the means of an example. Afterward, some general observations about the process of transformational analysis are given.

6.1 An Example: Text Editing Buffers

Text editing buffers[3] represent a state of a file being edited in a text editor. Text editing buffer caches the changes until user saves the text editing buffer into the file. Different text editing buffers employ different working set management

---

[3] The example discussed here is an adapted version of the text editing buffers example from [3].

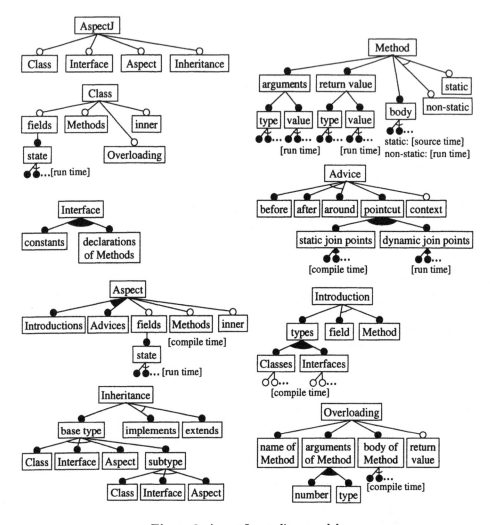

Figure 3. AspectJ paradigm model.

schemes and use different character sets. All text editing buffers load and save their contents into the file, maintain a record of the number of lines and characters, the cursor position, etc. The text editing buffer feature diagram is presented in Fig. 4. In the text, the feature names are distinguished by typesetting in the *italics style*. For simplicity, binding time and instantiation were not considered.

Now that feature models of both application and solution domains are available, we can proceed with the transformational analysis. We start with the unchangeable part of the application domain, i.e. the topmost common features. At this level a basic class or classes might be expected. The features *number of lines*, *number of characters*, and *cursor position* correspond to fields of the **class** paradigm. On the other hand, *yield data*, *replace data*, *load file*, and *save file*

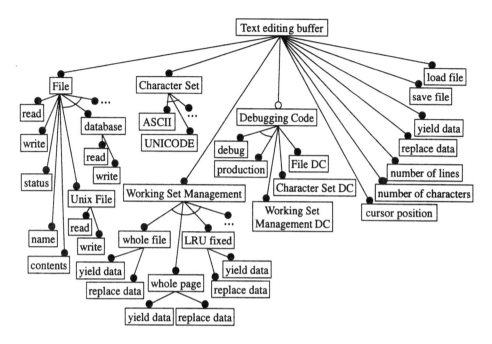

Figure 4. Text editing buffers feature diagram.

correspond to **method** paradigm. Accordingly, text editing buffer should be a class.

The rest of the topmost features are, apparently, variation points. The first one is *file*. All the files are read and written, but there are several file types and each one is read and written in a specific way. However, what is being read and written remains the same: *file name* and *contents*. We would probably expect to get the *status* of reading and writing. Thus we reached the leaves of the *file* subtree. If we compare these leaves to those of AspectJ feature diagram, they best match with arguments and return value. This brings us to **method** paradigm for *read* and *write* features.

We go up one level and discover that *database, RCS file, TTY,* and *Unix file* features match with the **class** paradigm. Accordingly, we expect that *file* would be a class too; so we match it with the **class** paradigm. The relationship between *file* and the file types matches with **inheritance**. Analogously, *character set* would be a class, and each type of it would be a subclass of that class.

The situation is similar with *working set management*: each type of *working set management* would be a class. But there is one difference: if we try to match it with **inheritance** further, we discover that we can match the whole *text editing buffer* with *base type* (because of *yield data, replace data*). So the *working set management* would be a primary differentiator.

Debugging code is somewhat special. It should be possible to turn it on and off easily (to obtain debug and production version, respectively). It is intended for *file, character set,* and *working set management* debugging; there is a special debugging code for each of those. For example, we would like to know when the file is being read from and written to. We already matched *file* with **class** and reading and writing with **method**, so it seems we must look for such a paradigm that can influence the execution of methods. There is only one such paradigm: **advice**. As **advice** is available only in **aspect** paradigm, the *file debugging code*, *character set debugging code*, and *working set management debugging code* will be aspects. *File debugging code* will provide two **advice**s, one for reading and the other for writing a file, and *character set debugging code* only one, as only a name of character set being used has to be announced.

Things are slightly more complicated with *working set management debugging code*, as we are interested in the general operations of working set management, as well as in the specific operations of each type of it (not displayed in the feature diagram). This points us to **inheritance**: *working set management debugging code* matches with a base aspect, while each of its or-subfeatures matches with a sub-aspect.

6.2 Transformational Analysis Outline

The text editing buffers example disclosed some regularities in the process of transformational analysis. The matching was performed starting at leaves towards the root. Rarely the leaves were considered alone. Mostly, a feature was considered together with its first-level subfeatures. Multiple nodes from the application domain can match with a single solution domain node if its name is in plural. Matching of nodes is done according to the type of the nodes, e.g. the overall match of mandatory or-nodes is successful if a match has been found for one or more leaves.

The matching is interdependent. If two features depend on each other, then it matters what paradigm the first feature was matched with. In other words, matching a feature with a paradigm constrains the further design.

Up to now, nothing has been said about how the actual matching of two nodes is performed. This can be compared to the matching between the domain commonality and parameters of variation from the variability table to the commonalities and variabilities from the family table. Two nodes match if they conceptually represent the same thing; do they—it is up to the developer to decide. However, a conceptual gap is significantly smaller than in the original MPD where developer was forced to make such decisions at a very high level of abstraction.

7 Conclusions and Further Research

The table representation of the application and solution domains used in multiparadigm design for C++ performs unsatisfactorily during the transformational analysis. Moreover, the C++ paradigm model is incomplete. The application of feature modeling instead of scope, commonality, variability, and relationship analysis leads to a more appropriate representation—the feature model—which enables to represent relationships between paradigms.

In this paper, such a paradigm model of AspectJ is proposed. The development of AspectJ paradigm model was based on an extensive comparison of feature modeling and multi-paradigm design (for C++) presented in Sect. 4. The use of the AspectJ paradigm model—a new transformational analysis—was demonstrated on text editing buffers example (Sect. 6) and then the outline of the process was drawn. The process of transformational analysis is more visible and easier to perform with feature models than with tables.

The AspectJ paradigm model presented in this paper provides a basis for further research on multi-paradigm design for AspectJ and its subsequent improvements are expected especially regarding the transformational analysis. The relationship of negative variability tables used in multi-paradigm design and feature modeling has to be investigated. Variability dependency graphs have to be incorporated into the transformational analysis. The transformational analysis results should be noted in a more appropriate form than a textual representation is. A graphical notation would be suitable here, which points to the need for a CASE tool. Besides these immediate issues, the discussion of scope, commonality, variability, and relationship analysis and feature modeling has tackled a deeper question of the relation of multi-paradigm design and generative programming [5].

References

[1] James Coplien, Daniel Hoffman, and David Weiss. Commonality and variability in software engineering. *IEEE Software*, 15(6), November 1998. Available at http://www.bell-labs.com/people/cope (accessed on May 14, 2001).

[2] James O. Coplien. Multi-paradigm design and implementation in C++. In *Proc. of GCSE'99*, Erfurt, Germany, September 1999. Presentation slides and notes. Published on CD. Available at http://www.bell-labs.com/people/cope (accessed on May 14, 2001).

[3] James O. Coplien. *Multi-Paradigm Design for C++*. Addison-Wesley, 1999.

[4] James O. Coplien. *Multi-Paradigm Design*. PhD thesis, Vrije Universiteit Brussel, Belgium, 2000. Available at http://www.bell-labs.com/people/cope (accessed on May 14, 2001).

[5] Krysztof Czarnecki and Ulrich Eisenecker. *Generative Programing: Principles, Techniques, and Tools*. Addison-Wesley, 2000.

[6] Gregor Kiczales et al. An overview of AspectJ. In *Proc. of ECOOP 2001—15th European Conf. on Object-Oriented Programming*, Budapest, Hungary, June 2001. Available at http://aspectj.org (accessed on May 14, 2001).

[7] Pavol Návrat. A closer look at programming expertise: Critical survey of some methodological issues. *Information and Software Technology*, 38(1):37–46, 1996.

[8] Valentino Vranić. Towards multi-pradigm software development. Submitted to CIT, 2001.

Aspect-Oriented Configuration and Adaptation of Component Communication

Dirk Heuzeroth[1], Welf Löwe[1], Andreas Ludwig[1], and Uwe Aßmann[2]

[1] Institut für Programmstrukturen und Datenorganisation, Universität Karlsruhe,
Germany
[2] PELAB, IDA, Linköpings Universitet, Sweden

Abstract. In order to compose components, we have to adapt them. Therefore, we pursue a transformational approach focusing on the communication view. We show how to separate the definition of communication from the definition of other system aspects, how to extract this definition from existing systems, and how to weave it back into the system. Our main concern is the reconfiguration of this aspect.

Keywords: Aspect-Oriented Programming, Component-Based Software Development, Program Transformation, Program Inversion

System *composition* aims at plugging modules [13] or components [15] together to construct systems. Composing modules means to establish interaction among them. Interaction essentially consists of service calls: components offer services to be called by other components and call themselves the services of other components. We can reduce this further to *communication* (transfer of data) and *coordination* (transfer of signals or control). With synchronized communication we model asynchronous communication (using buffers) as well as coordination /using synchronous communication without data transfer). Therefore, we focus on synchronous communication as a basis.

Components are often developed independently and hence, assumptions about the component environment are often violated. This is called a *mismatch*. For instance, the *signature* of a service call might not match the signature of the service definition in the component to be used. Or, interacting components might assume they are all *active* and responsible for initiating action. A component is *active* when it drives control of the system: it issues calls and triggers the actions of other components. Or, the component to be used might require a call *protocol* that does not match the needs of the client component.

In general, composition can only succeed when the system composer *adapts* the participating components accordingly. Adaptation is also necessary when the configuration of a system has to be changed due to some changed or new requirements. However, current modularization mechanisms do not allow to easily separate component interaction into modules as needed. Therefore, changing the interaction among components may involve changing all components taking part in the interaction. Hand-crafting the changes is then necessary on design level as well as on code level, which is both cumbersome and error-prone.

In the sequel, we demonstrate our technique to encapsulate communication aspects in modules. For now, we do not deal with protocol mismatches, which in general might lead to a complete rewrite of the algorithms concerned. Instead, we focus on the base communication mechanism and control of activity, as well as signature mismatches occuring in this context. Since we want to deal with existing software systems and the construction of new systems, our technique bases on a transformational approach that performs adaptions automatically, thus supporting the system composer. Essentially, we regard systems as consisting of several views and show how to define and integrate the communication view.

To demonstrate our approach, we present and analyze an example that illustrates the problems we outlined in the previous paragraphs. In Sect. 2 we describe our approach. This comprises our modularized communication view, the analyses necessary to cope with components and existing systems, the configuration and transformation steps, as well as system (re-)production. We also illustrate how to apply all these phases to our running example. Section 3 covers related work. In Sect. 4, we draw conclusions and outline future work.

1 Communication Scenario

Suppose, for a first try, we build a system essentially consisting of two building blocks, one to create the data, the other to process it, a producer-consumer scenario. Well known instances of this elementary scheme are workflow systems, compilers and to some degree client/server systems. Since we are only interested in the communication aspect, we regard this scenario abstractly, ignoring the details of a concrete instance. Suppose further that we have found two suitable components in our library that we would like to use; Figure 1 shows an example code in Java. On first glance, the use protocol requires to introduce a Producer p and a Consumer c to each other (p. setPartner (c); c. setPartner (p);) and to initiate action (p. start (); c. start ();).

Unfortunately, these components cannot interact in their present form. The producer assumes to be active and thus calls the consume method of consumer, transferring the Product data as parameter. The consume() method of the consumer, however, does not accept parameters, because the consumer assumes to be active, too. Thus, it calls the produce() method of the producer and expects a value returned from this method call. This signature mismatch is detected easily by the compiler or linker and is a consequence of the activity mismatch underneath. This kind of mismatch is rather frequent. It arises when mapping an object oriented design model to an implementation: in object oriented models, objects are usually considered active. The task of replacing communication mechanisms is also often found in reengineering scenarios.

To get rid of the mismatches, we have to adapt the participating components according to the following options: (1) We can make the producer active thus controlling communication and transform the consumer into a non-driving server component. (2) Instead, we can make the consumer the sole communication

```
public class Producer {                          public class Consumer {

  private Consumer consumer = null;                private Producer producer = null;

  public Producer() { }                            public Consumer() { }

  public Producer(Consumer c) {                    public Consumer(Producer p) {
    setPartner(c);                                   setPartner(p);
  }                                                }

  public void setPartner(Consumer c) {             public void setPartner(Producer p) {
    consumer = c;                                    producer = p;
  }                                                }

  public void produce() {                          public void consume() {
    Product p = new Product();                       Product p = producer.produce();
    System.out.println(p+"⎵produced.");             System.out.println(p+"⎵consumed.");
    consumer.consume(p);                           }
  }
                                                   public void start() {
  public void start() {                              for (int i = 10; i > 0; —i) {
    for (int i = 10; i > 0; —i) {                     consume();
      produce();                                     }
    }                                              }
  }                                              }
}
```

Fig. 1. A Producer and a Consumer Component

driver. (3) We can turn both components into non-driving ones that are driven by the using component. (4) We can leave both components driving control. This requires changing the communication from direct to indirect via a buffer acting as a mediator. Options (1), (2) and (3) are applications of a program transformation scheme called *program inversion* [6, 8].

The most severe case is changing from possibility (4) to any form of direct communication, since this comprises eliminating the buffer and therefore invasively changing every involved component: replace calls to the buffer by calls of services of the corresponding partner, then modify the initialization that makes the components know each other. This demonstrates that communication is not sufficiently encapsulated by current object oriented techniques.

2 Approach

Our task is to perform necessary adaptions of component interactions. Since the adaptions are invasive, it is dangerous and error-prone to perform them manually. We thus propose automatic adaptation driven by configuration information defining the setting to produce. To be useful for system construction and system composition, the system constructor must not be burdened with the invasive nature of adaptation but should only think and work in terms of adding or exchanging system properties. We have to hide the invasive nature of changes.

First, we define an abstract modularized communication model that allows to configure the desired communication pattern (Sect. 2.1). If we design from scratch, we could start with this abstract model. In reengineering or component-

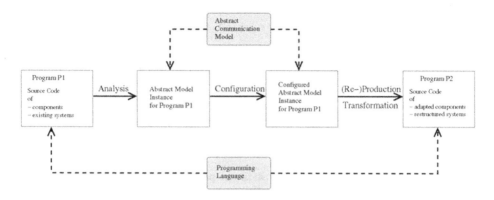

Fig. 2. Transformational System Configuration Approach

based scenarios, we construct this model using analyses that extract the relevant information from the sources (Sect. 2.2). Changing the abstract communication selects the actual communication pattern (Sect. 2.3). This step is independent of the programming language. Finally, the transformation step encodes the selected pattern in terms of the target programming language (Sect. 2.4). Figure 2 illustrates the whole process. In Sect. 2.4, we will show how to apply our approach to the example presented in Sect. 1.

2.1 Modularized Communication Model

As argued in the introduction and illustrated by the example in Sect. 1, calls of services are the relevant "hot spots", because these are responsible for interaction. We thus encapsulate calls that belong to the same communication relation of a module in a *port*. We explicitly represent communication by the communication primitives in() and out(). These are methods of an abstract *communication channel*, similar to CSP [5]. A channel connects communication partners and is a simple *connector* in the sense of architectural systems [4, 14]. Technically, a channel is an abstract data type at first.

```
public interface Channel<DataType> {
    DataType in ();
    void out(DataType c);
}
```

The communication primitive out() writes the data given as parameter to the channel; in() reads data from the channel and provides it as return value.

Both methods are synchronous in the sense of the Ada rendez-vous: A call to out() blocks until the corresponding call of in() and vice-versa. For an asynchronous out(), the channel acts as the receiver of data so that the caller can proceed immediately. The channel buffers the data. For an asynchronous in(), the channel stores the request for data but the receiver only blocks if the data is actually required.

The different kinds of semantics of a communication are determined by a concrete configuration. We deal with this in more detail in Sect. 2.3. On the

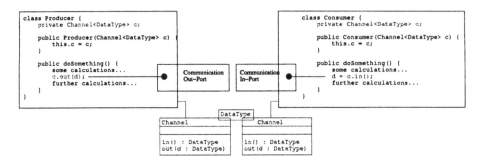

Fig. 3. Components with a communication out-port and an in-port, respectively.

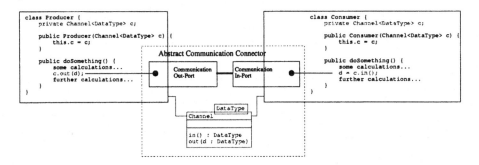

Fig. 4. Two components connected via an abstract communication connector

current abstraction level, we only care about the most essential communication aspect, i. e., the kind of data (DataType) and the points where data is written or read respectively. We thus define:

Definition 1 (Abstract Communication Ports). *An* abstract communication in-port *of a component is the set of calls to the method in() of the same abstract channel. Its type is the return type of the in() method.*

An abstract communication out-port *of a component is the set of calls to the method out() of the same abstract channel. Its type is the type of the parameter of the out() method.*

The set of abstract communication ports of a component defines its abstract communication interface *and thus its abstract communication behavior.*

Since ports aggregate communication calls that belong together, they allow their consistent change and management. Components indicate via their ports that data of a certain type is transmitted to or received from another component. Thus, the identity of a communication partner may be unknown until the component is composed. The concept of communication ports is illustrated in Fig. 3. Component Producer is equipped with a communication out-port and component Consumer with a communication in-port. Both components indicate their communication needs and requirements, but are not yet connected to each other. Hence, they can be used in different communication contexts. This leads to our definition of the term component:

Definition 2 (Component). *A component is a module with an interface that is prepared to exchange the communication coupling of the component via ports.*

We now want to specify that component Producer communicates with component Consumer by transferring data of type DataType. To express this, we introduce the notion of an *abstract communication connector.*

Definition 3 (Abstract Communication Connector). *An* (abstract) communication connector *is a relation among communication out-ports and communication in-ports that emit or accept data of the same data type.*

The relation establishes a connection between components by associating corresponding in- and out-ports to the same abstract channel. Figure 4 shows the result of applying an abstract communication connector to the components of Fig. 3. Components, ports and connectors are the elements of the abstract communication layer in our modularized communication view model.

2.2 Analyses

Analyses should detect the essential communication in a program, i. e., the in- and out-ports as designed. Let us assume for a first try that out-ports are parameters of method calls and return calls, and in-ports are formal parameters of methods and return points. Then it is trivial to detect in- and out-ports by static analyses.

Although this approach works for most practical cases, it fails for popular idioms like call-backs and events. In these architectures, the initial call only identifies the callee for the actual communication. Even worse: usually, a container captures the event listeners. If an event is fired, an iterator over this container delivers abstract event listener objects that receive the event object, which is the essential communication. This cannot be detected by static analyses, in general.

In order to detect the essential communications in a program we ought to merge static and dynamic analysis results. The VizzAnalyzer is a Java framework designed to perform such analyses. It consists of a package for the static analysis called COMPOST and a package for dynamic analysis and result visualization called VizzEditor.

The COMPOST [2, 11] framework performs static analyses and program transformations. The architecture is actually tailored to automate source code transformations. It consists of a compiler front-end, a pretty-printer as a back-end, and a library of small analyses, program generators and transformations. Currently, the front-end tool supports Java sources only, but the architecture works fine for other programming languages as well. The front-end performs syntactic and semantic analysis including name and type analysis and provides a convenient API to access the results. Except for trivial cases, it is not statically computable which method or attribute is actually called or accessed at run time and how often. Even data flow analyses cannot predict all branches and loop iterations. Similarly, it is not statically computable which concrete method is called on a polymorph call. An additional problem is the detection of implicit method calls as they occur if a default constructor of a base class is called. As objects are created at run time, relations over objects are dynamic by nature. All these relations can only be computed dynamically for a concrete program run.

The VizzEditor [10] framework provides run time information and visualization. Therefore, it accesses a debug interface and maps the obtained data to graphical imaging tools. The information to visualize is accessed at predefined program points such as method entries and exits or read/write accesses to variables (local variables and attributes), and at user defined breakpoints. The results of the dynamic analyses are displayed by the imaging tools. The package contains views for class, inheritance and call graphs.

In order to find event source - event handler pairs, we perform static analyses. COMPOST computes the class, inheritance and call graphs. Here, we easily find the program parts conforming to the event handler and source patterns. For these program parts (classes) we enable method calls for the dynamic analysis by the VizzEditor. We track the actual object identifiers sent to the potential event source and the calls back to these objects. Only those parts that match the dynamic pattern for event source - event handler pairs are finally displayed.

The method is not complete. Program parts that are not executed at run time cannot be refined. However, one may argue that parts that are less frequently executed are also less critical for restructuring. Still, we achieve an advantage compared to approaches depending on naming conventions: naming conventions can be broken and often are, especially in legacy programs requiring a re-engineering.

2.3 Configuration

Having specified the behavior of components in the abstract communication layer, we now substantiate communication by specifying different kinds of interaction patterns of calls to in() and out(), such as buffering, coordination, and destructive/non-destructive reading. Additionally, we specify activity and distribution patterns and communication mechanisms. We offer several connectors for common instances of the above configurations. Users may add further connectors by implementing the Channel interface. It is also possible to add further mechanisms to the above categories.

Substantiating the Semantics of the Abstract Channel The definitions of in() and out() in the abstract communication layer leave the interaction of calls to these methods open. This means, we did not specify the result of for example out(p1) out(p2) p3 = in() p4 = in(). If p3.equals(p2) and p4.equals(p1) hold, then the channel acts as a LIFO store (a stack). If p3.equals(p1) and p4.equals(p2) hold, then the channel acts as a FIFO store (a queue).

The next point to determine is the coordination behavior of in() and out(). For asynchronous calls, the channel needs to buffer the data. Otherwise, it must synchronize its clients. The last point concerns the kind of reading: Does calling the in() method destroy stored data or not? This distinction is important in case a piece of data shall be communicated to a set of components in a multi-cast. If the first read access destroys the piece of data, it cannot be delivered to all components except if it were stored in the buffer in a sufficient amount.

Activity and Distribution In our running example from Sect. 1, we illustrated the effects of marking components active. A component may act as a driver in one relation involving a set of methods and as a server in another relation involving another set of methods. Therefore, we assign an *activity property* to every *method* of a component.

The *distribution aspect* maps components to machines. It influences the actual communication mechanism that can be employed.

Communication Mechanisms There are different mechanisms that can be used to transfer data from one place to another. The principle of all mechanisms is to make data available in a storage location that the receiver can access. There are different forms of data transfer that follow this principle. Firstly, data may be written to and read from a *shared memory* location by direct memory access. Secondly, data may be sent from one location to another: either it is stored in buffers, directly transfered into the address space or local memory of the receiver, or passed as a parameter of a procedure call.

Procedure calls include communication and coordination. Depending on the distribution aspect, procedure calls can be local or remote. If two components are to communicate that are configured to run on different machines, a local procedure call cannot be employed. Of course, transfering data into a buffer may also involve procedure calls and parameter passing. We distinguish these cases nevertheless, because we regard buffered communication as indirect communication and passing data via a parameter to its recipient as direct communication. The above aspects lead to the following definition:

Definition 4 (Communication Configurator). *A communication configurator is a connector that defines the concrete semantics of the methods in() and out().*

A configurator is a metaprogram that defines a concrete class or object for the Channel interface for every communication relation. Moreover, it contains the communication mechanism to employ: buffered communication, direct memory transfer, or parameter passing via procedure calls. It adapts the concerned components and their use contexts accordingly.

Together with the activity and distribution aspects, the complete semantics of a communication is given. A communication configurator takes these aspects into account when they are mixed in. Fig. 5 illustrates a communication configurator.

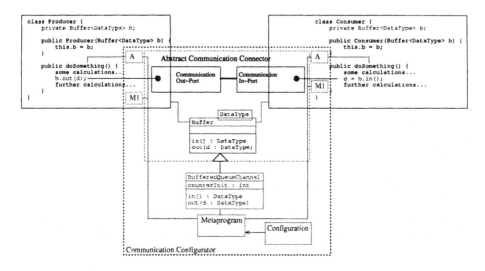

Fig. 5. A Configured Communication

Generalization More generally, ports and connectors are aspects in the sense of aspect-oriented programming [9], since they encapsulate code that cross-cuts the class structure of a system. We thus define:

Definition 5 (Aspect). *An* aspect *is a meta-object where 1. the* data part *contains the links to the concerned components, and 2. the* program part *is a (meta)program that adapts the concerned components identified by the data part according to configuration information.*

Since aspects are (meta-)objects, they can be regarded as components, too. Ports are aspects with empty program part. Connectors are components.

2.4 System (Re-)Production

The last step is to reproduce the source code of the working system. This is the task of the metaprograms contained in the connectors and includes the mapping of the configuration to a concrete programming language. Since we are not interested in cross-language transformations, we always retain the component programming language.

Example Revisited Reconfiguring our initial example so that the producer component drives control and communicates with the consumer as server component via a local procedure call would normally require to invasively change both components. Instead, we just feed our communication configurator with this configuration information and trigger system reproduction. The result is shown in Fig. 6.

```
public class Producer {                    public class Consumer {

  private Consumer consumer = null;          public Consumer() { }

  public Producer() { }
                                             public void consume(Product p) {
  public Producer(Consumer c) {                System.out.println(p+"⎵consumed.");
    setPartner(c);                           }
  }                                        }

  public void setPartner(Consumer c) {
    consumer = c;
  }

  public void produce() {
    Product p = new Product();
    System.out.println(p+"⎵produced.");
    consumer.consume(p);
  }

  public void start() {
    for (int i = 10; i > 0; —i) {
      produce();
    }
  }
}
```

Fig. 6. Initial example reconfigured

The out-port of the producer component coalesces with the activiation of the consumer component via the call to `consume`. It is thus represented as actual parameter to the call. The in-port of the consumer component is represented by the formal parameter of the `consume` method. Since we consistently generated these adaptions from the configuration information, we resolved the signature mismatch due to control violation presented in Sect. 1.

3 Related Work

The different techniques to realize modules like for example object-orientation did not succeed to encapsulate all items of change, especially interaction. This has also been noticed by other researches who proposed new techniques or concepts.

Architectural systems [4, 14] employ ports and connectors to encapsulate communication, too. These systems cannot handle existing code. Further, they only offer means to wrap building blocks, thus missing the power of invasive changes. Grey box connectors introduced in [1] try to alleviate the shortcomings of architectural systems. To reconstruct module connections, this approach requires the system composer to explicitly mark ports by special hooks. This restricts the applicability of the approach compared to our approach.

The work on communicating sequential processes (CSP) [5] constitutes the basis of our communication model. A shortcoming of the original work concerns the encapsulation of communication. Connectors must be realized by separate processes. The basic adaptation technique is wrapping. Relationships between a process interface and its internal structure are not considered. No effort is made to deal with existing code.

Several other approaches criticize modules as inadequate to encapsulate all items of change. Aspect-Oriented programming [9] introduces the notion of *cross-cut*: Code that cannot be encapsulated in modules. This approach collects cross-cuts in so-called aspects. Similar approaches introduce subjects [3] or hyper-slices [12]. These approaches claim to introduce new encapsulation concepts. In fact, these concepts are equivalent to modules but introduce new mechanisms. Compared to those, our ports are hyperslices as well as aspects. Our connectors are aspects. These approaches are too general to attack the source of mismatches and ignore that cross-cutting only occurs when systems are mapped to implementations. Cross-cutting is not a problem of the module concept, but the implementation facilities. Since current mechanisms (especially object-orientation) are obviously useful, we choose to enhance them to overcome the interaction encapsulation shortcoming. This allows us to cope with existing code and is thus preferable to inventing a new language. No matter what language we could have defined, it would not be able to overcome all mismatches.

4 Conclusions and Future Work

Our communication model allows to hide the invasive nature of changes, since changing communication behavior now means to give a corresponding configuration, add or exchange ports and connectors. Internal changes of components are hidden in the metaprograms of the connectors (aspects). Moreover, the model is independent of a certain programming language. The source code parsing and analysis phase allows to deal with existing systems or components. The configuration phase enables adapting components and restructuring of systems. Since we reproduce source code, the configuration and transformation results can be further processed by other tools.

Our procedure allows to execute desired changes (semi-)automatically and consistently. Thus, it supports the system composer and prevents errors which a human would probably introduce when performing changes manually. Hence, we meet our initial requirements.

We left some problems open. We did not discuss methods with side effects that are mapped to direct calls to perform the communication. In this case we must split communication from the side effect computation. Our simplified view may nevertheless be constructed by normalizing the code first [11]. Moreover, we only sketched the difficulties of retrieving all necessary information by static and dynamic analyses. Version management issues have been left out completely.

An issue of further research is the scalability problem: the numerous ports in an existing system require a recursive approach. Fortunately, components can be composed to larger components which, in turn, may be composed again. This should enable us to apply our method also to larger systems. Currently, we apply our approach to Linux components [7] within the scope of IBM´s SawMill-Linux project.

References

1. U. Aßmann, T. Genßler, and H. Bär. Meta-programming Grey-box Connectors. In *Proceedings of the 33rd TOOLS (Europe) conference*, 2000.
2. Uwe Aßmann, Andreas Ludwig, Rainer Neumann, and Dirk Heuzeroth. The COMPOST project main page. http://i44www.info.uni-karlsruhe.de/~compost.
3. Siobhan Clarke, William Harrison, Harold Oshher, and Peri Tarr. Subject-Oriented Design: Towards Improved Alignment of Requirements, Design, and Code. In *OOPSLA*, volume 34, pages 325–339. ACM SIGPLAN, ACM, Oct 1999.
4. David Garlan and Mary Shaw. An introduction to software architecture. In V. Ambriola and G. Tortora, editors, *Advances in Software Engineering and Knowledge Engineering*, volume 1, pages 1–40, Singapore, 1993. World Scientific Publishing Company.
5. C. A. R. Hoare. *Communicating Sequential Processes*. Prentice-Hall, 1985.
6. Michael A. Jackson. *Principles of Program Design*. Academic Press, 1975.
7. Trent Jaeger, Dirk Heuzeroth, and Uwe Aßmann. Automating the management of reusable system components. In *Proceedings of the 7th HotOS-Workshop*, 2001.
8. Tutorial JSD/JSP. http://cisx2.uma.maine.edu/NickTemp/JSP&JSDLec/jsd.html.
9. Gregor Kiczales, John Irwin, John Lamping, Jean-Marc Loingtier, Cristina Videira Lopes, Chris Maeda, and Anurag Mendhekar. Aspect-oriented Programming. In *ECOOP'97*, pages 220–242. Springer-Verlag, 1997.
10. Welf Löwe, Andreas Ludwig, and Andreas Schwind. Understanding software - static and dynamic aspects. submitted to 17th International Conference on Advanced Science and Technology, 2001.
11. Andreas Ludwig and Dirk Heuzeroth. Metaprogramming in the Large. In *Net.ObjectDays 2000 Tagungsband, 2nd International Conference on Generative and Component-Based Software-Engineering*, pages 443–452, October 2000.
12. Harold Ossher and Peri Tarr. Multi-Dimensional Separation of Concerns in Hyperspace. Technical report, IBM T. J. Watson Research Center, April 1999.
13. D. L. Parnas. On the Criteria To Be Used in Decomposing Systems into Modules. *Communications of the ACM*, 15(12):1053–1058, December 1972.
14. Mary Shaw and Paul Clements. Toward boxology: Preliminary classification of architectural styles. In *Joint Proceedings of the Second International Software Architecture Workshop and International Workshop on Multiple Perspectives in Software Development*, pages 50–54, 1996.
15. Clemens Szyperski. *Component Software, Beyond Object-Oriented Programming*. Addison Wesley, November 1997.

A Version Model for Aspect Dependency Management

Elke Pulvermüller[1], Andreas Speck[2], and James O. Coplien[3]

[1] Institut für Programmstrukturen und Datenorganisation,
Universitaet Karlsruhe,
D-76128 Karlsruhe, Germany
pulvermueller@acm.org
[2] Intershop Research Jena
D-07740 Jena, Germany
andreas.speck@intershop.com
[3] Bell Laboratories Lucent,
Naperville IL, USA
cope@research.bell-labs.com

Abstract. With Aspect-Oriented Programming (AOP) a new type of system units is introduced (aspects). One observed characteristic of AOP is that it results in a large number of additional (coarse-grained to fine-grained) system units (aspects) ready to be composed to the final application. With this growing number of system units the dependencies between them become vast and tangling. This results in the necessity of an improved management of the dependencies between these system units. Our paper investigates this problem, proposes a more general model (version model) to capture different facettes of AOP as well as a partial solution towards unit consistency based on versions.

1 Introduction and Problem

Aspect-oriented programming (AOP) extends the potential of common (e.g. object-oriented) software engineering allowing an improved realization of the "Separation of Concerns" principle [26]. Besides classes and objects, aspects are an additional type of system units. They serve to localize any cross-cutting code, i.e. code which cannot be encapsulated within one class but which is tangled over several classes [20]. Therefore, an aspect is a specific type of concern, namely a cross-cutting concern [19].

Beyond the identification and definition of aspects a further problem arises: How can an aspect configuration be verified and how can the correctness of their mutual dependencies and interactions be proved? The more aspects available the more complex and error-prone their combination if manually practiced. The importance of this problem in the context of aspect-oriented programming has already been detected in research as may be observed in [32], [31] and [28].

Examples of dependencies in practice are:

– Telecommunication domain:
A telephone switching station has to provide many different services. Some of them are cross-cutting and may be captured in aspects. Inserting aspects into the running system to extend the functionality may lead to interactions between the newly inserted units and the system units already part of the system. Research exists dealing with that problem (but still without employing supportive AOP concepts) [12].

– Aspects in distributed systems [27]:
In CORBA systems the communication code is strongly interwoven with the application code. In order to keep an application independent from the communication technique the communication code may be separated in aspects. When a client wants to access a service exposed by a specific server the client has to obtain an initial reference to the server. This can be done either via a name server or via a file-based solution (the reference is stored as a string in a file which is accessible for clients and server). Aspects realizing one of these two alternatives are exclusive. This is already known at design and implementation time.

– Cross-cuts in embedded systems [30]:
In the growing market of small embedded systems software is often reused when the same control hardware is modified in order to perform similar services. In the growing market of small embedded systems the industry aims at reusing both control hardware (with small adaptations to perform the specific services) and the corresponding software. The same microcontroller with a core software may be used in digital I/O devices or analogue I/O devices as well as in incremental resolvers. Except to a few statements (handling the internal data-flow) the software may be the same for all these devices. Besides a few adaptations of the software statements the software for all these devices may be reused. These statements may be ideally realized as aspects. The problem here is to assert that an aspect set woven into a specific base code is complete and that there are no data-flow statements missing (especially with respect to security and error handling code). Similar problems may be found when the systems have to be adapted to different often very similar field-bus protocols.

– In the AOP workshop at Rennes [19] L. Seiturier presented a Virtual Virtual Machine (VVM) [6]. A VVM is a micro-VM loading VMlets. A VMlet is similar to an Applet but describes an execution environment instead of an application. This technology provides an open virtual machine, a (micro) runtime, where each domain expert may build his/her specific execution environment adding or modifying functionality (by means of VMlets). Some of the VMlets may be aspects. The VVM, therefore, weaves aspects into a base system.

However, no coordinator or similar technology is implemented to avoid clashes between the separately loaded VMlets. If a VMlet is dependent (e.g. via initialization) from another one an error occurs.

In the remainder of the paper we introduce a version model and show how it captures and extends the idea of AOP in a more general way and, moreover, how it provides a means to preserve consistency and correctness. The approach presented is not limited to AOP but may be employed for any kind of feature composition. Section 3 examines the consistency and correctness conditions in more detail. Some related work may be found in section 4.

2 Version Model

Aspects may cross-cut object systems [20] on various levels of granularity: For instance, entire architectures may contain tangling classes or methods, classes may be cross-cut by methods or attributes and methods may be intersected by single statements.

Our approach for the aspect dependency problem is based on a broader viewpoint onto the different granularity levels of aspects: a version model. The version model integrates consistency and dependency management in a natural way. It allows the description of the internal structure of an aspect as well as the dependencies between aspects of a set.

The versions we discuss in our approach may be stored in versioning systems as elaborated e.g. in [13], [23] or [5]. Note that in contrast to that work, we do not focus on the administration and storage of different versions of software systems. In our approach versions are issues of system construction with aspects. However such versioning systems may be applied to manage the versions of our approach. The described version model and existing systems or research in the area of versioning systems, respectively, may complement one another.

A version model is a model explaining the construction of software systems using the notation of versions. A version describes a software core which may contain other versions and has to consist of a valid set of conditions.

Definition: (*Version*)
The symbol reflecting a version is V_i^k where k represents the granularity (0 stands for the most low-level granularity) and i gives the index distinguishing between versions on the same level of granularity.

Now we can inductively define the construction of versions:

$$Version\ V_i^0\ =\ 1\ \wedge\ Cond_i^0$$

where $Cond_i^0$ represents the condition [1] that has to be true for one version V_i^0 on level 0. $V_i^0 \in V^0$ where

$$V^0\ =\ \{\bigcup_{j=1}^{\infty} V_j^0\}$$

is the set of all versions on level 0.

---

[1] Several conditions may be unified in one condition.

Similarly we can define the induction step:

$$Version\ V_i^{(n+1)}\ =\ \bigwedge_{j=1}^{m} V_j^n\ \wedge\ Cond_i^{(n+1)}$$

with

$$Cond_i^{(n+1)}\ is\ true,$$
$$1 \leq l \leq m \leq |V^n|,$$
$$V_j^n \in V^n$$

□

In other words: a version is a set of conditions (a unification of the particular conditions of a certain version and all conditions of the subversions contained in the version). A condition is expressed as boolean expression (cf. section 3).

The operands in such an expression are conjunction, disjunction, negation. An example for a condition may be:

$$V2 \wedge (\neg C3 \vee C4) \wedge (V3 \wedge C3)$$

where $C3$, $C4$ represent some defined conditions (e.g. $C3$ represents something like "This version is only reasonable if used in France since the dialogues are in French language.")

The condition Vn (in the example: $n = 2$ or $n = 3$) means that a version V_i^k for one possible k and i with name Vn is part of the (partial) system.

We now use this version model to model both individual aspects as well as sets of aspects forming a valid configuration (i.e. resulting in a valid and reasonable system when woven). In fact, the border between these two poles is not fixed but is viewpoint respectively design dependent.

Some of the atomic conditions (in the first case), for instance, have the following appearance: $C1 = $ "Statement 1 (code line 1) has to be in the aspect" $= S1$, $C4 = $ "Statement 4 has to be in the aspect" $= S4$. These atomic conditions filter (and thus structure) some part of the total code into aspects.

Atomic conditions in the second case (i.e. the modeling of valid aspect sets based on versions) are, for instance: $A1 = $ "Aspect with name $A1$ has to be part of the system", $A2 = $ "Aspect with ID $A2$ has to be part of the system". There are different possibilities to uniquely identify an aspect (e.g. by name or by unique identifier).

Figure 1 shows an example for the second problem discussed in section 1. We demonstrate the usage of versions to model the construction:

- **Example for modeling individual aspects (fine-grained):**
  Based on a file containing statements (lines of code) as depicted in figure 1 a version reflecting an individual aspect may be constructed as follows.

$$Version\ V_1^1\ =\ 1 \wedge C_1^1$$

with $C_1^1 = C1 \wedge C2 \wedge \neg C7$ and the atomic conditions $Cn = $ "Statement n has to be part of the aspect" $= Sn$, $n \in \{1, 2\}$ and $C7 = $ "System is built for France" (additional condition).

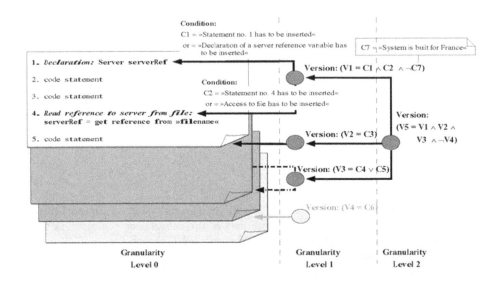

Fig. 1. Versions in a Distributed System

Note that we start with granularity 1 in this case. Granularity level 0 reflects single statements or their existence respectively.

Besides the construction of aspects, the version model also serves to express the proper combination of aspects which is a logical and consistent continuation of the first case but on a higher granularity (cf. the following example).

- **Example for modeling a set of aspects forming a valid configuration (coarse-grained):**
  Figure 1 contains a version ($V5$ respectively V_5^2) for a distributed system built from individual aspects. V_5^2 consists of V_1^1 and V_2^1 and V_3^1 but excludes V_4^1. In other words V_5^2 is valid when all the expressions or conditions of V_1^1, V_2^1 and V_3^1 are true and V_4^1 is false. Note that the versions of granularity level 1 also contain conditions which have to be true otherwise these versions are not valid. E.g. V_1^1 may represent the file-based reference of the server (expressed by C_1^1 and C_2^1) from non-French systems (represented by $\neg C_7^1$).

The version model, therefore, provides a consistent support for the software developer giving aid in producing semantic reasonable aspects and aspect combinations. It is independent of the underlying implementation language and technique realizing the concrete aspects and software system (e.g. AspectJ [1], HyperJ [3], meta-programming approaches or transformation systems [15], [24], [2], [10], respectively). The advantage of this formalization is that it provides a base for automatic configuration and checking. Having defined all relevant conditions it becomes possible to evaluate these boolean expressions and to find combinations which are semantically wrong (then the boolean expression of the version is false).

3 Conditions

There are several issues to be considered with respect to conditions: The classification, detection, collection, storage and evaluation of conditions as well as the different ways to express conditions in a formal way (allowing automatic evaluation). Each is an area of research by itself and in this paper we only touch some of these issues.

The concrete conditions are application dependent which means that they appear during the problem analysis and design of a system. Storing the conditions, i.e. the versions, in a repository results in a better reuse [21]. Besides the reuse of the aspects and additional system issues it becomes possible to use existing condition information to decide whether the reuse is semantically reasonable in a certain context.

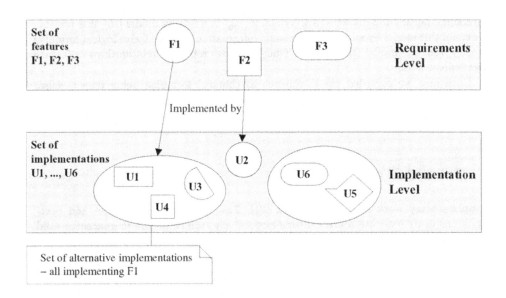

Fig. 2. Relationship between Requirements and Implementation Level

Following the traditional model for software development we can distinguish between two levels of semantic knowledge: Conditions referring to the high-level requirements and features and conditions on the level of the individual implementation. There is a clear connection between these two levels as exposed in figure 2.

Formally the relationship can be expressed as follows:
$U1, U2 \in Set1$; $F1, F2 \in Set2$ where $Set1$ is the set of implementation units and $Set2$ is the set of features on the requirements level. Let us assume that $U1$ implements (besides others) feature $F1$ and $U2$ implements $F2$ then the following property holds:

$$valid(U1, U2) \Rightarrow valid(F1, F2)$$
$$valid(F1, F2) \not\Rightarrow valid(U1, U2)$$

with function

$$valid(X,Y) = \begin{cases} 1 & : \text{X and Y form a} \\ & \quad \text{valid combination} \\ 0 & : \text{X and Y form an} \\ & \quad \text{invalid combination} \end{cases}$$

Function $valid(X,Y)$ may be calculated by evaluating the binary condition expressions.

The distinction between requirements and implementation level is not only limited to the development phase of a system or aspects but also exists in the maintenance phase where additional conditions may appear. This is due to the fact that it is impossible to capture all relevant dependencies and conditions from beginning. Additional conditions are added as needed or detected in a piece-meal growth manner [14].

Domain engineering [16] is a powerful means to detect and capture reoccurring and thus reusable conditions on the requirements level for a certain domain. While modeling the commonalities and differences of a domain, e.g. in a feature model [16], it is possible to extend this model by additional semantic information or even derive logical formulae directly from the model (the model already captures semantic relationships as feature interdependencies).

Until now we regarded the conditions as (binary) formulae being true or false. Though this is the first step for a mathematical foundation it does not yet reflect all the facettes of the reality. An extended version model also considers values between 0 and 1, temporal and contextual information and dependencies.

4 Related Work

Complementary work may be found in [21]. The Hoare triples (or pre- and post-conditions as its realization mechanisms respectively) are employed to guarantee valid aspect combinations during the combination process. While [21] concentrates on the checking mechanism and assumes given aspect combination rules without focusing on the rules themselves the approach in this paper provides a version model to structure the rules or conditions respectively. This is a step towards improved mathematical support dealing with a complex set of rules and also towards their (partial) automatic processing.

Related work may be found in all aspect-oriented and related approaches like subject-oriented programming [18], adaptive programming [22], adaptive plug & play components [25], composition filters [7] or also transformation systems [10].

Common to all these approaches is the goal to divide a system into smaller units in a more natural way aiming at reducing the gap between code and reality and managing the inherent complexity.

The proposed version model is orthogonal to these approaches as it provides a means to describe the system units in a more abstract way on different levels of granularity (in the form of a construction instruction). With the definition of versions it is possible to extract different views (i.e. versions) onto one unit. The most important difference is that the version model integrates (even focuses on) consistency and dependency management in a natural way.

With respect to composition validation further work may be found in [9]. In the GenVoca model composition is described with type equations. A design rule checking mechanism detects illegal combinations. GenVoca is a powerful layered model and thus mainly layered composition is considered.

Prior work at Bell Laboratories and in [29] about versioning has influenced the proposed version model approach.

Generative programming [16] is another related field which may augment the version model. The version notation may serve as an input for generators. Especially domain engineering as one part of the generative programming approach is, vice-versa, a means to detect, collect and describe semantic conditions. Feature models may be an important technique in this context.

Requirements engineering methods in general bear a potential to detect and explore semantic knowledge which is needed in the version model and captured in the conditions.

Also, AI technologies like expert systems may be used. [17] describes a way to use expert systems to support reuse of object-oriented frameworks by means of explicitly encoded design knowledge and user interaction. Aspect composition conditions are one type of such semantic design knowledge.

An alternative approach using logic to describe aspect dependencies may be found in [11].

University of Twente currently conducts research on fuzzy quantification of domain knowledge which is a promising complement to the presented work [8].

5 Summary and Conclusion

The version model proposed in this paper allows both, to describe the internal structure of an aspect and to define valid clusters of aspects. Using binary logical formulae for that purpose provides, moreover, a mathematical foundation to prove correctness of composition. This opens the field of logic and all its algorithms.

An extended version model also considers condition values in the range from 0 to 1. Semantic conditions may have a value in a range of discrete or analogue values. Currently, further research is going on in this area together with University of Twente in the context of the European project EASYCOMP [4].

References

1. *AspectJ - Aspectj-Oriented Programming (AOP) for Java.* http://www.aspectj.org, 2001.
2. *COMPOST Homepage.* http://i44w3.info.uni-karlsruhe.de/~compost/, 2001.
3. *HyperJ: another alphaWorks technology.* http://www.alphaworks.ibm/tech/hyperj, 2001.
4. *IST Project 1999-14191 EASYCOMP.* http://www.easycomp.org, 2001.
5. *RCE, VRCE, BDE; RCE: the Revision Control Engine.* http://wwwipd.ira.uka.de/~RCE/, 2001.
6. *Virtual Virtual Machines.* http://www-sor.inria.fr/projects/vvm/, 2001.
7. M. Aksit. Composition and Separation of Concerns in the Object-Oriented Model. *ACM Computing Surveys*, 28(4), December 1996.
8. Tekinerdogan B. Design and Experimentation of a Fuzzy Logic Controller for Evaluating Domain Knowledge. In *Proceedings of Second International Workshop on Softcomputing Applied to Software Engineering (SCASE)*, 2001.

9. D. Batory and B.J. Geraci. Composition Validation and Subjectivity in GenVoca Generators. In *IEEE Transactions on Software Engineering*, pages 67 – 82, 1997.
10. I. Baxter. Design Maintenance Systems. *Communications of the ACM*, 35(4):73 – 89, April 1992.
11. J. Brichau. Declarative Composable Aspects. In *Proceedings of Workshop on Advanced Separation of Concerns, OOPSLA*, 2000.
12. M. Calder and E. Magill. Proceedings of Sixth International Workshop on Feature Interactions in Telecommunications and Software Systems. IOS Press, 2000.
13. R. Conradi and B. Westfechtel. Version Models for Software Configuration Management. *ACM Computing Surveys*, 30(2):232 – 282, 1998.
14. J.O. Coplien. Re-evaluating the Architectural Metaphor: Towards Piecemeal Growth. Guest editor introduction to IEEE Software Special Issue. *IEEE Software Special Issue on Architecture Design*, 16(5):40 – 44, September 1999.
15. K. Czarnecki and U.W. Eisenecker. Synthesizing Objects. In *Proceedings of ECOOP'99, European Conference on Object-Oriented Programming*, LNCS 1628, pages 18 – 42. Springer-Verlag, June 1999.
16. K. Czarnecki and U.W. Eisenecker. *Generative Programming - Methods, Tools, and Applications*. Addison-Wesley, 2000.
17. W.D. De Meuter, M. D'Hondt, S. Goderis, and T. D'Hondt. Reasoning with Design Knowledge for Interactively Supporting Framework Reuse. In *SCASE*. http://progwww.vub.ac.be/Research/ ResearchPublicationsDetail2.asp?paperID=81, February 2001.
18. Ossher H. and P. Tarr. Using Subject-Oriented Programming to overcome common Problems in Object-Oriented Software Development/Evolution. In *Proceedings of the 1999 International Conference on Software Engineering*, pages 687 – 688, May 1999.
19. IRISA/IFSIC. Workshop on Aspect Oriented Programming, co-located with OCM, Objets, Composants et Modeles. Rennes, France, May 2001. http://www.irisa.fr/coo/OCM2001/programAOP.htm.
20. G. Kiczales, J. Lamping, A. Mendhekar, C. Maeda, C.V. Lopes, J.-M. Loingtier, and J. Irwin. Aspect-Oriented Programming. In *LNCS 1241*, ECOOP. Springer-Verlag, June 1997.
21. H. Klaeren, E. Pulvermüller, A. Rashid, and A. Speck. Aspect Composition applying the Design by Contract Principle. In *Proceedings of the GCSE'00, Second International Symposium on Generative and Component-Based Software Engineering*, LNCS, Erfurt, Germany, September 2000. Springer. to appear.
22. K. J. Lieberherr. *Adaptive Object-Oriented Software: The Demeter Method with Propagation Patterns*. PWS Publishing Company, 1996.
23. E. Lippe and G. Florijn. Implementation Techniques for Integral Version Management. In *Proceedings of ECOOP'91, European Conference on Object-Oriented Programming*, LNCS 512. Springer, 1991.
24. A. Ludwig and D. Heuzeroth. Metaprogramming in the Large. In *Proceedings of the GCSE'00, Second International Symposium on Generative and Component-Based Software Engineering*, LNCS, Erfurt, Germany, September 2000. Springer. to appear.
25. M. Mezini and K.J. Lieberherr. Adaptive Plug-and-Play Components for Evolutionary Software Development. In *ACM SIGPLAN notices*, volume 33, October 1998.
26. D.L. Parnas. On The Criteria To Be Used in Decomposing Systems into Modules. *Communications of the ACM*, 15(12):1053 – 1058, December 1972.

27. E. Pulvermüller, H. Klaeren, and A. Speck. Aspects in Distributed Environments. In K. Czarnecki and U. W. Eisenecker, editors, *Proceedings of the GCSE'99, First International Symposium on Generative and Component-Based Software Engineering*, LNCS 1799, Erfurt, Germany, September 2000. Springer.

28. E. Pulvermüller, A. Speck, M. D'Hondt, W.D. De Meuter, and J.O. Coplien. Workshop on Feature Interaction in Composed Systems, ECOOP 2001. Budapest, Hungary, June 2001. http://i44w3.info.uni-karlsruhe.de/~pulvermu/workshops/ecoop2001/. To be held.

29. M.J. Rochkind. The Source Code Control System. *IEEE Transactions on Software Engineering*, SE-1(4):364 – 370, December 1975.

30. A. Speck, E. Pulvermüller, and M. Mezini. Reusability of Concerns. In C. V. Lopes, L. Bergmans, M. D'Hondt, and P. Tarr, editors, *Proceedings of the Aspects and Dimensions of Concerns Workshop, ECOOP2000*, Sophia Antipolis and Cannes, France, June 2000.

31. P. Tarr, L. Bergmans, M. Griss, and H. Ossher. Workshop on Advanced Separation of Concerns, OOPSLA 2000. Minneapolis, USA, October 2000. http://trese.cs.utwente.nl/Workshops/OOPSLA2000/.

32. P. Tarr, M. D'Hondt, L. Bergmans, and C.V. Lopes. Workshop on Aspects and Dimensions of Concerns: Requirements on, and Challenge Problems for, Advanced Separation of Concerns, ECOOP 2000. In J. Malenfant, S. Moisan, and A. Moreira, editors, *ECOOP 2000 Workshop Reader*, LNCS 1964, page 203 ff., Sophia Antipolis and Cannes, France, June 2000.

An Object Model for General-Purpose Aspect Languages

Stefan Hanenberg, Boris Bachmendo, Rainer Unland

Institute for Computer Science
University of Essen, D - 45117 Essen
{shanenbe, bachmendo, unlandR}@cs.uni-essen.de

Abstract. Aspect-Oriented Programming on the one hand supports a separate treatment of different concerns in software development. On the other hand it provides "weaving" technologies for knitting together such individual concerns in software systems. Since the aspect-oriented approach is an extension of the classical OO-paradigm it requires an enhancement of well-known language constructs on the meta level. Although some general-purpose aspect languages (GPAL) are available in the meantime, no commonly accepted object model has yet been proposed. Consequently a common terminology is still not available what substantially hinders the spread of good and useful concepts. This paper proposes an object model, which represents the foundation of the GPAL *Sally*. We compare our model in respect to AspectJ which is by far the most popular and well-established aspect language and, therefore used by a wide community.

1 Introduction

The development of complex software systems requires to consider and individually treat multiple *concerns* and their relationships. Examples of concerns are not only the functionality of a system but also non-functional issues such as failure handling, communication, coordination strategies, memory reference locality, etc. (cf. [7]).

Object-oriented programming (OOP) technologies provide for issues like separation of concerns mechanisms like delegation and inheritance. However, these techniques are inadequate to handle concerns whose behavior *crosscuts* the program structure - concerns that require the programmer to explicitly insert fragments of code into the primary application functionality. This produces *tangled code* and, consequently, software systems that are difficult to understand and to maintain.

Aspect-Oriented Programming (AOP, [9]) has been emerging as a technology for expressing multiple concerns in software development, along with "weaving" technologies for knitting together different concerns in software systems. This is mainly achieved by handling the *tangled-code phenomenon* which is a result of the so-called *tyranny of dominant decomposition*.

In the meantime several general-purpose aspect languages (GPAL) are available. Nevertheless, no commonly accepted object model has yet been proposed. This currently leads to a lack of a common terminology and decreases the identification of common concepts in GPALs. This paper proposes an object model which forms the backbone of the GPAL *Sally*.

Aspect-orientation has mainly been influenced by AspectJ [8] which has been developed at the Xerox Palo Alto Research Center. It is by far the most popular and best-established aspect language and, therefore, is widely used. For this reason we will introduce our model and compare it to AspectJ.

The remainder of this paper is structured as follows. Section 2 introduces the basic concepts of aspect languages. Section 3 discusses the model of AspectJ and identifies main weaknesses. Section 4 discusses the proposed object model and introduces our GPAL Sally. Section 5 compares our approach to related work. Finally, section 6, summarizes and concludes this paper.

2 Motivation

The core elements of object-oriented approaches are objects, classes and inheritance (cf. [13]). Classes are templates from which objects can be deduced. Moreover, they define interfaces for their objects and encapsulate, respectively hide their implementations as well as their data structures. Objects collaborate by sending messages to each other. Every message sent to a certain object has to match a corresponding signature of its underlying class. Classes consist of attributes and methods. Inheritance is a mechanism for deriving new class definitions from existing ones, which means that an existing class is taken as a basis and adapted to the new needs by adding new and/or overriding existing attributes and methods; i.e. inheritance means to extend existing classes to achieve new ones that better fit to the underlying needs. Inheritance is discussed in some detail in [12].

Object-oriented software development heavily relies on inheritance. Whenever utilizing instances of existing classes cannot solve a problem at hand an appropriate class has to be extended in a way that it meets the expected requirements. Changing the behavior of objects means to extend a class and to override the implementation of one or more methods. However, since the implementation of a method is encapsulated, it is not possible to replace only a part of it. Instead, a new class has to be derived from the existing one. Then a new one that fits the needs at hand can override the original method. Well-known design patterns like *template method* or *strategy* (cf. [5]) can be used to realize varied behavior. However, using these patterns assumes that the software developer already knows which part of the implementation is to be modified. Such a fortunate situation is not given if some software has to be extended by certain aspects that were not yet treated in the development process.

In summary one can say, that object-orientation is a very crude technique when behavior has to be adapted to new demands.

Aspect-Oriented Programming permits to treat different aspects or concerns separately. Typical concerns of this kind are concurrency or persistency (cf. [7]). Adding

82

a certain new aspect to existing code usually means to add crosscutting code. In order to overcome the rigid and inflexible approach of object-oriented technology towards the change of behavior general-purpose aspect languages like *AspectJ* [8] or *Sally* [11] introduced an additional extension point: *interaction*.

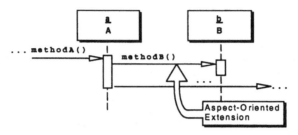

Fig. 1. Extending interactions using AOP

Figure 1 shows how an instance of A in methodA() interacts with other objects. The object-oriented approach would just permit to reuse the method-implementation "as is". With the aspect-oriented approach the interaction between A and B can be adapted by adding some code to this specific interaction. Whenever the specified interaction happens this additional code is executed. For this purpose the participants of the interaction and the code which is supposed to be executed need to be specified. In this context we use the term *aspectual invocation*, because the code is executed although it is not directly embedded in A. Such code, that can be used for an arbitrary number of different interactions, is called *crosscutting code*.

The intention of the here proposed model is to give a clear understanding of the ingredients a GPAL should consist of to support the extension of interactions. Thereto we will first discuss AspectJ in the next section and afterward suggest an alternative model the GPAL Sally is based on.

3   AspectJ

AspectJ [8] from the Xerox Palo Alto Research Center is currently the most popular GPAL. In this section we will shortly introduce the model AspectJ and discuss its weaknesses. We will introduce the model "bottom-up" what means, that we show how interaction can be specified before we explain what aspects consist of.

3.1   Join Points

[8] introduces *join points* as "principled points in the execution of the program" which means that they refer to situations where certain interactions take place. AspectJ provides different kinds of join points, like *method call join points* or *method call reception join points*. They are used for expressing the actions "calling a method" or "receiving a method call".

For example, `receptions(void methodB())` is a valid join point in AspectJ. It specifies the actions of receiving a method call `methodB()`. This join point can be used in combination with the join point `instanceof(B)`. This combination describes the action "an instance of B receives a method call `methodB()`".

In this example a combination of two join points is needed in order to specify the receiver of the method call. However, it is not possible to specify the caller. Furthermore, we need to know how join points can be combined and what combinations are valid.

The complexity of declaring and combining join points this way is immense. Furthermore, it augments the number of keywords of the language substantially. In AspectJ each join point only specifies one part of an interaction and therefore needs to be combined with other join points in order to describe a complete interaction.

3.2 Pointcuts

Pointcuts are named combinations of join points. In AspectJ these combinations need to be defined as boolean expressions. For example, a valid pointcut definition is:

```
pointcut callB():  instanceof(B) &&
                   receptions(void methodB())
```

This pointcut is named `callB` and describes, that an instance of class B receives a message `methodB()`. A pointcut is *activated* whenever the execution of a program reaches a point that matches this specified pointcut.

While this pointcut definition just permits to specify the receiver of an interaction, other combinations allow to specify the caller. Usually AspectJ does not handle caller and receiver at the same time. But since an aspect logically belongs to both participants of an interaction there is often a need to treat both participants at the same time. By regarding only callers or receivers AspectJ is very similar to the approach of composition filters [1].

Additionally there is the problem to determine whether a pointcut is valid. For example a pointcut like `(instanceof(B) && instanceof(A))` will never be valid, if none of those classes extends the other.

3.3 Advice

An *advice* specifies the code that is to be executed whenever a certain interaction occurs. Therefore, it represents the crosscutting code because it may be executed at several execution points in the program.

The declaration of an advice needs to specify at what pointcuts it is meant to be executed, i.e. every advice refers to one or more pointcuts. Additionally, it must specify at what point in time it is supposed to be executed: an advice may either be executed *before* or *after* a certain interaction happens or may even *replace* it.

In AspectJ pointcut methods are defined as follows:

```
before(): aPointcut() {...do something...}
```

This pointcut method is executed before the pointcut aPointcut is activated (the modifier before() is responsible for deciding, at which point of the interaction the method should be invoked).

AspectJ does not permit to name advices. We regard this as a disadvantage because an advice is a special method which is invoked whenever a pointcut is activated. If advices cannot be named and, therefore, cannot be treated as special methods then pointcuts cannot have advices as interaction participants.

3.4 Aspects

In general-purpose aspect languages aspects are constructs that represent those fragments of code which crosscut several decomposition units or modules. [4] defines aspects as follows: "A model is an aspect of another model if it crosscuts its structure".

Lieberherr et al. call this in [10] the *aspectual paradoxon*: the nature of an aspect is that it cannot be decomposed into separate modules. Although this argument seems to be obvious, it neglects one important thing: aspects cannot be decomposed as long as there is no mechanism like aspectual invocation.

On the implementation level aspects are constructs which consist of attributes, methods, pointcuts, and advices. Join points are not part of the aspect in AspectJ, however, part of the pointcut.

AspectJ distinguishes between classes and aspects. Classes describe components (the term component is used in [9] to differentiate units of a system's functional decomposition from aspects) and aspects are statically woven into them (cf. [2]).

Distinguishing classes and aspects has some severe disadvantages: a developer always has to be aware of two different views on his system: the object-oriented view and the aspect-oriented view. While the first can be extended by aspects, the second can hardly be adapted to new needs, e.g. advices cannot be extended.

Another critical point is the static weaving in AspectJ. After the weaving process the original information like pointcuts and advices is lost. So it is not possible to analyze a compiled aspect in order to find out what parts of the object-oriented system are influenced by this particular aspect.

Extending Aspects

Classes and aspects are very similar in AspectJ, e.g. it is allows to extend abstract aspects via inheritance. On the other hand it is neither allowed, that an aspect extends a class via inheritance, nor to extend non-abstract aspects via inheritance. Extending a concrete aspect is also not allows. In this way the instructions for extending classes and aspects are quite complex.

3.5 Creating Aspect Instances

In AspectJ instantiating aspects is realized differently from the object-oriented approach where developers have to create instances explicitly. Instead, the aspect declaration specifies how aspect instances are created during run-time. For example, the aspect declaration

```
aspect X of eachobject(instanceof(B)) {
    pointcut callB(): instanceof(B) &&
                      receptions(void methodB())
    before():callB (){...}}
```

specifies, that for every instance of B a new instance of X is created. In fact, the result of this declaration consists of two steps: first, defining, at what time a new aspect instance will arise, and second, to which object this instance will be bound to.

The first step can be handled by the mechanism of aspectual extension, because a new aspect instance will be created whenever the interaction "someone calls a constructor of B" occurs.

The problem of the second step is that it directly influences the semantic of the aspect. In the example above an instance of aspect X is created for each instance of B. As a result instanceof(B) in pointcut callB() just refers to *that* instance. If the aspect does not contain such an eachobject-declaration instanceof(B) would refer to every instance of B.

While the first step is a redundant language feature, because it can be realized via aspectual extension, the second step leads to some confusion: the meaning of pointcuts defined in an abstract aspect without an eachobject-clause is changed if subaspects introduce such a clause.

In summary we can say, that this kind of creating aspect instances unnecessarily increases the complexity of the language.

All the above-mentioned weaknesses reduce the flexibility of the aspect-oriented approach and reduce the possibility to maintain aspect-oriented systems.

4 Object Model of Sally

The following model forms the foundation for our GPAL Sally. The model will be introduced "bottom-up". The terms used are mainly based on AspectJ.

4.1 Join Points

Our point of view differs from the AspectJ join point model. The intention is to make the join point declaration as easy as possible without the need for operations to combine them. A join point based on our model is a complete specification of a participant in an interaction. Provided that corresponding get() and set()-methods exist for every attribute a join point is always a method belonging to a certain class. So a join point specification is a 4-tuple consisting of the following elements:

- class identifier
- return type identifier
- method identifier and
- parameter type identifiers.

A valid join point declaration in Sally is:

```
joinpoint j1 {B, void, methodB, null}.
```

This join point declaration differs from the approach in AspectJ in several ways:

- A join point describes just one participant of an interaction.
- A join point describes the participant entirely; its description includes information like the class identifier, the return type identifier, the method name, and the parameter type identifiers.
- A join point is described on a neutral level; i.e. it contains no information about the context (as a caller or receiver of a message) in which it may be used.
- A join point is always named.

This model offers a number of essential advantages in comparison to AspectJ. The usage of join points is much easier, because neither additional keywords are needed nor operations to combine join points, because Sally does not distinguish between different types of join points. Hence a join point is named it can be used for different interactions and as caller or receiver.

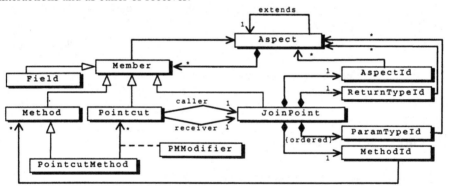

Fig. 2.: GPAL Object Model (extract)

While join points just specify one participant in an interaction, the following section describes how to specify the entire interaction.

4.2 Pointcuts

For specifying interactions it is sufficient to define a pointcut as a tuple consisting of two join points as shown in figure 2: one join point for the caller and one for the receiver.

For example, specifying a pointcut for the interaction between methodA() of an instance of A and methodB() of an instance of B can be done in Sally as follows:

```
joinpoint c {A, void, methodA, null};
joinpoint r {B, void, methodB, null};
pointcut p1 {c, r};
```

This defines two join points c and r, and a pointcut p1, which defines c as the caller and r as the receiver. Although there is an additional effort to define each named join point the advantage of this approach is that every join point can be used in an arbitrary number of pointcuts without the need to redefine it.

4.3 Advices / Pointcut Methods

We argued in section 3.3 that in AspectJ advices are not named and can therefore not be used as extension points for further aspects. Furthermore advices are lost after weaving.

To avoid such problems advices in Sally are special methods and therefore are called *pointcut methods*. On the meta level it means that the metaclass Pointcut-Method extends the metaclass Method (fig. 2). So, the Sally definition of the point-cut method corresponding to the advice in section 3.2 is:

```
public void beforeAPointcut() before aPointcut {
   ...do something... }
```

The pointcut method modifier (keyword "before" in our example) is an attribute of the relationship between pointcut methods and pointcuts (fig. 2) and declares at what point in time in relation to the interaction a pointcut method is invoked. Because a pointcut method is a special method, it can be addressed by join points and, in this way, can be extended in an aspect-oriented way.

4.4 Aspects

On the implementation level aspects are constructs which consist (in Sally) of attributes, methods, join points, pointcuts, and pointcut methods (fig. 2).

Based on that model it is possible to distinguish between classes and aspects. An aspect has in addition to attributes and methods join points, pointcuts, and pointcut methods. So, the metaclass Aspect is supposed to extend the metaclass Class. The question arises whether both metaclasses are to be considered in a general-purpose aspect language.

In 3.4 we argued that the distinction between classes and aspects leads to the problem that the developer always has to be aware of the object-oriented and the aspect-oriented view on the system. This requires to cleanly separate between aspects and classes in the entire development process. The main reason for it is, that classes and aspects in AspectJ are not extensible in the same way. On the other hand the benefit of aspect-oriented programming is that this approach allows to adapt existing systems. AspectJ does not follow this aim consequently, because concrete aspects cannot be extended using inheritance and its advices cannot be used as join points. [6] discusses the problem of adapting an aspect's behavior in more detail.

To support a higher degree of flexibility Sally does not differentiate between classes and aspects. This is possible since members of the construct Class (attribute, method) are a subset of the members of the construct Aspect (attribute, method, join point, pointcut, pointcut method). That means the classification of objects is realized using aspects. A traditional object-oriented model still remains the same, because it consists of aspects which have no join points, pointcuts and pointcut methods.

Extending Aspects

If aspect languages do not support classes any longer it has to be defined how aspects can be extended to cover inheritance between classes as well.

As long as aspects only consist of attributes and methods they are equivalent to a normal object-oriented class. In this case extending an aspect means, that the subaspect has the same methods and attributes as its parent. The question is, how the aspect-oriented elements behave with respect to inheritance.

In AspectJ inheritance between aspects behaves similar to object-oriented inheritance: join points, pointcuts, and pointcut methods defined in a super-aspect are also available on the level of the sub-aspects. It is also possible to define abstract aspects that may have abstract pointcuts. But as discussed above extending aspects is restricted to abstract aspects.

In Sally inheritance between aspects is similar to inheritance in AspectJ: a sub-aspect inherits all elements defined in its parent. It also allows to define abstract join points.

```
abstract aspect X {
  joinpoint j1 {A, void, methodA, null};
  abstract joinpoint j2 {, void, methodB, null};
  pointcut p1 {j1, j2};   ...}
abstract aspect Y extends X {
    joinpoint j2 {B,,,,};}
```

In the example above join point j2 is abstract because it leaves the definition of the aspect identifier to its sub-aspect. Pointcut methods relating to pointcut p1 will not be invoked as long as j2 is not concrete.

The aspect Y is a sub-aspect of X since it defines the aspect identifier as B. So, the pointcut p1 activated whenever an instance of B receives a message methodB() from a method methodA() from an instance of A.

Overriding methods and pointcut methods in an aspect is identical to the mechanism in Java. A method (or pointcut method) overrides another one in its super-aspect, if it has an identical signature.

4.5 Creating Aspect Instances

In 3.5 we argued, that the way aspect instantiation is realized in aspects is a redundant language property and unnecessarily increased the complexity of the language. Furthermore this declaration is responsible for the complex definition of inheritance in AspectJ.

Our model does not define how aspect instances are created, because we do not differentiate between aspects and classes. Therefore the developer needs to define at what time aspect instances should arise. After its creation an aspect instance can be bound to other aspects (or aspect instances) and, in that way, can react on their interactions. Binding a certain aspect instance to another is achieved by a common interface which is implemented on the root level.

```
abstract aspect X {
    joinpoint j3 {*, *, *, *};
    joinpoint j4 {B, B, new, *};
    joinpoint j1 {A, void, methodA, null};
    joinpoint j2 {B, void, methodB, null};
    pointcut p1 {j1, j2}; pointcut p2 {j3, j4};
    public static void createXInstances() after p2 {
        receiver.return.register(new X());}
    public void aPCMethod() before p1 {...}}
```

The code example above creates an instance of X every time a new instance of B is created. This is achieved by defining the pointcut pc2 which is activated whenever some caller sends a message to the constructor of B with arbitrary arguments (the wildcard * means "some", the method identifier new identifies the constructor). Then the static pointcut method createXInstances() is executed, which binds a new instance of X to the new instance of B. Within every pointcut method the special object receiver is available which itself has the variable return, which refers to the returning object of an interaction. The method register() is part of the root aspect and, therefore, is available in every aspect in Sally.

After this the pointcut method aPCMethod() of the newly created instance of X is executed whenever an instance of A sends in methodA() the message methodB() to the instance of B the new X is bound to.

5   Related Work

Our view on AOP was mainly influenced by AspectJ. As discussed above our model differs in some ways from AspectJ: the join point and pointcut model in AspectJ allows to react to incoming or outgoing messages, i.e. it is very similar to the composition filters approach [1]. Our approach explicitly supports a two-way interaction in which the caller as well as the receiver can be specified. Furthermore we argue that pointcut methods are special kinds of methods and aspects are special classes.

On the implementation level the main difference between Sally and AspectJ is the process of weaving. In Sally weaving is realized in a different way than discussed in

[2]: it is neither pure static nor pure dynamic. Static weaving abandons the structure of aspects by inserting the aspect code into the original code. Because of that it is not possible to apply reflection to woven aspects. Also, pure dynamic weaving cannot be achieved as long as static pointcut methods exist which need to relate aspects to each other on the aspect level and not on the instance level. In Sally an aspect that contains one or more pointcuts is registered at all receivers of the specified interaction at compile time using some trivial byte code transformation. Because of this Sally, in contrast to AspectJ, does not need to transform source code every time a new aspect is introduced. Instances of aspects have to be assigned at run-time. So the structure of aspects is preserved in Sally and allows to analyze aspects and aspect instances during run-time using a provided reflection API.

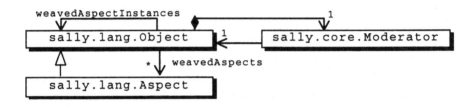

Fig. 3. : **sally.lang.Object**

There are some similarities between Sally and the Aspect Moderator Framework [3]: in Sally every aspect inherits from a certain class (`sally.lang.Object`) which refers to a certain moderator-object (fig. 3). This moderator is responsible for activating pointcuts of registered aspects. In contrast to [3] we think that the moderator should be embedded in the GPAL instead of being a construct at the design time of a software system. Using the aspect moderator framework implies, that the developer has to be aware of certain aspects, that may change the systems behavior in the future. But as explained in the beginning this is usually not the case.

6 Conclusion and Further Work

We proposed an object model for general-purpose aspect languages and proved its applicability and usefulness by taking this model as a basis for the implementation of our aspect language Sally. The object model helps the developers to get a common understanding of what elements an aspect language should consist of and how AOP extends the object-oriented approach. We discussed the mechanism of aspectual invocation and explained, how this can be achieved using the AOP-specific elements.

We critically analyzed the model underlying AspectJ. It turned out that is suffers from a number of severe flaws with respect to reuse and extension of aspects. Moreover, AspectJ requires to treat the object-oriented and the aspect-oriented view as two different views whose relationship have to be coordinated very carefully during the software development process. Our model eliminates these flaws and treats both perspectives uniformly in one view.

The proposed model can be directly used to support reflective properties of a GPAL. To achieve this we abandoned the use of static weaving.

Currently we investigate how the mechanism of synchronizing different aspects can be applied to our model and implemented in Sally.

References

1. Aksit, M., Wakita, K., Bosch, J., Bergmans, L., Yonezawa, A.. Abstracting Object-Interactions Using Composition-Filters. In: object-based distributed processing, R. Guerraoui, O. Nierstrasz and M. Riveill (Eds.), LNCS, Springer-Verlag, (1993) 152-184,
2. Böllert, K.: On Weaving Aspects. Position paper at the ECOOP '99 Workshop on Aspect-Oriented Programming, (1999)
3. Constantinides, C., Bader, A., Elrad, T., Netinant, P., Fayad, M.: Designing an Aspect-Oriented Framework in an Object-Oriented Environment. ACM Computing Surveys, Volume 32 , No. 1es, (2000)
4. Czarnecki, K., Eisenecker, U.: Generative Programming: Methods, Tools, and Application. Addison-Wesley, (2000)
5. Gamma, E., Helm, R., Johnson, R., Vlissides, J.: Design Patterns: Elements of Reusable Object-Oriented Software. Addison-Wesley, (1995)
6. Hanenberg, S., Unland, R.: Concerning AOP and Inheritance. In: Mehner, K., Mezini, M., Pulvermüller, E., Speck, A. (Eds.): Aspektorientierung - Workshop der GI-Fachgruppe 2.1.9 Objektorientierte Software-Entwicklung. Paderborn, 3./4. Mai 2001, Technischer Bericht der Universität Paderborn tr-ri-01-223. (2001)
7. Hürsch, W., Lopes, C.: Separation of Concerns. Northeastern University, Technical Report, no. NU-CCS-95-03, (1995)
8. Kiczales, G., Hilsdale, E., Hugunin, J., Kersten, M., Palm, J., Griswold, W.. An Overview of AspectJ. Appears in ECOOP 2001 (2001)
9. Kiczales, G., Lamping, J., Mendhekar, A., Maeda, C., Lopes, C., Loingtier, J., Irwing, J.. Aspect-Oriented Programming. Proceedings of ECOOP '97, LNCS 1241, Springer-Verlag, (1997) 220-242
10. Lieberherr, K., Lorenz, D., Mezini M.: Programming with Aspectual Components, Technical Report, NU-CCS-99-01, Northeastern University, Boston (1999)
11. Sally: A   General-Purpose   Aspect   Language,   http://www.cs.uni-essen.de/dawis/research/aop/sally/, January 2001
12. Taivalsaari, A.: On the Notion of Inheritance. In: ACM Computing Surveys, Vol. 28, No. 3, (1996) 439-479
13. Wegner, P.: Dimensions of object-based language design. In: N. Meyrowitz (Ed.), Proceedings of OOPSLA '87, SIGPLAN Notices 22, 12, (1987) 168-182

Generic Visitor Framework
Computing Statistical Estimators

Jean-Daniel Nicolet

403, Route de Matailly, F 74520 Valleiry, France
web site: www.linkvest.com/jdn/index.htm
email: jean-daniel.nicolet@linkvest.com

Abstract. This paper presents a concrete application of template meta-programming techniques to provide a generic, efficient and type-safe implementation of statistical estimator computation using visitors.

Introduction

This paper shows a concrete use of template meta-programming techniques to deal with a concrete problem often encountered when building financial or other statistically oriented reports. The problem itself is thus not new. The innovative part is the technique used to solve it both in a generic and type-safe way. Meta-programming ways that are now popular among the community are put to good use to achieve both flexibility and efficiency.

The chosen concept (recursive template inheritance) has been fully modeled and documented in UML[1], thus allowing the reader to understand the numerous pieces involved in the construction of the puzzle and their relations. The corresponding code skeleton has been generated automatically with the help of the modeling tool Rational Rose®[2]. The resulting implementation is very efficient and economical in code size.

Problem Description

The handled problem is commonly arising when dealing with financial data in order to compute statistically oriented reports. Statistics is viewed here in a broad sense to include several common operations one may apply to a data series to obtain some analytical result summarizing a series' properties. The involved operations correspond roughly to the summarizing operators found in the SQL database language (count, sum, average, etc.).

These standard SQL operations may be extended with additional statistical operations we will explain here in more details, like standard deviation, skewness and excess, which constitute the core of our framework, and were also important to show the way toward a generic solution.

---

[1] Unified Modeling Language, see [OMG 00]

[2] http://www.rational.com

All these statistical operations are based on so-called statistical moments mathematically defined as follows. For a discrete random variable ξ, the kth moment at location c is given by:

$$m(\xi - c)^k = \sum_{i=1}^{n} (x_i - c)^k P_i \tag{1}$$

The x_i are the data values and the P_i their probability of occurrence. The first interesting moment is for $c = 0$ and $k = 1$. It is called "mean" and corresponds to the usual average of a data series. It is designed by the Greek letter μ. Other interesting moments are obtained for higher exponents (the k value) and for c being precisely equal to the mean. One speaks then of centered moments (centered around the mean). The 2nd order moment is called the variance and is a measure of the scattering of the data around the mean. The third moment allows for computing the so-called skewness, which gives an idea of the asymmetry of the data around the mean, and the fourth moment leads to the excess, measuring the narrowness of the data around the mean.

Mathematical properties of these moments that we don't want to explain further allow to compute them in one pass when receiving the data as input, thus avoiding a first pass on the data to compute the mean (the moment's center), followed by a second pass to compute the corresponding power sum. This is especially important when dealing with big data sets. Moreover, doing all computations at once is usually more efficient.

The computation of, say, the excess implies not only computing the 4th moment, but also all the smaller order ones. Said otherwise: if you have invested the effort to be able to compute the excess, then all other interesting estimators come essentially for free. This recursive property is at the core of our solution.

The data item type may vary, but it must support the fundamental arithmetic properties. The other degree of freedom is constituted by the kind of statistical operation to apply.

The Visitor Pattern

The above situation (double polymorphy) is usually best handled with the help of the visitor pattern [GHJ+ 98]. The main hierarchy contains the classes of the objects to manipulate and the operations are reified into visitor classes applying to the data objects' classes. The computation of an operation on a data series may then be implemented by the following steps:

1. Instantiate and initialize a visitor object according to the requested operation.
2. Iterate over the data series
3. Apply the visitor to each data item.
4. Extract the final result from the visitor object

This pattern suffers from some well-known limitations. If it is relatively easy to add a new visitor, the work involved is much bigger when adding a new kind of data item, because the whole visitor hierarchy must then be extended. There are more sophisticated variants, as described in [Ree 98], that mitigate somehow these inconveniences, but they are not completely eliminated.

In the financial world we are interested in, the situation leans precisely over the bad side. It is much more common to add a new kind of data item than a new kind of statistical operation. Instead of having a data item hierarchy, we'll use static polymorphism instead. This means concretely that we don't impose hierarchical constraints on the data items but rather templatize our visitors with the data item type. Various data item types are rarely to never mixed in practice, so this decision is perfectly acceptable. Let's call this template parameter "T" and name it the fundamental data type.

Just as for any template parameter, we must precise the behavioral properties we expect from the actual types being substituted during template instantiation. They must be default-constructible, assignable, equality-comparable and less-than-comparable, as defined in the SGI standard template library documentation[3]. They must also have fundamental arithmetic properties, described in the following table:

Table 1. Fundamental type arithmetic requirements

Name	Example	Post-condition
Construction from a number	`T t( 3 )`	
Default constructor, should behave like a construction with 0	`T t;`	The same as `T t( 0 )`
Arithmetic operation	`u + v;`	Convertible to T

These requirements are quite natural for types that should behave like numbers. The second one is just a matter of comfort. The ability to build an object from a (whole) number without additional information is required, because statistical computation formulas need such multiplicative constants. Multiplicative constants could be of a different class than the data item itself. A traits template parameter bound to the fundamental type T would then be required. This would also imply mixed arithmetical operators offering the appropriate combinations, but we ignore these extensions in the rest of this document.

An efficient Power Algorithm

The first sub-problem to solve is of mathematical nature. Computing statistical moments implies first being able to compute integral powers of data items. Because we plan to design a generic solution, we need a generic way of computing integral powers efficiently. The corresponding meta-function has obviously two parameters: our fundamental type T and the integral power exponent, called n that we require to be positive. Negative values could be handled too, but it is simpler to deal with that

---

[3] see www.sgi.com/tech/stl/DefaultConstructible.html, www.sgi.com/tech/stl/Assignable.html, www.../EqualityComparable.html and www.../LessThanComparable.htmlfor more details

case elsewhere, as we will see. The best choice is to define a functor class, implementing the power computation as function operator. This leads us to the following UML class diagram:

The intermediate class appearing in this diagram, with the <<Place holder>> stereotype, is an artifact of UML to allow the exact specification of the template parameters in the inheritance relation. It is also a way to make the parameter substitution apparent on the diagram. Its stereotype, as well as the absence of colors is there to remind the reader that it does not contribute to generate C++ code

The naïve power implementation would simply use a for loop to multiply the function argument x n times by itself, but this is knowingly far from optimal. For example, x^4 can be computed by squaring x twice, thus using only two multiplications instead of three.

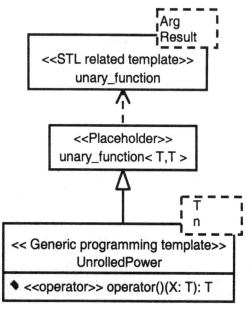

Fig. 1. The unrolled power meta-function template

The optimum computation is still an open problem in general [Knu 81], but there exists a nearly optimal solution simple enough to implement it easily. It is based on the binary decomposition of n. If we express this algorithm in its conventional form, it looks as follows:

```
for(T v = x; n > 1U; n >>= 1)
{
  v*= v;
  if (odd( n ))
    v*= x;
}
```

The above algorithm is not absolutely correct. The case n == 0 should be handled specifically, but we ignore this detail here. When switching to template meta-programming, we must recall that only n is constant. The T argument x is variable. It actually corresponds to the data item we will extract from our data series. Hence, the computation cannot be completely done at compile-time. The best we can hope for is to use template meta-programming to unroll the loop and compute the additional multiplication by x contained in the if clause based on the parity of n. Hence the named "UnrolledPower" we have given to this template, to distinguish if from a fully static version, where the x argument is also fixed.

The odd meta-function is simple to implement and belongs to every template meta-programming toolkit, as follows:

```
Template< unsigned long n >
struct Odd
{
   enum {IsTrue = bool( n & 0x1 ), IsFalse = !IsTrue };
};
```

We are using a now classic (anonymous) enumeration type to force the compiler to evaluate the boolean result at compile-time. Using a boolean inside an enumeration value is also perfectly legal, because we have a guaranteed conversion to an integral type and the enumeration construct must accommodate every integral type by requirement of the C++ standard.

We now have all we need to implement the power meta-function. The for loop is implemented with the help of a recursive template and a partial template specialization to stop it, as follows:

```
template< typename T, unsigned int n >
struct UnrolledPower : public std::unary_function< T ,
T >
{
   T operator()( T x ) const
     { return (Odd< n >::isTrue ? x : T( 1 )) *
           sqr( UnrolledPower< T, (n >> 1) >()( x ) ); }
};

template< typename T >
struct UnrolledPower< T, 0U >
{
   T operator()( T x ) const
     { return T( 1 ); }
};
```

The sqr function used in the recursive expression is a helper mathematical template function computing the square of its argument. One could have used another recursive instance of the UnrolledPower template with a value of 2 for n, but this would have made the expression less readable.

The if statement testing the oddity of n is replaced here by the classical ternary ? operator using an invocation of the Odd meta-function explained before. The if statement testing the oddity of n is replaced here by the classical ternary ? operator and an invocation of the Odd meta-function explained before. Note that if n is even, we multiply by 1 instead of x, hence the need for the T's constructor accepting a simple constant as argument. One could argue that a multiplication by a factor of 1 is not very optimal, and a tighter version could have been devised, but again this would have made the whole expression much less understandable.

Moreover, such meta-functions are not devised to be used as-is. In order to obtain efficient code, the most aggressive compiler's optimization options must be used, and the result is actually very effective: all templates, constructors, destructors, recursion and function calls disappear. Only the series of multiplication and storage operations remain.

As is usual with such template meta-functions, we declare the following accompanying template function as syntactic sugar:

```
template< typename T, int n >
inline T Power( T value )
{ return n > 0 ?    UnrolledPower< T,  n >()( value )
           : T( 1 ) / UnrolledPower< T, -n >()( value ); }
```

This allows for two things: First, we may now express a computation whilst dropping the constructor pair of parentheses, and second negative power arguments are now possible (the second template parameter is not unsigned anymore):

```
double y = Power< double, -9 >( x )
```

The above ideas are not new. They now belong to the classical paraphernalia in the template meta-programming field. They were presented in [Vel] (see also [CzE 00] for a systematic exposition).

The Summator Template

Now that we are equipped with a powerful(!) template, we can envision the next step. The computation of statistical moments implies that we sum various powers of the data items. So we need a kind of accumulator allowing this summation. The minimum needed to achieve this is the following:

1. A variable of type T, holding the summation's result and initialized properly (to 0 in the simplest case)
2. A function acting on the received data item to compute the value to accumulate (our power function in the statistical estimator case)
3. The accumulation operation itself (usually the += operator)

The resulting pseudo-code would look like this:

```
Accumulate function( arg ) to result;
```

If we go back to our original problem, our intention was actually broader than computing just the statistical moments. We would like to also have visitors computing the minimum and maximum of a given data series, but this requires another kind of "accumulation". Instead of the traditional operator += we need a kind of "min=" operator. This means that we need some parameterization on the accumulate function too. The following template presents the retained approach.

As can be seen in the UML diagram below, we now have 3 template parameters. Our fundamental type T, our data item functor F, and the accumulation operator O. Moreover, the starting operand value must now be passed as constructor argument to allow the special case when this value is different from the default. The template name has become more general too, because this template may accomplish more than a mere accumulation.

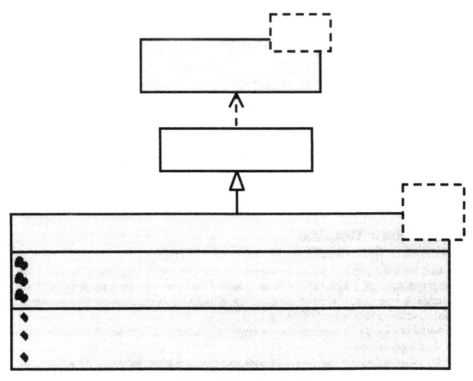

Fig. 2. The transformator template

The accumulation operators we need are implemented as follows:

```
template< typename T >
struct PlusAssign : binary_function< T, T, void >
{ void operator()( T& arg1, const T& arg2 ) const
    { arg1 += arg2; }
};
template< typename T >
struct MinAssign: binary_function< T, T, void >
{
    static const T startValue;
    void operator()( T& arg1, const T& arg2 ) const
    { if (arg2 < arg1) arg1 = arg2; }
};

template< typename T > const T MinAssign< T >
::startValue = numeric_limits< T >::max()
```

The first template is the exact pendant of the standard "plus" functor encapsulating the global addition operator. A point to notice it that the function operator does not return its result as usual, but on the first argument instead, that must be declared as a non-const reference to allow it.

The second template is our "min=" operator. To help later with the starting value in the transformator template, we declare an embedded static constant that can be used for this purpose. It is initialized here with the help of the standard template `numeric_limits` traits class, available for all built-in types. It should thus be provided for the additional data item types we plan to use with our framework. Note that we only need the "max" (for the `MinAssign`) and "min" value (for the `MaxAssign` operator).

We are now able to express a special case of our transformator, by fixing its accumulation operator to be the usual `+= operator`, called an "Accumulator"

From a conceptual point of view, this accumulator could be seen as a kind of partially specialized `typedef`, although there is no direct way to express this concept in C++. One is forced to resort to one of the following constructs instead:
1. A template partial specialization.
2. Another descendant class, as we have done it here.
3. A typedef encapsulated within a template.

The minimum and maximum computation using the "`min=`" respectively "`max=`" accumulation operators will not be explained further in this abridged document.

The Resultor Class

We are now nearly ready for the most complicated step: the recursive computation of the statistical moments. We want first go one step further in the specialization of the accumulator class. After having fixed the accumulation operator, we'll fix its functor. As already explained before, we need to compute the cumulative sums of the powers of the data items for which we want a given statistical moment. Our power meta-function (`UnrolledPower`) will just do that.

The resulting specialization must itself be parameterized by the power exponent, besides our now pervasive fundamental type T. We name that further specialization `NthPowerSummator`. It may be viewed as a templatized typedef (parameterized on both T and n), for the same reasons as the Accumulator itself.

This time we chose to encapsulate a usual typedef within a template class, as shown on the UML diagram on the next page. Note that the vertical dashed arrows have actually two different meanings. The up-arrows are bounding relations (going from a place-holder or a `typedef` to a template) whilst the down arrow is a simple dependency relationship (the `NthPowerSummator` typedef makes use of the `UnrolledPower` template class to instantiate the `Accumulator`).

We have taken advantage of our `typedef` encapsulating `SummatorHolder` being a first class(!) citizen to add a few extras. It derives from the `unary_function` standard template (this feature is not directly used here, but it is always a good idea to be compliant with some pre-defined standard). Thus, the main operation we are interested in (that will later be the core of our visit operation) is implemented as a function operator.

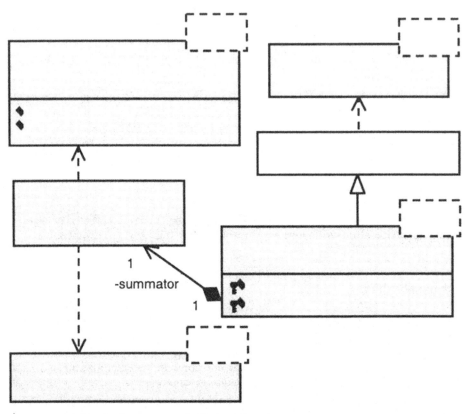

Fig. 3. The summator holder template class for statistical visitors

Why don't we use inheritance between the summator holder and the accumulator ? Public inheritance would actually not be necessary, because we only want to reuse part of the accumulator functor. Private inheritance would do, but there is no virtual method to redefine. Hence, aggregation introduces the least coupling. Our summator holder class has a member of its own nested `typedef` type, visible on the above diagram as a composition relationship.

We are now fully equipped to define the core template class of the whole system. A summator holder holds the sum of the nth powers of the data items it receives. A statistical estimator of order n needs also all sums of smaller order. The idea is to compose them all using recursive template inheritance, as shown hereafter:

The most striking point on the diagram is the recursive inheritance relation illustrated by the bounding relation coming down under the template itself. One sees how useful the placeholder class may be in such a diagram to help understanding the recursion correctly, especially the template parameter mapping. The other inheritance relation is toward our summator holder class. Hence, the resultor hierarchy builds a kind of trunk with summator holder branches. The higher the ladder bar, the lower the power exponent

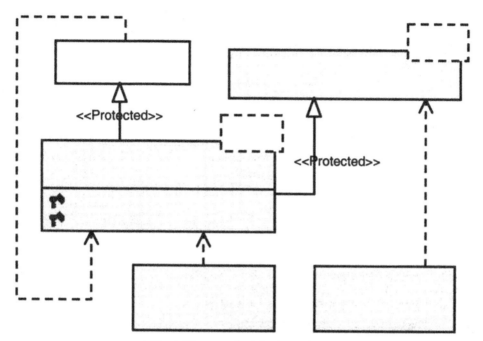

Fig. 4. The recursive inheritance ladder

Note also that both inheritance paths are protected inheritance. We don't need public inheritance and private would be too strict, because each stage must have access to the whole ladder. This is an interesting case where both multiple and protected inheritance are combined. Such a case is rare enough to be underlined[4].

There are finally two nested typedefs corresponding to the classical "inherited" trick, to simplify reference to the ancestor classes (see [Str 94]). These aliases are needed to disambiguate the inherited methods, because the recursive inheritance automatically brings with it an overriding of all the inherited methods. Because we need to access both the methods defined at a given stage and all the overridden ones, it is necessary to use explicit class references. The language luckily has enough scoping power to allow full disambiguation.

Note also that such constructs are a challenge for the modeling tool. It must support both the recursive inheritance relation drawing and have enough tuning possibilities to be able to generate the correct code. We recall that all source files are generated automatically from the model. This encompasses all classes' declarations, constants, enums, methods skeletons and typedef declarations, but in such generative template contexts, this corresponds to about 80% of the final code.

Like all recursions, the one presented above must be stopped somehow. This is achieved with the help of partial template specialization (on the parameter n) of the resultor template. A single specialization (for n == 0) would be sufficient to solve the

---

[4] The UML specification (see [OMG 00]) does actually not authorize direct inheritance between templates, although our modeling tool does. An implicit bounding class must be thought, mapping <T, n> to <T, n>. We used that simplified form to make the diagram lighter.

recursion problem, but one aspect remains that we have not yet discussed: the actual computation of the estimator results based on the various power sums. Further specializations will help us implementing it. Here is the recursion stopping specialization:

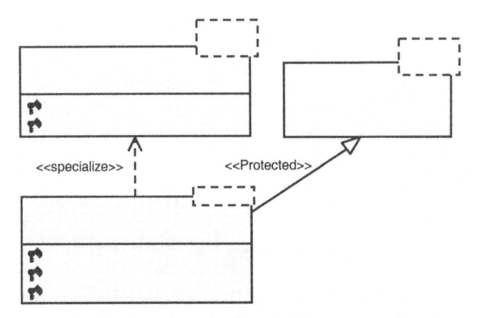

Fig. 5. Partial resultor specialization of order 0 stopping the inheritance recursion

One word about the additional "getCount" method. It is actually a simple alias of the "getResult" method. Its presence simplifies the result picking amidst the overridden "getResult" methods by introducing a more typical name. In this case, at the 0th level, this is the same as the total extracted from the summator holder:

```
const T& getCount() const
    { return getSummator().getTotal(); }
```

Note that the generic power functor gives the correct result: accumulating the 0th power of all data items is precisely the same as just counting them. One could be tempted to handle this counting result as an integer number, but this is not a good idea. Not only would it constitute a special case that should be handled specially in our generic construction, but the equivalent expressed in our fundamental type T is needed anyway by the higher order resultors to do their computations.

Beware that this resultor specialization only inherits from the summator holder of order 0. Remember, we must stop the recursion! This is the highest branch in our recursion tree.

The visit method is also trivial at this level:

```
void visit( const T& arg )
    { inherited::operator()( arg ); }
```

Where we have defined the usual "inherited" typedef. In the general case, the visit method should delegate to its both ancestors, that is to the summator holder side branch (for the nth power sum) and along the trunk for the recursion:

```
void visit( const T& arg )
   { inherited1::operator()( arg );
     inherited2::visit( arg ); }
```

Let's now consider the specialization of order 2 (order 1 is not very different and a little less interesting). Note that this time, the specialization actually both specializes and inherits from the general resultor template. It inherits actually from the order 1, which is itself a specialization, but this is irrelevant here.

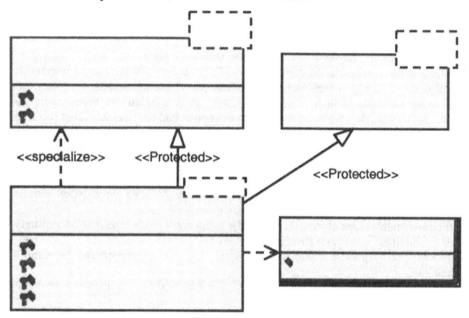

Fig. 6. The second order resultor specialization

The visit method is implemented just as discussed above (general case). Note the appearance of the new "getSquareSum" method, just delegating to the summator holder of order 2 (its direct right ancestor). This is again a help in disambiguating the entangled overridden names. Moreover, this makes the computation of the variance clearer, as can be seen hereafter:

```
T getVariance() const
   { return getSquareSum() / getCount()
       - sqr( getMean() ); }
```

No need here to use class scoping to choose the correct version of a particular method. We are rather using the traditional, specialized names. Note that the above computation makes use of the helper mathematical square function presented earlier.

Two additional resultor specializations are defined: for order 3 (computing the so-called skewness) and for order 4 (computing the excess). They are defined in a similar way, with "getCubeSum" and "getBiSquareSum" methods respectively. The "getSkewness" and "getExcess" method implements the actual result computation, and they are a little more complicated than the variance computation. They both make use of our power template again to compute the cube, respectively the fourth power of the mean that are needed in the calculation.

These methods are the reason why an actual specialization is needed. The computation of the nth order statistical estimator is not expressible directly through a closed formula. An alternating power series expansion is needed as well as additional specific coefficients. This would make a more generic computation too cumbersome. Anyway, Statistical moments beyond order 4 are never used in practice.

Implementing the Interface

We are not totally finished yet. We must still implement the "Estimatable" interface, corresponding to the contract we will offer to our clients. Like all interfaces, this abstract class has virtual methods defining our visitor operations. One may ask why using virtuality with a framework where all is templatized, hence static by nature. Moreover, the combination of the two implies that the interface must itself be a template parameterized by the fundamental type (or one of its ancestors!) This is actually the point. It could be possible with minor modifications to use the framework in a polymorphic context should it be needed. This would definitely require the use of an accompanying traits template. The idea would then be to have different, but related, types bound together in the traits template. At least three types can be distinguished:
1. the fundamental type corresponding to the estimator's result type (and accordingly to the interface's template parameter).
2. The internal type used within the estimators to do the summation and the result's calculus.
3. The type used to build constants needed when multiplying an intermediate result by a whole number.
   In our simplified case, all three types coincide, making the traits class unnecessary.

Having defined an interface with virtual functions, we need a coupling class between the recursive resultor classes and the interface. This is achieved with a glue template class called "NthEstimator", inheriting privately from the resultor and publicly from the interface to realize it.

Packing all together

We now have all needed elements to build our statistical framework. What fails is a good packaging. Clearly enough, all of the above templates should be instantiated with the same fundamental type in a given context, although with different power exponents (and functor variants for the minimum and maximum computation). The final types we want to offer would be best presented as templatized tpyedefs. Because it is not directly possible in C++, we have chosen the solution of the encapsulating template, called "Statistic visitor". It is actually nothing more than a parameterized namespace encapsulating the various estimator `typedefs`.

The practical use of our framework is quite amusing: the simple declaration of the visitor computing the standard deviation implies the direct or indirect instantiation of no less than 21 templates, of whom some are used more than once, like the `Odd` meta-function. The most complicated estimator, the "`Excessor`", stretches this number till 28. This illustrates the extreme fine granularity of the template meta-programming approach. The final visitor template class is composed of a lots of small tidbits classes, like in a game of virtual Lego. This extreme granularity also implies a corresponding amount of work for the compiler, rendered more difficult by the extensive use of template partial specializations. The one we used (GNU) was nonetheless able to tackle that ambitious goal.

Conclusion

Recursive inheritance is yet another interesting and flexible tool offered to template meta-programmers to implement solutions to inherently recursive problems.

References

[BRJ 98] "The Unified Modeling Language User Guide", by Grady Booch, James Rumbaugh and Ivar Jacobson, 1998, ISBN 0-201-57168-4

[Ree 98] "Indirect visitor" & "The (B)Leading Edge: Yet Another Visitor Pattern", by Jack Reeves, The C++ Report, Vol. 10, No. 3, March 1998, No. 5, May 1998 and No. 7, July 1998

[GHJ+ 98] "Design Patterns" by Erich Gamma, Richard Helm, Ralph Johnson, John Vlissides, January 1995, ISBN 0-201-63361-2

[Knu 81] "The art of computer programming", by Donald Knuth, 1981, Vol. II, § 4.6.3, p. 441-462, ISBN 0-201-03822-6

[Vel] "Template meta-programs", by Todd Veldhuizen,
http://extreme.indiana.edu/~tveldhui/papers/Template-Metaprograms/meta-art.html

[CzE 00] "Generative Programming: Methods, Tools, and Applications", by Krzysztof Czarnecki and Ulrich Eisenecker, June 2000, ISBN 0-201-30977-7

[Str 94] "The Design and Evolution of C++", by Bjarne Stroustrup, January 1994, ISBN 0-201-54330-3

[OMG 00] "Unified Modeling Specification", version 1.3, March 200, http://www.omg.org/

Base Class Injection

Douglas Gregor, Sibylle Schupp, and David Musser

Computer Science Department
Rensselaer Polytechnic Institute
{gregod,schupp,musser}@cs.rpi.edu

Abstract. Class hierarchies, though theoretically reusable, have generally not seen much practical reuse in applications, due in part to the inflexibility of the inheritance relationship. We present a technique, base class injection, that allows the creation of generative class hierarchies that may be adapted by adding new methods, data members, and ancestor classes without modification to the class library code; an implementation of this technique in the C++ language is given.

1   Introduction

Inheritance is a powerful yet inflexible tool for program construction in object-oriented programming languages [22]. Inheritance is intended to convey the hierarchical structure of data and code and to foster a large degree of code reuse. While proper design of inheritance hierarchies has been successful in conveying the structure of data, the much-touted reusability of class hierarchies has not occurred [7, 9, 16].

The limited reuse of class hierarchies is due to many factors, one of which is the inextensibility of inheritance. The direct ancestors of a given class are chosen at the design time of that class, and are not changed barring a source code rewrite. While this is often reasonable—a class's parents define much of what that class is—it is inflexible, in that certain relationships may exist between two independently developed class hierarchies that cannot be expressed through inheritance without modifying either class hierarchy. Essentially, the limitation to reusability of class hierarchies is that they may only be extended by creating a new leaf in the inheritance graph.

To foster reuse of class hierarchies, we must make them extensible beyond the limited benefit of creating a new leaf in the inheritance graph and instead allow the class hierarchy to be customized at all levels. Extensibility in this case means that we must be able to express relationships between classes and hierarchies that were unknown or nonexistent at class hierarchy design time, but come into existence because of a particular usage of the class hierarchy. Such relationships occur when a class hierarchy is adapted to a particular program environment that requires certain global properties such as persistence, reflection, or garbage collection; they may also occur when two independently developed libraries are found to have common properties that could be exploited if only the libraries shared the same interface.

We will present a motivating example in Section 2 along with a sketch of our solution using a technique we call *base class injection*. Section 3 will highlight the requirements of a base class injection system, along with the basic language requirements needed to implement such a scheme, and Section 4 details the implementation of base class injection in Standard C++. Complete source for a base class injection library is listed in the appendix and we are planning a submission to Boost [11] for formal review.

2 Adapting to New Interfaces

We start our example considering an application developed with a hypothetical graphical user interface widget library named GOOEY. The GOOEY library handles the usual widgets, including buttons, menus, and text entry fields. For reference, we will assume it is implemented as an object-oriented hierarchy similar to that in Figure 1.

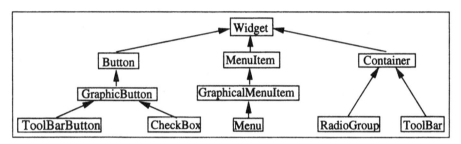

Fig. 1. Inheritance hierarchy for the hypothetical widget library, GOOEY

Late in the development of our application, it is determined that our customers require an interface that also suits visually impaired users. While much of the information required for an audible interface exists in the instances of widgets used in the user interface, the information is not accessible in the form necessary for an audible interface. For instance, the label of a Button conveys the functionality of the button and could be used in conjunction with a text-to-speech synthesizer and, similarly, a RadioGroup may have a caption describing its function and a CheckBox would convey both its label and whether it is selected or not. Had we designed the GOOEY widgets with an audible interface in mind, we would have provided a common interface to the audible description of each widget. Each widget would provide an implementation appropriate for the style of widget: a Button would convey the functionality of a button press, and a CheckBox would customize a Button to include whether it is selected or not.

Given that we are unable to directly modify the GOOEY library, how can we include the audible description interface in each widget of the GOOEY library, customizing the access methods for any widget? One common technique is to wrap the functionality of the GOOEY library in a set of wrapper classes that each implement the audible description interface. This method is tedious and error-prone and is also brittle: changes in the GOOEY library will have to be reflected in the wrapper classes. We present a more natural and resilient solution based on base class injection.

With base class injection, we create an audible description interface class and then inject it into the GOOEY class hierarchy as a base class of Widget. Then, we use base class injection to override the methods of the audible description interface in subclasses of Widget that require a specific audible interface. Our application remains unchanged by the addition of this code, but we now possess the capability to access the audible listener interface of any widget. Figure 2 illustrates a portion of the resulting GOOEY hierarchy with the injection of the AudibleDescription interface at the root, with overrides injected for the Button and CheckBox subclasses. We have essentially customized the entire GOOEY class hierarchy without requiring a change to the GOOEY library source code by injecting an additional interface (and its implementation) into the preexisting hierarchy. Note also that the injections are performed without regard to the intervening class hierarchy, so this solution does not suffer from the same brittleness experienced with wrapper approaches. Furthermore, additional interfaces—such as one for handheld computers—could be developed independently of the audible interface, and at compile time the appropriate set of interfaces could be selected, essentially giving the developer the power to generate a class hierarchy specific to the needs of the given application but without requiring hooks into the actual class hierarchy source code.

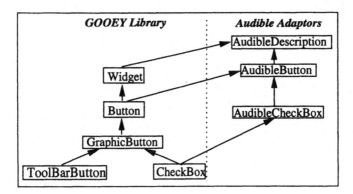

Fig. 2. The GOOEY class hierarchy with the AudibleDescription interface injected at the root class Widget and later reimplemented for the Button and CheckBox classes.

3 Base Class Injection

Base class injection may be characterized by the extension and augmentation of existing class libraries at any point in the class hierarchy without the need for rewriting library source code. We now enumerate the exact requirements of a base class injection implementation to better understand its capabilities:

1. It should allow arbitrary classes to be prepared to receive injections. Once prepared any class can be injected into that class without modifying the source code for the class receiving the injection.
2. It should not change the type of the class receiving the injection, so that no code modifications are necessary after the injection.
3. Common object-oriented features, such as virtual method invocation, encapsulation, and polymorphism, should be available with respect to the injected base class and its members.
4. It should minimize additional run-time overhead.

We see from our example in the previous section that all of the properties are necessary to augment the GOOEY library with an interface for the visually impaired. We inject an interface class AudibleDescription not known at the time the GOOEY class library was designed (Property #1), without changing the types of any of the classes in the GOOEY library so that only recompilation is required to access the new functionality (#2); finally, we use virtual function overriding to customize the implementation of the AudibleDescription interface for different classes in the GOOEY class library (#3) and, although it was not explicitly stated, we assume polymorphic behavior from the augmented class hierarchy, that is, we can rely on the ability of any Widget to be viewed as an implementation of the AudibleDescription interface. The final requirement (#4) is one of efficiency—for an organizational technique to be adopted it must clearly have little negative impact on the run-time efficiency of the system.

It is beneficial to understand the key language features required for an implementation of base class injection. It is clear that we are considering object-oriented or hybrid languages with inheritance. We restrict our discussion to statically typed languages; similar techniques for the dynamically typed languages Ruby and Smalltalk are discussed in Section 5. We now isolate the language requirements for base class injection:

1. It must support multiple inheritance or, more generally, allow for a given class to extend two classes neither one of which is derived from the other.
2. It must support a method of specifying the base classes to inject for a given class, and statically collect this list of base classes.
3. It must support a method of delaying the full definition of a class until all of its base classes are known.

The first requirement is obvious; the second essentially requires the ability to specify a list of base classes that a given class must inherit. For a statically typed language, this list must be built statically. The third requirement is the most interesting; it requires that a class be developed with no knowledge of the base classes that may later be injected, but the language must not prohibit references to the class prior to its full definition. Forward referencing minimally fits this requirement, though it places an unfortunate burden on the library developer and user to provide declarations and definitions in entirely different areas, with base class injections declared after forward declarations, but before definitions.

It is worth noting that such a system could be constructed from a very type-strict and non-generic language such as Java [4] only with the assistance of external programs. For instance, a source code preprocessor or source-to-source translator that scans an auxiliary database and adds additional implements clauses and methods could be used to satisfy the second and third language requirements (Java interfaces support multiple inheritance).

We next illustrate that the C++ language [3] already meets or exceeds these requirements and stress that no extensions to the language are necessary to support base class injection.

4 Implementation

Our C++ implementation relies on some advanced features of the C++ language and on techniques well-known in the C++ community. Most prominently, we will use C++ templates to meet the second and third language requirements for base class injection, using partial specialization, traits [5], and template metaprogramming [10, 21]. Templates will also allow us to delay the actual definition of a class until it is absolutely necessary, thereby allowing the user a large degree of freedom in the timing of class injections.

We will explore the implementation of base class injection first from the user's perspective, covering injection of base classes and overriding virtual methods in injected classes in Sections 4.1 and 4.2, then move to the interface used by the library designer to build a class hierarchy that can accept injections in Section 4.3. Finally, we explain the implementation of a base class injection library in Section 4.4.

To avoid any ambiguity regarding the actual class being injected and the class receiving the injection, we will call the class receiving the injection the *receiver*. The class that is being injected into the receiver will be called the *injected base class*. Therefore, in our example from Figure 2, Widget, Button, and CheckBox are all receivers, while AudibleDescription, AudibleButton, and AudibleCheckBox are all injected base classes.

4.1 Injecting a Base Class into a Receiver

Injecting an arbitrary base class into a receiver is performed by specializing one of two template classes, base_class or virtual_base_class. Figure 3 illustrates the injection of the base classes AudibleDescription, AudibleButton, and AudibleCheckBox into the receiver classes Widget, Button, and CheckBox, respectively. The Tag template parameter is essential to the C++ implementation of base class injection and is explained in Section 4.3.

From Figure 3, we see that virtual_base_class is parameterized by two template parameters. The first parameter is the name of the receiver, and the second is an index value. For the first injection into a given receiver, this value

```
template<typename Tag> struct virtual_base_class<Widget<Tag>, 0>
  { typedef AudibleDescription base; };

template<typename Tag> struct virtual_base_class<Button<Tag>, 0>
  { typedef AudibleButton base; };

template<typename Tag> struct virtual_base_class<CheckBox<Tag>, 0>
  { typedef AudibleCheckBox base; };
```

Fig. 3. Injecting the base classes `AudibleDescription`, `AudibleButton`, and `AudibleCheckBox` into the GOOEY library classes `Widget`, `Button`, and `CheckBox`

should be zero; for the second injection into that receiver, it should be one, and so on (each receiver has its own counter). The member type `base` declares the base class to be injected. The template classes `base_class` and `virtual_base_class` differ only in the method used to derive from the injected base class—`base_class` defines base classes that will be injected into the receiver via nonvirtual public inheritance, whereas `virtual_base_class` defines base classes injected via virtual public inheritance. For those unfamiliar with C++ terminology, a given class A that is inherited nonvirtually a certain number of times in a hierarchy will show up that many times in a hierarchy. However, if all inheritance of A in a hierarchy is virtual, it will appear only once. We will use this powerful feature later when describing the overriding of virtual functions introduced through base class injection in Section 4.2.

4.2 Overriding Virtual Function Injections

Our injected base classes may declare virtual functions and it is essential that we be able to override these virtual functions at a later point in the hierarchy. Figure 4 illustrates the definition of the `AudibleDescription` class and its descendants, including the virtual function `getAudioText` that is overridden in each descendant.

The only point of interest in the overriding of injected virtual functions is the `virtual` keyword that specifies virtual inheritance of the `AudibleDescription` and `AudibleButton` classes. Revisiting Figure 2, we see that we had assumed virtual inheritance of the injected classes in the construction of our inheritance lattice—without it, both `AudibleButton` and `AudibleCheckBox` would have their own distinct copies of the `AudibleDescription` interface, causing conflicts during name resolution on the `AudibleDescription` interface.

4.3 Preparing the Receiver

Preparing a receiver class to accept injections requires only a few small changes to the definition of the receiver class. The receiver will publicly derive from a class **bases** that represents the unknown set of base classes, specializing it based on the name of the receiver, as is illustrated in Figure 5. This is reminiscent of

112

```
class AudibleDescription
  { public: virtual AudioText getAudioText(); };

class AudibleButton : virtual public AudibleDescription
  { public: virtual AudioText getAudioText(); };

class AudibleCheckBox : virtual public AudibleButton
  { public: virtual AudioText getAudioText(); };
```

Fig. 4. Injecting and overriding virtual methods with base class injection

the well-known B & N trick [5] that customizes the ancestors of a class based on the descendant class as a method of supporting multiple implementations of a common interface through a common base class template while preserving static bindings.

```
template<typename Tag = default_tag>
class Widget : public bases< Widget<Tag> > { /* ... */ };
```

Fig. 5. Preparing a receiver for base class injection

The explanation of the Tag parameter delves deep into the intricacies of the C++ language. The so-called One Definition Rule [3] states that any entity may only be defined once. A non-template class is defined when its class body is defined, therefore non-template receiver classes give us no chance to inject injectable base classes because they are immediately defined. Template classes, on the other hand, are not fully defined until they are instantiated with a given set of template parameters. By adding the Tag template parameter we ensure that our receiver class is a template class and is therefore not fully defined before user code requires a definition. In effect, this allows the receiver class to be written without regard to the base classes that may be injected later. The injected base classes may then be included up until the first concrete usage (i.e., one that requires knowledge of the size of the class or accesses its member variables).

The Tag parameter has an additional usage allowing multiple distinct hierarchies in a single translation unit. The tag denotes a specific set of injections, e.g., Audible or Handheld. Figure 6 illustrates that Widget can be injected with either an AudibleDescription class or a HandheldDescription class, depending on whether the tag is Audible or Handheld.

4.4 Collecting Injected Base Classes

Moving to the implementation of a base class injection library, we present a technique for collecting the set of injected base classes and deriving from each

```
template<typename Tag> struct virtual_base_class<Widget<Tag>, 0>
   { typedef placeholder_base_class base; };

template<> struct virtual_base_class<Widget<Audible>, 0>
   { typedef AudibleDescription base; };

template<> struct virtual_base_class<Widget<Handheld>, 0>
   { typedef HandheldDescription base; };

template<typename Tag> struct virtual_base_class<Widget<Tag>, 1>
   { typedef GarbageCollected base; };
```

Fig. 6. Using tags to allow multiple versions of a hierarchy to coexist in a translation unit. All **Widgets** will derive from **GarbageCollected**

of them. We use template metaprogramming to traverse the list of injected base classes and create an inheritance chain containing all injected base classes.

We refer again to Figure 3 and note that the second template parameter of **base_class**, the index value, mimics the familiar concept of an array index. Essentially, **base_class** is a compile-time resizeable array: to insert elements, we specialize **base_class** given the next index value; the **base** member type is the value of the element at the given position in the array. This linearization does not hamper base class injection in any way: injected base classes parameterized by their receivers may access extensions made by other injected base classes regardless of base class ordering.

Iteration through such a data structure is clear: starting a counter at zero, we access the **base** type to get the element value and increment the count to access the next element, but how do we know when to terminate iteration? C++ contains the notion of a *primary* template, that is, a template that will be selected if no (partial) specialization matches the given set of arguments. We therefore define a sentinel type **end** and a primary template for our compile-time array **base_class** that contains **end** as its value; then, our iteration construct terminates when it finds that the current element is **end**. Figure 7 illustrates the **end** class, the primary template for **base_class**, and the class **gather_bases** that creates the derivation chain including all injected base classes.

5   Related Work

Our work is most similar to work done by Ossher and Harrison [19] where object systems were extended by combining *base* hierarchies (e.g., the GOOEY library) with *extension* hierarchies (e.g., the audible and handheld hierarchies). Ossher and Harrison discuss extension by adding new superclasses, but opted to use composition operators within a new language because adding new superclasses "changes the structure of the inheritance hierarchy at an internal node, a type of change that is usually poorly supported by object-oriented systems" and which,

```
struct end {};

template<typename Receiver, int Index = 0>
struct base_class { typedef end base; };

template<
  typename Receiver,
  int Index = 0,
  typename Base = typename base_class<Receiver, Index>::base>
struct gather_bases : public Base,
                      public gather_bases<Receiver, Index+1> {};

template<typename Receiver, int Index>
struct gather_bases<Receiver, Index, end> {};
```

Fig. 7. Implementation of a template class to manage the derivation from any number of injected base classes, along with the default definition of the base_class class

they assumed, "requires editing the original class." While this assumption was probably valid for all programming languages (including C++) at the time of writing, our technique demonstrates how modern C++ fully supports such changes in the inheritance hierarchy without source code editing.

Our view of the reusability problems with class hierarchies can be likened to the motivations behind aspect-oriented programming [15, 14] in that class hierarchies that are conceptually distinct often have common roots that express basic system-wide properties. In aspect-oriented programming terminology, these common base classes implement functionality that cross-cuts the hierarchies, and the resulting implementation that joins them tangles the two hierarchies together in an unnatural way. Our technique is supportive of aspect-oriented programming in that it provides another method for keeping conceptually distinct hierarchies distinct in design, and joining them only when necessary by injecting base classes developed separately to form a single hierarchy. In this way, base class injection can be seen as a restricted implementation of the weaving process—one for which, in C++ at least, one does not need any additional tools to implement.

A technique apparently similar to our own is that of mixin classes [8, 13], which are (often abstract) classes that are intended only as base classes to be "mixed in" to a class as it is used. In most languages mixins are limited in that they can only generate a new leaf in the inheritance hierarchy. Therefore the use of mixins requires system-wide changes and, for extensive hierarchy modifications, necessitates something similar to the wrapping approach described above because inheritance relationships between the newly-created leaves will need to be specified manually.

Ruby [1] is a dynamically typed, object-oriented scripting language in which mixins can be injected at any level of a class hierarchy through reopening of class definitions. Thus in Ruby, even though it only has single inheritance among classes, one can use mixins to extend a class hierarchy at all levels without modifying its source code. Unfortunately, in its unrestricted form in Ruby, the ability to reopen class definitions breaks encapsulation. This problem could perhaps be fixed by disallowing access to data members when classes are reopened, but another drawback to implementing base class injection in this way in Ruby is that only one extension of a given class hierarchy can exist within a single program, whereas our C++ injection library supports coexistence of multiple extensions.

In Smalltalk, which is also dynamically typed, a technique that could be described as a limited form of base class injection was introduced by Kent Beck [6]. This technique allows extending an *instance* of a class without changing the source code of the class. However, it only allows modifying a particular instance of a leaf node.

Work in the refactoring of inheritance hierarchies [18, 12] is rooted in the same realization that at some point in the lifetime of a class hierarchy inheritance becomes too inflexible. Refactoring itself is very different—it relies on source code transformations and changing inheritance relationships among classes already in a given class hierarchy. Since base class injection allows reorganization with minimal code change, it may be preferable to refactoring in some situations, such as independent development of classes by different programmers. Refactoring may, however, help identify classes that would best be abstracted outside of the class hierarchy and later injected.

6 Conclusion

Inheritance is a powerful and essential feature of object-oriented languages, but its ability to foster reuse is degraded by its inflexibility. One limitation to class hierarchy reuse across applications is that extensibility of class hierarchies is confined to extension by new leaves.

Base class injection overcomes this significant limitation to the reusability of class hierarchies by enabling the injection of new base classes and new functionality into a class hierarchy. Such a capability enables class libraries to better adapt to specific uses, whether it be to environmental requirements such as base classes common to all class types (e.g., for reflection, persistence, or synchronization) in a system or through the injection of new interfaces. Base class injection is a tool for increasing the adaptability of a class hierarchy, overcoming limitations in inheritance and resulting in more reusable class hierarchies.

The appendix contains source code for a complete C++ base class injection library. Though the implementation of base class injection requires in-depth knowledge of the C++ language, its application is easily grasped by non-experts. The examples given in Figs. 3 and 5 may be reused substituting only class names and index numbers, making base class injection practical for all programmers.

We have successfully employed the base class injection technique in the Algebra library [20] as part of the Simplicissimus [2] project, where concepts—sets of abstractions—are represented as C++ template classes as a way of expressing concept lattices such as those defined by the Tecton language [17]. Concept refinement is expressed as class inheritance, but some refinement relations are not known at library design time and are introduced only later in user code—as a counterpart of Tecton lemmas, which establish refinement relations between previously defined concepts. Base class injection allows us to model such lemmas without modifying the library source code.

References

1. Ruby: a gem of a language. http://www.ruby-lang.org.
2. Simplicissimus. http://www.cs.rpi.edu/research/gpg/Simplicissimus.
3. ANSI-ISO-IEC. *C++ Standard, ISO/IEC 14882:1998*, ANSI standards for information technology edition, 1998.
4. K. Arnold and J. Gosling. *The Java Programming Language*. Addison-Wesley, Reading, MA, 1998.
5. J. J. Barton and L. R. Nackman. *Scientific and Engineering C++: An introduction with advanced techniques and examples*. Addison-Wesley, 1994.
6. K. Beck. Instance specific behavior: How and why. *Smalltalk Report*, 6(2), 1993.
7. J. M. Bieman and J. X. Zhao. Reuse through inheritance: A quantitative study of C++ software. In *ACM SIGSOFT Symposium on Software Reusability*, pages 47–52, 1995.
8. G. Bracha and W. Cook. Mixin-based inheritance. In N. Meyrowitz, editor, *Proceedings of the Conference on Object-Oriented Programming: Systems, Languages, and Applications / Proceedings of the European Conference on Object-Oriented Programming*, pages 303–311, Ottawa, Canada, 1990. ACM Press.
9. S. R. Chidamber and C. F. Kemerer. A metrics suite for object oriented design. *IEEE Transactions on Software Engineering*, 20(6):476–493, June 1994.
10. K. Czarnecki and U. W. Eisenecker. *Generative Programming—Towards a New Paradigm of Software Engineering*. Addison Wesley Longman, 2000.
11. B. Dawes and D. Abrahams. Boost. http://www.boost.org.
12. G. Fischer, D. Redmiles, L. Williams, G. I. Puhr, A. Aoki, and K. Nakakoji. Beyond Object-Oriented Technology: Where Current Approaches Fall Short. *Human-Computer Interaction*, 10:79–119, 1995.
13. M. Flatt, S. Krishnamurthi, and M. Felleisen. Classes and mixins. In *Conference Record of POPL 98: The 25TH ACM SIGPLAN-SIGACT Symposium on Principles of Programming Languages, San Diego, California*, pages 171–183, New York, NY, 1998.
14. G. Kiczales, E. Hisdale, J. Hugunin, M. Kersten, J. Palm, and W. Griswold. An overview of AspectJ. In *European Conference on Object-Oriented Programming (ECOOP'01)*, 2001.
15. G. Kiczales, J. Lamping, A. Mendhekar, C. Maeda, C. V. Lopes, J.-M. Loingtier, and J. Irwi. Aspect-oriented programming. In *European Conference on Object-Oriented Programming (ECOOP'97)*, 1997.
16. A. Lake and C. Cook. A software complexity metric for C++. Technical Report 92-60-03, Computer Science Dept., Oregon State University, 1992.
17. D. R. Musser. The Tecton Concept Description Language. http://www.cs.rpi.edu/~musser/gp/tecton/tecton1.ps.gz, July 1998.
18. W. F. Opdyke and R. J. Johnson. Refactoring: An Aid in Designing Application Frameworks. In *Proceedings of the Symposium on Object-Oriented Programming emphasizing Practical Applications*, pages 145–160, 1990.

19. H. Ossher and W. Harrison. Combination of inheritance hierarchies. In A. Paepcke, editor, *Proceedings of the Conference on Object-Oriented Programming Systems, Languages, and Applications (OOPSLA)*, volume 27, pages 25–40, New York, NY, 1992. ACM Press.
20. S. Schupp, D. P. Gregor, and D. Musser. Algebraic concepts represented in C++. Technical Report TR-00-8, Rensselaer Polytechnic Institute, 2000.
21. T. Veldhuizen. Using C++ template metaprograms. *C++ Report*, 7(4), 1995.
22. P. Wegner. Dimensions of object-based language design. In N. Meyrowitz, editor, *Proceedings of the Conference on Object-Oriented Programming Systems, Languages, and Applications (OOPSLA)*, volume 22, pages 168–182, New York, NY, 1987. ACM Press.

Injection Library Source

```
struct default_tag {};
struct end {};


// Users add nonvirtual base classes to this list
template<typename T, int Index = 0>
struct base_class { typedef end base; };


// Users add virtual base classes to this list
template<typename T, int Index = 0>
struct virtual_base_class { typedef end base; };


template<typename T,
         int      Index = 0,
         typename Base  = typename base_class<T, Index>::base>
struct gather_bases : public Base, public gather_bases<T, Index+1> {};


template<typename T, int Index>
struct gather_bases<T, Index, end> {};


template<typename T,
         int      Index = 0,
         typename Base  = typename virtual_base_class<T, Index>::base>
struct gather_virtual_bases :
  virtual public Base, public gather_virtual_bases<T, Index+1> {};


template<typename T, int Index>
struct gather_virtual_bases<T, Index, end> {};


// Receiver classes derive from this
template<typename T>
struct bases : public gather_bases<T>,
               public gather_virtual_bases<T> {};
```

Reflection Support
by Means of Template Metaprogramming

Giuseppe Attardi, Antonio Cisternino

Dipartimento di Informatica, corso Italia 40, I-56125 Pisa, Italy
{attardi,cisterni}@di.unipi.it

Abstract. The C++ language has only a limited runtime type information system, which doesn't provide full reflection capabilities. We present a general mechanism to support reflection, exploiting template metaprogramming techniques. Two solutions are presented: a static one where metaclass information is only available at compile time to produce class specific code; and a dynamic one where metaclass objects exist at runtime. As a case study of technique we show how to build an object interface to relational database tables. By just annotating a class definition with meta information, such as storage attributes or index properties of fields, a programmer can define objects that can be stored, fetched or searched in a database table. This approach has been used in building a high-performance, full text search engine.

1 Introduction

When building generic components, capable of handling a variety of object types, not yet known, the programmer is faced by a number of possibilities:

1. produce a library totally unaware of the specific kind of objects used by applications of the library. This is typical of C-based libraries, where parameters are passed as arrays of raw bytes (i.e. void*). The application programmer must supply custom code required for converting back and forth the parameters between the library and the application.
2. provide a multiple variant API, for a certain programming language, which includes one special function for each basic type, used to inform the component of each specific supplied parameter [5, 6, 8, 10]. Consider for instance database interfaces like ODBC, graphic libraries like OpenGL. The component in this case has more information available on parameters and can perform optimizations and provide higher-level services. The programmer must write sequences of invocations whenever complex parameters are involved.
3. extend the application programming language with ad-hoc primitives for interacting with the component, and supply a code generator or preprocessors which performs source to source code transformations, producing specific code for each application. For instance embedded-SQL allows inserting SQL-like statements within an ordinary program: a preprocessor translates embedded SQL into suitable database system calls.

4. develop a special purpose language for programming the component: e.g. Macromedia Lingo, PL/SQL [10], etc.
5. exploit reflection [1]. Using reflection the library can inspect the parameter types and optional traits and determine the proper way to handle them, e.g. converting them or handling them with the most appropriate specific code.

Reflection is the most advanced and powerful solution, since it does not involve external tools from the programming language, relieves the application programmer from low level interface coding, and enables a variety of domain optimization by the component developer. Unfortunately reflection is not generally available in most programming languages: most notable exceptions are Java, C#, CLOS, Smalltalk.

There are a few proposals for extending C++ with support for reflection. In [14, 15, 16] keywords are added to the language for specifying the location of meta-information. A preprocessor generates C++ source code containing the appropriate classes that reflects program's types. In [13] a similar approach is presented which avoids the use of special keywords but still uses a preprocessor.

OpenC++ instead extends the C++ compiler providing support for reflection during program compilation [17].

As pointed out in [12] the ability of handle reflective information at compile time leads to more efficient and usable reflection-oriented programs. Nevertheless the capability of accessing meta-information at runtime is fundamental for supporting dynamic binding.

We present how to implement the technique of reflection in C++ by means of template metaprogramming, which allows executing code at compile time which accesses type information without involving a preprocessor. It is supported in standard C++ and can be used with any recent C++ compiler.

While reflection is normally available and used by a program at run time, our approach provides reflection support also to metaprograms at compile time. This allows generating a specific version of the program or library, optimized to the special kind of parameters in the application.

As a case study of the use of reflection, we show how to build an object interface to a relational database table. The metaclass for objects to be stored in the table can be annotated with custom information about methods and attributes, useful for instance to express specialized traits, like indexing properties and size for a database column.

2   C++ Template Metaprogramming

C++ supports generic programming through the *template* mechanism, which allows defining parameterized classes and functions. Templates together with other C++ features constitute a Turing-complete, compile-time sublanguage of C++. C++ can be considered as a two-level language [2] since a C++ program may contain both static code, which is evaluated at compile time, and dynamic code, which is executed at runtime. Template meta-programs [2] are the part of a C++ source that is executed during compilation. Moreover a meta-program can access information about types not generally available to ordinary programs – with the exception of the limited facilities provided by the Run Time Type Identification (RTTI) [3].

Template metaprogramming exploits the computation performed by the type checker to execute code at compile time. This technique is used mostly for code selection and code generation at compile time. Its applications are mainly code configuration, especially in libraries, and code optimization [2].

Partial evaluation can be used to produce optimized code, specialized for a particular combination of the arguments, allowing, for example, the development of generic libraries that are specialized for each particular type used in an application.

In the examples below we use some useful meta-functions for testing types and perform other common metaprogramming tasks [9], for instance, `If<Condition, Then, Else>`, `IsClass<T>`, `IsPointer<T>`, `IsConst<T>`, `Equals<T, U>`, `IsA<T, U>`.

We exploited metaprogramming for providing an introspection facility for C++.

3   C++ Reflection

Throughout the paper we will use the following example of a C++ class, named `DocInfo`, which contains information about a collection of documents. The class definition is enriched with meta-information, as follows:

```
class DocInfo {
    char const*     name;
    char const*     title;
    char const*     type;
    int             date;

    META(DocInfo,
         (VARKEY(name, 2048, Field::unique),
          VARFIELD(title, 2048),
          VARFIELD(type, 32)),
          KEY(date));
};
```

`META` is a macro which exploits template metaprogramming for creating a metaclass for the class, as described later. Such annotation is the only effort required to a programmer for being able to use reflection on a certain class. The type of each attribute is in fact deduced from the class definition, using template metaprogramming. Macros `VARKEY` and `VARFIELD` allow supplying attribute traits: `2048` and `Field::unique` for instance express storage properties of the attribute in our application: in particular the maximum byte size and the kind of indexing for the column.

Using introspection capabilities we can define the template class `Table` that implements a persistent table containing objects of a specified class:

```
Table<DocInfo> table("db/table");
```

The table can be queried through a cursor created on the results of the query, which behaves essentially like an iterator on a list of objects.

Reflection involves creating a metaclass cointaining information about each class. We describe how to provide interospection and intercession capabilities both to metaprograms, through a metaclass type (*static reflection*), and to programs, through metaclass objects present at runtime (*dynamic reflection*).

We limit our discussion to how to handle reflection on attributes of classes: constructors and methods may be dealt similarly.

Static reflection

In static reflection, the metaclass of a particular class (Foo), is defined by a corresponding class (MetaFoo). The latter class stores information about the described class in static members. For instance, let us consider the following class:

```
class Foo {
  int attr1;
  char* attr2;
};
```

The associated metaclass is the following:

```
struct MetaFoo {
 typedef ctype class;
 typedef Reflection::End _curr_type0;
 static char* const name = "Foo";
 // Field attr1
 struct attr1_name { static char* const name = "attr1"; };
 typedef Reflection::Field<attr1_name, class,
  (int)&(((class*)0)->attr1), int, _curr_type0> _curr_type1;
 // Field attr2
 struct attr2_name { static char* const name = "attr2"; };
 typedef Reflection::Field<attr2_name, class,
  (int)&(((class*)0)->attr2), char*, _curr_type1> _curr_type2;
  typedef _curr_type2 attributes;
};
```

The metaclass describes the attributes and methods using a template list. An attribute is described by the following class:

```
template<class name_, class cont, int offs, class h_,
         class t_ = End,
         class traits_ = Reflection::defaultTraits>
struct Field {
  typedef cont memberof;
  typedef h_ attr_type;
  typedef t_ Tail;
  typedef traits_ traits;
  enum { size = sizeof(attr_type), offset = offs };
  static char * const name = name_::name;
};
```

A class field is described by suitable template parameters: t_ represents the tail of the list, End the end of the list, h_ the type of the attribute which is stored in a typedef within the class, cont is the class containing the field.

Without going into the details of the implementation, we just mention that the metaclass provides informations like these:

```
MetaFoo::class;              // the type Foo
MetaFoo::name;               // the string "Foo"
MetaFoo::attributes::type;   // type char*
MetaFoo::attributes::name;   // the string "attr2"
```

The static metaclass can be used either by meta-functions or by standard code. In the former case all computation is performed at compile time, while in the latter case types and constants defined in the metaclass can be used at runtime.

The generic template metafunction Serialize for instance produces code for serializing an object of a given type. This is the base case for the function:

```
template <class T>
struct SerializeBase {
  static void serialize(T *p, byte* buffer) {} };
```

SerializeBase is called for the End type terminating the recursion through the list of attributes of a class. The general case is the following:

```
template <class T>
struct Serialize {
  static void serialize(typename T::memberof *p,
                        byte* s) {
    typedef Reflection::If<
      !Reflection::Equals<typename T::Tail,
                          typename Reflection::End>::VAL,
      Serialize<typename T::Tail>,
      SerializeBase<typename T::memberof> >::VAL next;
    next::serialize(p, s);

    typename T::type *m =
      (typename T::type *)((char*)p + T::offset);
    *(T*)m = *(T*)s;
  }
};
```

Method serialize() generates the appropriate sequence of assignments for storing each field of the object, by recurring over the list of attributes of the metaclass. At each step, serialize() gets called on the type of the next attribute. This generates the serialization code for the following attributes. The current attribute gets serialized by knowing the base pointer of the object and the attribute offset. An object foo can be serialized to a location dest as follows:

```
Serialize<MetaFoo::attributes>::serialize(foo);
```

Static reflection does not handle subtype polymorphism: a metaprogram can only know the formal parameter type, not the actual type.

Dynamic reflection

Dynamic reflection uses an instance of class MetaClass for describing a class. Each class holds a static reference to its metaclass. The META construct for class Foo produces the following code:

```
class Foo {
  int attr1;
  char* attr2;

  typedef Foo _CLASS_;
  static Field* _createFields() {
    return &(
      createField("attr1", (int)&((_CLASS_*)0)->attr1,
        0, Field::unique, &((_CLASS_*)0)->attr1),
      createField("attr2", (int)&((_CLASS_*)0)->attr2,
        1024, Field::None, &((_CLASS_*)0)->attr2),
      ); }
  static MetaClass metaClass;
};
MetaClass Foo::_metaClass("Foo", Foo::_createFields());
```

Method createFields() builds the list of fields for the class. Function create-Field() creates an object of class Field with the specified attributes: the name of the attribute, its offset, the size of the field, whether the field must be indexed and a pointer to the attribute used to determine the type with template metaprogramming. The operator, () for class Field has been overloaded to create a linked list of Fields. The metaclass is initialized with its name and the list of fields. The same approach can be extended to methods and constructors.

Function createField() uses template metaprogramming to build the proper Field object and it is defined as follows:

```
template <class T>
inline Field& createField(char_t const *name, size_t
  offs, size_t maxLength,
  Field::IndexType indexType, T*) {
MetaClass* mc = If<isClass<T>::VAL,
                    getMetaClass<T>,
                    noMetaClass>::VAL::get();
  return
    If< isPointer<T>::VAL,
        FieldBuilder<VarField<deref<T>::VAL> >,
        If< isClass<T>::VAL,
            CompositeBuilder<T>,
            FieldBuilder<FixedField<T>
            > >::VAL
```

```
        >::VAL::factory(name, offs, maxLength, indexType, mc);
}
```

Class `Field` is abstract and can be specialized for different kinds of fields, in particular: `VarField`, `FixedField` and `CompositeField`. `FixedField` is used to represent an attribute of fixed size such as a number or a pointer. `VarField` is used to represent a variable length type such as a C string. `CompositeField` is

Template classes derived from `Field` provide a method `store()` for storing the field of an object in a table row. Here is the case for `FixedField`:

```
template <class T>
byte* FixedField<T>::store(byte*& row, byte* src) {
    *(T*)row = *(T*)src;
    return row + sizeof(T);
}
```

The serialization of an object `foo` of class `Foo` is performed by the static method `serialize()` in Foo's metaclass `Foo::metaClass`:

```
Foo::metaClass.serialize(row, &(byte*)foo);
```

which is defined as follows:

```
byte* MetaClass::serialize(byte*& row, byte* src) {
    for (Field* fd = columns; fd != NULL; fd = fd->next)
        row = fd->store(row, src + fd->offset);
    return row;
}
```

This method simply iterates over the list of fields and for each field calls its virtual `store()` method.

Static vs. dynamic reflection

When using dynamic reflection, having a metaclass is sufficient to manipulate objects of the corresponding class, hence it is possible to define classes dynamically assembling the field descriptions and other information. For instance, the metaclass for `Foo` can be created like this:

```
MetaClass metaFoo("Foo",
    createField("attr1", 0, 0, Field::unique, (int*)0,
    createField("attr2", 4, 1024, Field::None,
                (char**)0)));
```

Our framework provides class `AnyObject` to represent instances produced from such metaclasses, and class `DynamicTable` for using them in tables:

```
AnyObject any(metaFoo);
any.field<int>(0) = 5;
any.field<char*>(1) = "value for attr2";
DynamicTable table("/tmp/foo", metaFoo);
table.insert(&any);
```

DynamicTable is just a variant of class Table and defines the same tables, provided the same metaclass is used. For instance an SQL interpreter needs to use the DynamicTable interface in order to access a table created with C++ classes, since the classes it will use are not known at compile time.

Certain methods used with dynamic reflection involve some runtime computations for interpreting the metaclass information, while with static reflection the body of such methods is expanded at compile time into code specific for the class. For example, the dynamic version of method serialize() iterates through the fields of the class and calls methods for storing each field. Instead the static version of serialize() consists of a sequence of store operations of the appropriate type for each field: there is no iteration nor invocation of virtual methods.

On the other hand dynamic reflection can use virtual methods, which cannot be dealt instead with static reflection.

Both solutions suffer for a minor drawback: namespace pollution, since they introduce classes or types (e.g. MetaFoo, Foo::_CLASS) that might conflict with names present in the user program.

4   Case study: a relational object table

An object oriented interface library to a relational table must be capable of storing objects of any class in rows of a relational table. Therefore the library must know the structure of the class of the objects in order to perform serialization when storing the object. The table schema is often extracted from the database itself, which was created separately or by means of SQL constructs like "create table". For fetching or updating objects from a table, the library needs only to provide methods for accessing the individual fields of a row: the programmer must know and specify the type of each field being accessed and he is also responsible of storing values of the correct type into the fields of the object. Table schema definition and table usage are independent operations, of which the compiler is totally unaware: none of the information involved in such operations is available to it, in particular type information.

On the other hand, if the programming language used to implement the interface library supports introspection [1], the library can exploit it for determining the attributes of a class and their types. Through intercession [1] the library is then capable of modifying the object's attributes by accessing the description of the class.

An interface library built with introspection can provide a higher-level interface to programmers, relieving them from the burden of reconstructing an object fetched form a table or supplying detailed information about the class of the object.

We present the design for such an object interface to relational tables. The interface goes beyond the ability to store flat objects, corresponding to relational rows, and allows storing composite objects, containing other objects. A full object-oriented database can be build with limited effort on top of this interface.

The relational table interface has been inspired by GigaBase [7], but exploits metaprogramming in order to produce a suitable metaclass, capable of handling for instance various kinds of attribute traits. The interface has been used in implementing IXE, a fully featured, high performance class library for building customized, full-text search engines.

Class Table implements a relational table stored on disk on a Berkeley Database [4]. The template parameter to this class defines the structure of the table and must provide a metaclass through the META construct. Various kind of indexing can be specified through attributes traits, including inverted indexes and full-text indexes.

A program can load the data into the table as follows:

```
Table<DocInfo> table(table_file);
DocInfo aDocinfo(…);
table.insert(aDocInfo);
```

A query on the table can be performed as follows:

```
Query query(query_string);
QueryCursor<DocInfo> cursor(table, query);
while (cursor.hasNext()) {
  DocInfo docInfo = cursor.get();
  // use docInfo
}
```

Differently from traditional interfaces to database systems [5, 6, 8], here the cursor returns a real object, built from database row data using reflection. The cursor is capable of accepting complex boolean queries, involving full-text searches on full-text columns and other typical SQL conditions on other columns.

IXE uses dynamic reflection, which is required for dynamic class creation, a necessary feature for building an SQL interpreter. In future versions of the library we will combine static and dynamic reflection to exploit the efficiency of static reflection.

5 Conclusions

We have presented a general technique based on template metaprogramming for supporting reflection in C++. Metaprogramming is crucial to the solution since it allows accessing type information from the compiler and inaccessible otherwise.

We have shown how to use reflection to define a generic component for storing objects in a relational table. The component can be specialized to any class of objects. Such component has been used in developing the search engine library IXE. The application programmer can insert C++ objects directly into the table, without any conversion. Search the table is done through a cursor interface that allows scanning the results returned as C++ objects. The IXE library has proven effective in building several customized search engines and its performance is superior to similar commercial products.

Future work includes combining static and dynamic reflection. Static reflection would be the preferred choice with fall-back on dynamic reflection when sufficient type information is not available.

References

1. R.G. Gabriel, D.G. Bobrow, J.L. White, *CLOS in Context – The Shape of the Design Space*. In *Object Oriented Programming – The CLOS perspective*. The MIT Press, Cambridge, MA, 1993, pp. 29-61.
2. K. Czarnecki, U.W. Eisenacker, *Generative Programming – Methods, Tools, and Applications*. Addison Wesley, Reading, MA, 2000.
3. B. Stroustrup, *The Design and Evolution of C++*. Addison Wesley, Reading, MA, 1994.
4. Sleepycat Software, *The Berkeley Database*, http://www.sleepycat.com.
5. MySQL, *MySQL*, http://www.mysql.com.
6. Microsoft, *ActiveX Data Objects*, http://msdn.microsoft.com/library/psdk/dasdk/adot9elu.htm.
7. K.A. Knizhnik, *The GigaBASE Object-Relational database system*, http://www.ispras.ru/~knizhnik.
8. Sun Microsystems, Java Database Connectivity, http://java.sun.com/.
9. Petter Urkedal, *Tools for Template Metaprogramming*, http://matfys.lth.se/~petter/src/more/metad.
10. R. Sunderraman, *Oracle8™ Programming: a primer*, Addison-Wesley, MA, 2000.
11. P. J. Plauger, A. Stepanov, M. Lee, D. Musser, *The Standard Template Library*, Prentice-Hall, 2000.
12. J. Malenfant, M. Jaques, and F.-N. Demers, *A tutorial on behavioral reflection and its implementation*. Proceedings of the Reflection 96 Conference, Gregor Kiczales, editor, pp. 1-20, San Francisco, California, USA, April 1996.
13. Tyng-Ruey Chuang and Y. S. Kuo and Chien-Min Wang, *Non-Intrusive Object Introspection in C++: Architecture and Application*. Proceedings of the 20th Int. Conference on Software Engineering, IEEE Computer Society Press, pp. 312-321, 1998
14. Peter W. Madany, Nayeem Islam, Panos Kougiouris, and Roy H. Campbell, *Reification and reflection in C++: An operating systems perspective*. Technical Report UIUCDCS-R-92-1736, Dept. of Computer Science, University of Illinois at Urbana-Champaign, March 1992.
15. Yutaka Ishikawa, Atsushi Hori, Mitsuhisa Sato, Motohiko Matsuda, J. Nolte, Hiroshi Tezuka, Hiroki Konaka, Munenori Maeda, and Kazuto Kubota, *Design and Implementation of metalevel architecture in C++ – MPC++ approach*. Proceedings of the Reflection 96 Conference, Gregor Kiczales, editor, pages 153-166, San Francisco, California, USA, April 1996.
16. B. Gowing and V. Cahill, *Meta-Object Protocols for C++: The Iguana Approach*. Proc. Reflection '96, San Francisco, California, 1996, pp. 137-152.
17. Shigeru Chiba. *A metaobject protocol for C++*. Conference Proceedings of Object-Oriented Programming Systems, Languages and Applications, pp. 285-299, ACM Press, 1995.

Scenario-Based Generation and Evaluation of Software Architectures

Hans de Bruin and Hans van Vliet

Vrije Universiteit
Mathematics and Computer Science Department
De Boelelaan 1081a, 1081 HV Amsterdam, The Netherlands
{hansdb,hans}@cs.vu.nl

Abstract. Architecture conception is a difficult and time consuming process, requiring advanced skills from the software architect. The tasks of an architect are alleviated if means can be provided to generate architectures that can be evaluated with respect to functional and non-functional requirements. This paper discusses an approach for doing so. It centers around a rich feature-solution graph which captures the evolving knowledge about requirements and solution fragments. This graph is used to guide an iterative architecture development process.

1 Introduction

The architecture of a software system captures early design decisions. These early design decisions reflect major quality concerns, including functionality. We would obviously like to design our systems such that they fulfill the quality requirements set for them. Unfortunately, we in general do not succeed in doing so in a straightforward way. For that reason, we develop an initial architecture, meanwhile making tradeoffs between quality concerns. We next assess the architecture with respect to its qualities, as far as such is feasible. If necessary, the architecture is next adapted, and the assessment/adapt cycle is repeated.

This paper is concerned with supporting this iterative process. In particular, we propose to use a rich feature-solution graph to capture the evolving knowledge about quality requirements and solution fragments. This graph is next used to guide the iterative architecture development process.

Our approach to generating and evaluating software architectures combines and extends the following, widely accepted ideas:

Architectural patterns. By capturing structural and behavioral aspects of (partial) design solutions together with their quality properties, we may hope to be able to design and reason about architectural solutions and their quality attributes. Attribute-Based Architectural Styles (ABASs) have been proposed as a means to do so. An ABAS combines an architectural style (such as a layered style) with certain quality characteristics (such as portability) [11].

Scenario-based evaluation. Architecture evaluation is most often scenario-based. Different stakeholders are then asked to come up with scenarios of anticipated use. These scenarios may concern the present set of requirements as well as possible future extensions or changes. The latter are especially useful to assess the architecture with respect to structural aspects such as flexibility or modifiability. Well-known architecture assessment methods are SAAM (Software Architecture Analysis Method) [7] and its successor ATAM (Architecture Tradeoff Analysis Method) [8]. The emphasis in ATAM is on identifying interactions between various quality attributes in a system. So called tradeoff points, i.e. architectural elements to which multiple quality attributes are sensitive, require to be analyzed carefully.

In later publications on ATAM, e.g. [9], attention has shifted from (ex-post) quality assessments to (ex-ante) architectural approaches with known quality properties, captured in ABASs.

Goal-oriented requirements engineering. Early approaches to requirements engineering focussed on eliciting and documenting the requirements sec, and not the reasons for them. In goal-oriented requirements engineering, the relation between goals and requirements is represented explicitly. Since goals may conflict, this requires resolution strategies to obtain a satisfactory compromise [12, 13]. Recently, representation schemes used in goal-oriented requirements engineering have also been used to represent dependencies between quality goals and architectural styles [5].

In our approach, the generation of a software architecture is based on a rich feature-solution graph, which connects quality requirements with solution fragments at the architectural level. The structure of this feature-solution graph resembles that of the goal-hierarchy in goal-oriented requirements engineering. The solution fragments included in this graph have much in common with ABASs. This approach is made concrete as follows (see also Figure 1):

Scenario-based architecture description. Software architectures are described using a scenario-based modeling technique called Use Case Maps (UCM) [4, 3]. UCM is a diagrammatic modeling technique to describe behavioral and to a lesser extent structural aspects of a system at a high (e.g., architectural) level of abstraction. UCM provides stubs (i.e., hooks) where the behavior of a system can be varied statically at construction time as well as dynamically at run time. These stubs provide the basis for generating alternative software architectures with so called *architectural snippets*, which are basically small, reusable UCM scenarios.

Architecture generator. An architecture generator generates a candidate software architecture. It does so on the basis of the feature-solution graph that establishes the connection between quality requirements and solutions. The generator uses the graph to fill in UCM stubs with appropriate architectural snippets. This can be seen as the equivalent of an aspect weaver found in aspect-oriented programming systems [10].

Scenario-based evaluation. Once an architecture has been generated, it must be evaluated on the basis of UCM scenarios to assess whether they meet non-functional requirements. For a number of quality attributes, this can be done automatically. Other attributes require the expert eye of a software architect.

But do not stop here. An interesting extension to the above scheme is to automatically refine architectures on the basis of evaluation outcomes. Suppose, for example, that a certain non-functional requirement has not been met in the current architectural solution. By consulting the feature-solution graph, we might come up with several solutions that can be applied to remedy the shortcoming. Thus, in principle, the outcome of the evaluation phase can be used to drive the architecture generation process in the next iteration. That is, the generator selects a solution and then generates a refined architecture, which is evaluated in its turn. This process is repeated until all requirements are met or we run out of potential solutions.

The idea to generate architectures driven by functional as well as non-functional requirements is not new. Work in frame technology [1], the framework for non-functional requirements discussed in [15], GenVoca generators [2], and aspect-oriented programming [10], have similar objectives. What sets our approach apart is that we use a scenario-based modeling technique in combination with a rich feature-solution graph. Generated architectures are evaluated using scenario-based evaluation techniques. The evaluations might trigger further optimizations in the generated architectures, using the knowledge captured in the feature-solution graph. These optimizations are then evaluated again using the same set of scenarios. In this way, we get a closed loop process, occasionally requiring the architect's expertise.

In this paper, we restrict ourselves mostly to behavioral aspects such as functionality, security, and performance. There are no principal reasons for not supporting

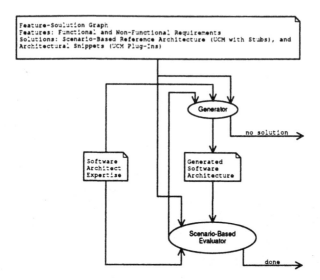

Fig. 1. The process of generating and evaluating architectures.

structural aspects, such as flexibility, integrability, and modifiability, as well. However, the notation that we use for architecture description needs to be extended to cater for the latter aspects.

This paper is organized as follows. Section 2 introduces a running example used to illustrate our approach. The major architectural design dimensions for this problem are discussed in section 3. A feature-solution graph for the example system is given in section 4. We discuss how the graph is used to generate and evaluate architectures. Section 5 then elaborates several candidate architectures for the example system, using the knowledge captured in the feature-solution graph. Finally, section 6 gives our conclusions.

2   Running Example: Resource Management (RM) System

A generic Resource Management (RM) system is used as a running example. The conceptual model of the RM system is depicted in Figure 2. The basic idea is that a *customer* can *reserve* a *resource* that can be taken up later on. *Resources* are being described in *resource types*. The RM system can be seen as an abstraction for a collection of information systems that all share the concept of claiming resources. For instance, in a hotel reservation system, the resources are rooms, whereas in a car rental system, the resources are cars.

Typically, a RM system provides the following, basic functionality:

– Make/Cancel/Amend/Take-up Reservation;
– Add/Remove/Amend Resource or ResourceType.

A RM system is not necessarily restricted to serve one company. It is perfectly possible to share resources amongst companies, or alternatively to acquire resources from other companies as in the case of Business-to-Business (B2B) applications. A resource type object can then include functionality for locating resources outside the scope of a company. Yet another possibility is that a resource type object acts as a broker or connects to a broker to find the best offer amongst a number of resource providers.

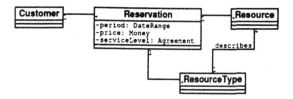

Fig. 2. Conceptual model of the Resource Management System.

3 Exploring Design Dimensions for the RM System

The 3-tier reference architecture is frequently used as a starting point in devising architectures for classes of information systems, such as the RM system. As the name suggests, the 3-tier reference architecture is composed of three layers:

- User Interface (UI) layer, alternatively called presentation or medium layer;
- Business Logic (BL) layer, alternatively called transaction or workflow layer;
- Data Management (DM), alternatively called application or abstraction layer.

The characteristics of the 3-tier architecture are flexibility, scalability, user independence, availability, and low upgrade costs. On the downside, the architecture can suffer from performance problems and may involve high initial costs [17].

Frequently, the layers are further divided, resulting in a $n(> 3)$-tier architecture. These decompositions depend on both functional and non-functional requirements. We will now discuss a number of alternatives for each layer. The intent is not to show every conceivable alternative, but rather to indicate that even in a relatively simple system, the design choices grow rapidly. In addition, we show that a decomposition in one layer might have an impact on other layers. Hence we need a kind of architecture generator to assure that the effects of a decomposition are properly effectuated in other layers as well. This can be seen as the counterpart of aspect weaving in aspect-oriented programming systems.

3.1 User Interface (UI) Layer

The UI layer is responsible for interacting with the user. The term user should be interpreted in a broad sense. It could be a real user, interacting with, for instance, a Graphical UI (GUI) or a Command Line Interface (CLI). In case of B2B interaction, it could also be another system that manipulates reservations for particular resources maintained by the system. A typical technique for B2B interaction is XML.

The logical UI layer may be split in two physical layers for WEB enabling. One side runs the WEB browser, whereas the other side generates HTML pages and reacts to HTTP requests. Offering public access to the system by using Internet technology (e.g., XML and HTML) typically imposes non-functional requirements in the areas of security and performance. As a result, the UI layer must be further refined to deal with these aspects.

3.2 Business Logic (BL) Layer

The BL layer manages the interactions between the UI and the DM layer. It can be thought of as a workflow layer, realizing the automated business processes. The BL layer abstracts away from media peculiarities, which are handled by the UI layer. It rather provides media independent workflow and dialogue handlers (sometimes called system services) with hooks to connect to the UI layer. The BL layer is built on the abstractions provided by the DM layer. Typically, the interface to the DM layer is composed of an OO class model (e.g., a slightly less abstract class model than shown in Figure 2) and a number of elementary, system services (e.g., elementary use cases for basic object manipulations).

There is not always a real need for a BL layer. For simple applications that support only elementary services, the BL layer can be skipped. In that case, the UI layer calls on the OO abstractions provided by the DM layer directly, and vice versa. Even if complex services are provided by the system, the BL layer can be virtually non-existent. That is, the BL and DM layer are effectively merged into one layer. This is typically the case when a "pure" object-oriented approach is followed, where data and business logic are tightly integrated into objects.

3.3 Data Management (DM) Layer

Many degrees of freedom exist for realizing the DM layer, to name a few:

- interface with a relational or object DBMS;
- use the persistency features of a programming language or library;
- read from and write to flat files.

The objects in the DM layer do not necessarily reside in the same system. As discussed before, resources may be shared (temporarily) amongst a number of systems, as is the case in B2B applications. An object like *resource type* then fulfills the role of resource locator or broker. The extended interpretation of *resource type* has impact on other layers. For instance, a broker can request several resource providers to come up with an offer within a certain period. In that case, a user will not get an immediate response, but rather a notification (e.g., an e-mail) after the bidding period has been elapsed. To put it differently, implementing broker functionality crosscuts the functionality offered in the various layers.

4 Generating and Evaluating Architectures

The starting point for generating and evaluating architectures is first to derive feature dependencies, which in their turn spark of solutions in the form of architectural snippets to be placed in UCM stubs. The feature-solution dependencies are captured in the feature-solution graph. We make a clear distinction between features (i.e., requirements) and the design particles that provide solutions by defining the following two spaces:

Feature space describes the desired properties of the system as expressed by the user.
Solution space contains the internal system decomposition in the form of a reference architecture composed of components. In addition, the solution space may also contain general applicable solutions that can be selected to meet certain non-functional requirements.

A feature-solution graph for the RM system is given in Figure 3. It is composed of the usual AND-OR decompositions to denote combinations and alternatives of features and solutions. We use an AND decomposition to denote that all constituents are included, an OR to select an arbitrary number of constituents, and an EXOR to select exactly one constituent. Besides the AND-OR relationships, the graph contains directed *selection* edges (represented by a solid curve that ends with a hollow pointer) to establish the connection between features and solutions. Thus, a feature in the feature space selects a solution in the solution space. A solution may be connected by selection edges to more detailed, general applicable solutions (e.g., design patterns). That is, solutions are found by determining the transitive closure of selection edges originating from the feature space.

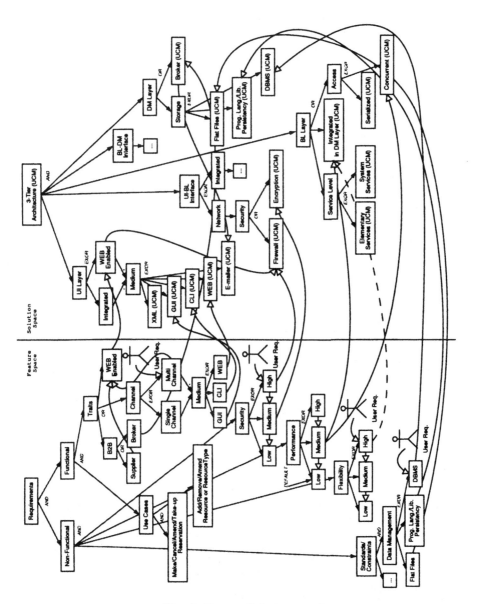

Fig. 3. Feature-Solution graph.

In some cases, it is useful to outrule a solution explicitly. This is done with *negative selection* edges (represented by a dashed curve that ends with a hollow pointer). For example, if we want high flexibility, then the BL layer should *not* be integrated in the DM layer, since merging both layers makes it more difficult to adapt the business logic.

It is interesting to observe that the feature-solution graph contains tradeoff knowledge. For example, the features "high flexibility" and "medium and high performance" give rise to a clash in the sense that for flexibility reasons the BL and DM layer should be separated, whereas for performance reasons they should be integrated. Other indications of tradeoff points can be found when two or more solutions in an OR decomposition are selected simultaneously, that is, their selection stems from distinct feature choices.

For understanding the process of generating and evaluating architectures, recall the scheme given in Figure 1. The architecture generator is driven by the feature-solution graph. Some features can be selected directly on the basis of the requirements. For instance, we might require a high level of flexibility. As a result, the non-functional requirement "Flexibility" in the feature space is set to "High". The implication of this decision is that the BL and DM layer may *not* be merged. For some requirements, the required level of support is harder to determine. Consider, for example, performance. A performance requirement might be that a "Make Reservation" takes less than a second. However, it is not clear from the outset which performance level in the feature-solution graph will satisfy the performance requirement. So as an initial guess, we set the performance to "Low", since this results in less constraints on the design than higher performance levels. The software architecture then has to be evaluated in order to assess whether the performance requirement is satisfied or not. If not, the outcome of the evaluation process will result in setting the performance to a next level (i.e., "Medium"). The next step is to generate a new architecture, and so on, until all requirements are satisfied, or we reach the conclusion that the requirements are too strict.

To summarize the closed-loop process: The non-functional features can be set to a required level, in our example ranging over "Low", "Medium", and "High". A level for a particular feature selects solutions, providing the basis for generating a candidate software architecture. The required level of some features (e.g., flexibility in our example) can be determined directly from the requirements, whereas others must be determined from evaluations (e.g., performance). To put it differently, the feature levels are the knobs with which the architecture can be fine-tuned. Notice that the feature-solution graph is typically underspecified in the sense that not all (EX)OR decompositions are necessarily connected by selection edges. In this way, we have created degrees of freedom for generating design alternatives.

5 Elaborating Architectures for the RM System

In previous sections, we have sketched design dimensions and we have shown how requirements and design alternatives can be connected in a feature-solution graph. We are now in the position to show how the graph can be applied to actually generate architectures for the RM system. To this end, we need some kind of architectural description language, ideally a diagrammatic language that focuses on the larger, architectural issues. The Use Case Map (UCM) notation suits this purpose well. It is a scenario-based technique for capturing behavioral and to a lesser extent structural aspects of an architecture. UCMs can be used for analysis purposes. For instance, in [16] a method is discussed for performance evaluations, and [6] discusses a scenario-based approach for assessing behavioral system properties such as deadlock and reachability.

In the solution space of the feature-solution graph, some solutions in the decomposition tree are marked as UCM. These solutions represent UCM stubs and plug-ins with which an candidate architecture is composed. The principles are demonstrated by taking the "Make Reservation" use case as an example.

5.1 Filling in the Layers

The 3-tier reference architecture is described in terms of a UCM, which is composed of 5 stubs (see Figure 4). Three stubs correspond with the UI, BL, and DM layer, whereas the remaining two model the interface between the UI-BL and the BL-DM layer. As discussed before, a stub can be seen as a placeholder where architectural snippets (i.e., UCM fragments) can be plugged in. The default plug-ins for the stubs do no implement functionality, they simply pass information from their start points to their end points.

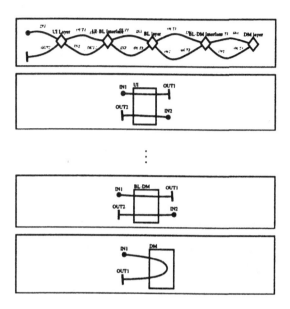

Fig. 4. Reference architecture.

UI layer We assume that a multi channel, WEB enabled UI is selected (see Figure 5). That is, multiple users may use the reservation system simultaneously.

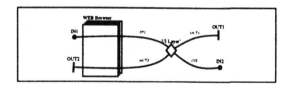

Fig. 5. User Interface Layer.

BL layer The business logic for making a reservation is quite simple. It basically passes on requests from the UI layer to the DM layer and vice versa. To put it differently, the default BL plug-in can be used for the time being.

DM Layer We will make use of a DBMS. For making a reservation, the DM layer first checks the database whether the resources can be acquired or not. If they can be acquired, the database is updated accordingly and the DM layer sends an acknowledgement as a result, otherwise a negative acknowledgement is returned immediately. These two scenarios are captured in the UCM shown in Figure 6.

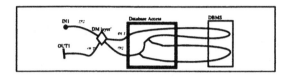

Fig. 6. Data Management layer.

5.2 Feature Interaction

Assume that we require a high level of security. According to the feature-solution graph, this translates into protecting access to the reservation system with a firewall and using encrypted messages between the UI layer and the rest of the system. The process of composing the UI-BL interface with encryption and a firewall is shown in Figure 7. In the first step, the UI-BL interface stub is replaced by encryption/decryption components and a stub called UI-BL interface'. The latter stub in its turn is replaced by a firewall component and the UI-BL interface" stub. The default behavior for a stub is to do nothing, that is, there is a path from IN1 to OUT1 and another one from IN2 to OUT2.

Notice that the order of substitution is important. The architecture generator must be prepared to generate different sequences. The approach of recursively replacing stubs with plug-ins resembles the concept of composition filters used in the programming language SINA [14]. The composition filter model consists of input and output filters that surround an object and affect the messages sent to and received by that object. Composition filters can be seen as objects in the role of proxies that perform additional pre- and post-processing.

Now that the UI-BL interface layer is secured, the new architecture can be evaluated to assess other non-functional requirements. Suppose that because of the security measures that have been taken the performance degrades to an unacceptable level. This means that the architecture must be enhanced in order to improve the performance. One option is to skip the BL layer altogether and to integrate it with the DM layer. But this has a negative impact on flexibility, and this solution is explicitly prohibited if a high level of flexibility is required. Another option is to increase the amount of parallelism in the BL layer, so that it can handle multiple requests simultaneously, instead of serializing them. This solution is shown in Figure 8.

5.3 Crosscutting Layers

Suppose we want to extend the reservation system with B2B functionality in the sense that resources may be acquired from other parties if they cannot be obtained from the system itself (see Figure 9).

In this example, a broker is used to select a best offer amongst the parties involved. This takes time, and for this reason, an AND-fork is introduced, with one branch sending back a reply immediately indicating that the broker process is in progress, and the other branch doing the actual brokering followed by updating the database if a resource has been acquired. Notice that this splitting has impact on the BL and

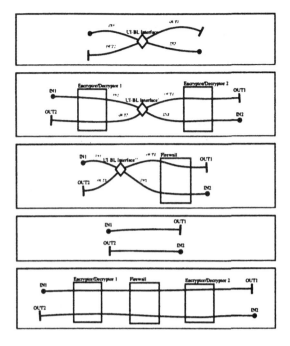

Fig. 7. Composition of design solutions.

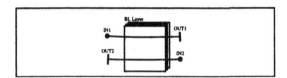

Fig. 8. Parallelizing the Business Logic layer.

UI layer. An advance "brokering-in-progress" message can be sent as an immediate response to the user, whereas the actual result of the broker process can be used for sending a notification to the user, for instance, in the form of an e-mail (see Figure 10).

6 Concluding Remarks and Future Work

We have discussed a closed loop process for generating and evaluating software architectures. At the heart of the process is the feature-solution graph, which combines AND-OR feature and solution decompositions with (negative) selection relationships. The feature-solution graph connects quality requirements with design alternatives. In addition, it can be used to pinpoint tradeoffs between quality attributes such as flexibility and performance, as shown in this paper.

The architectural description language that is being used to specify architectures is actually of secondary importance. In this paper, we make use of Use Case Maps (UCM) because of its scenario-based, visualization, and abstraction properties. Especially its abstraction mechanism in the form of stubs and plug-ins provides the means to specify extensible software architectures. Although UCMs are well-suited for modeling behavioral aspects of a system, they are less equipped for structural aspects. For this reason,

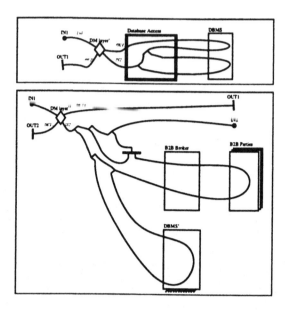

Fig. 9. Data Management layer extended with B2B broker functionality.

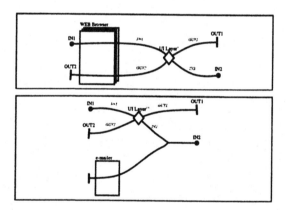

Fig. 10. User Interface layer extended with an e-mailer.

the notation has to be extended, or alternatively other notations should be used beside UCM, to cover the full spectrum of architectural description. Nevertheless, in our present work, UCM serves our purpose well and, in our opinion, it is only a minor step to add new relationships between components along with appropriate viewpoints to cater for yet unattended structural aspects.

In the near future, we want to investigate tool support for looping through the generate-evaluate cycle. One possible solution is to encode the feature-solution graph as Prolog facts, goals, and clauses. This requires that further attention is given to the precise semantics of the constructs in the feature-solution graph. We can use the resolution mechanism of Prolog to produce solutions, i.e., software architectures that satisfy the requirements set. To determine whether a certain Prolog goal is satisfied or not translates to architecture evaluation with respect to a corresponding quality attribute.

In addition, intelligent help can be provided to guide the architect in preparing the next iteration.

We envisage that the feature-solution graph can be further enriched with relationships and annotations to accurately capture domain and architectural knowledge and the connection between them. In this way, we build a body of knowledge that can be applied to similar problems.

References

1. Paul G. Basset. *Framing Software Reuse: Lessons from the Real World.* Prentice Hall, Upper Saddle River, New Jersey, 1996. Yourdon Press.
2. Don Batory, Gang Chen, and Tao Wang. Design wizards and visual programming environments for GenVoca generators. *IEEE Transactions on Software Engineering*, 26(5):441–452, May 1998.
3. R.J.A. Buhr. Use Case Maps as architecture entities for complex systems. *IEEE Transactions on Software Engineering*, 24(12):1131–1155, December 1998.
4. R.J.A. Buhr and R.S. Casselman. *Use CASE Maps for Object-Oriented Systems.* Prentice Hall, Upper Saddle River, New Jersey, 1996.
5. L. Chung, D. Gross, and E. Yu. Architectural design to meet stakeholder requirements. In P. Donohue, editor, *Software Architecture*, pages 545–564. Kluwer Academic Publishers, 1999.
6. Hans de Bruin. Scenario-based analysis of component compositions. In Greg Butler and Stan Jarzabek, editors, *Proceedings of the Second Symposium on Generative and Component-Based Software Engineering (GCSE'2000), Erfurt, Germany*, Lecture Notes in Computer Science (LNCS), pages 1–18, Berlin, Germany, October 9–12, 2000. Springer-Verlag.
7. R. Kazman, G. Abowd, L. Bass, and P. Clements. Scenario-based analysis of software architecture. *IEEE Software*, 13(6):47–56, 1996.
8. R. Kazman, M. Klein, M. Barbacci, T. Longstaff, H. Lipson, and J. Carriere. The architecture tradeoff analysis method. In *Proceedings of the 4th International Conference on Engineering of Complex Systems (ICECCS98)*, pages 68–78. IEEE CS Press, 1998.
9. R. Kazman, M. Klein, and P. Clements. ATAM: Method for architecture evaluation. Technical report, CMU/SEI-2000-TR-004, 2000.
10. Gregor Kiczales, John Lamping, Anurg Mendhekar, Chris Maeda, Cristina Videira Lopes, Jean-Marc Loingtier, and John Irwin. Aspect-oriented programming. In M. Askit and M. Matsuoka, editors, *Proceedings of 11th European Conference on Object-Oriented Programming (ECOOP'97), Finland*, volume 1241 of *Lecture Notes in Computer Science (LNCS)*, pages 220–242, Berlin, Germany, June 9–13, 1997. Springer-Verlag.
11. M.H. Klein, R. Kazman, L. Bass, J. Carriere, M. Barbacci, and H. Lipson. Attribute-based architectural styles. In P. Donohue, editor, *Software Architecture*, pages 225–244. Kluwer Academic Publishers, 1999.
12. Axel van Lamsweerde. Requirements engineering in the year 00: A research perspective. In *Conference Proceedings ICSE'00*, pages 5–19, Limerick, Ireland, 2000. ACM.
13. John Mylopoulos, Lawrence Chung, Stephen Liao, Huaiqing Wang, and Eric Yu. Exploring alternatives during requirements analysis. *IEEE Software*, 18(1):92–96, January 2001.
14. TRESE project. WWW: http://trese.cs.utwente.nl/sina/.
15. Nelson R. Rosa, George R.R. Justo, and Paulo R.F. Cunha. A framework for building non-functional software architectures. In *Proceedings of the 16th ACM Symposium on Applied Computing (SAC'2001)*, pages 141–147, Las Vegas, Nevada, USA, March 11–14, 2001.
16. W.C. Scratchley. *Evaluation and Diagnosis of Concurrency Architectures.* PhD thesis, Department of Systems and Computer Engineering, Carleton University, 2000.
17. A. Umar. *Object-Oriented Client/Server Internet Environments.* Prentice Hall, Englewood Cliffs, New Jersey, 1997.

The Role of Design Components in Test Plan Generation

Jaehyoun Kim and C. Robert Carlson

Department of Computer Science, Illinois Institute of Technology
201 East Loop Road, Wheaton, Illinois 60187, U.S.A
{kimjaeh | carlson}@iit.edu

Abstract. In this paper, we focus on the integration of a test plan generation technique in the context of a use case design methodology. The foundation for this approach lies in partitioning the design schemata into a layered architecture of functional components called design units together with action matrices that tabularly represent each use case scenario as a unique sequence of design units. Based on these two concepts, we demonstrate how test plan generation and software test metrics are developed. The action matrix with design unit boundaries provides the test engineer with a constructive framework to follow a bottom-up test process that proceeds from unit to integration and user acceptance testing. The proposed software testing metrics are employed to improve the productivity of the testing process through scenario prioritization. This approach supports effective test plan generation based on sound and systematic design procedures.

1. Introduction

As software systems have gotten more complicated, software development techniques have needed to improve to cope with this complexity. Software development methodologies [2, 7, 9, 18, 20] have been introduced to integrate design, code development and testing processes. Each methodology provides a different approach to software development. However, no single methodology provides a complete solution [19]. This means that a process is needed that integrates and extends existing methodologies.

One such effort is the Fusion Method [5] that combines and extends existing methodologies such as CRC [1], OMT [18] and OOD [2]. It provides a logical and systematic way of developing object-oriented software. Another effort is the Unified Modeling Language (UML) that combines the best notations used in the three most popular analysis and design methodologies, the Booch method [2], the Object Modeling Technique [18], and the Object-Oriented Software Engineering (OOSE) [7], to produce a single, universal modeling language that can be used with any method. It is regarded as a language for specifying, visualizing, and documenting object-oriented systems. However, these methodologies neglect the role of test specification during the design phase.

This paper supports the thesis that test activity and test plan generation should be initiated early in the design process to reduce the cost of testing and prevent problems from propagating later on. A component analysis technique is introduced which produces design units. Design units provide the framework to achieve a consistent integrated approach to design, code generation, and testing. By applying the design unit concept, we develop a bottom-up test plan generation process during design that automatically carries over to code testing. Bottom-up test plan generation uses a hierarchical action matrix that combines an action matrix and a design unit characterization of each unit. This hierarchical action matrix with design unit boundaries provides the test engineer with a constructive framework to generate a bottom-up testing process that follows from unit to integration and user acceptance testing. The test engineers can choose one or more of the design units based on their preference for testing techniques. In addition, this paper describes software testing metrics which the test engineers can use to guide the testing process.

This paper begins with a description of our software design methodology and the concept of design units which it employs. The design of *Withdraw Money* and *Deposit Money* use cases for an Automatic Teller Machine application are then specified using interaction diagrams. The design unit concept is presented and applied to interaction diagrams. A hierarchical action matrix is then introduced and a bottom-up testing process is described. Finally, two software testing metrics are described.

2. Software Development Methodology

Use cases have been well established as one of the fundamental techniques for object-oriented analysis and design. The use case driven approach has become popular as a software development technique because of its capacity for capturing functional requirements. It provides a powerful means of communication between different kinds of people participating in software development – users, analysts, designers, developers and testers. Carlson and Hurlbut [4, 6] proposed an adaptive use case methodology for software development that leads to semi-automatic processes for code generation and test plan generation. This methodology is enhanced by a test plan generation technique [8] that employs an action matrix containing a collection of the executable sequences of design units. This test plan generation approach improves the productivity of the testing process through use case scenario prioritization and unit decomposition.

This section briefly describes Carlson's software design methodology [4]. The methodology starts off with requirements analysis and produces a use case model in which actors and use cases are identified and represented graphically. Interaction diagrams are produced, one for each use case. The methodology then follows two collaborative paths each for a unique purpose. They are the code generation path and the test plan generation path, as illustrated in Figure 1. Both paths work from interaction diagrams and employ the design unit concept as their standardizing, coordinating and tracking element. The code generation path produces event-state tables that describe the behavioral changes of an object. Both interaction diagrams and event-state tables are the key design elements used to generate a code skeleton.

The test plan generation path produces an action matrix that helps generate a preliminary test plan and test scheme. The action matrix is intended to tabularly represent each scenario as a unique sequence of design units. A key consideration of this methodology is the notion of requirements tracking throughout the software development process based on the modular design unit concepts introduced in the next section.

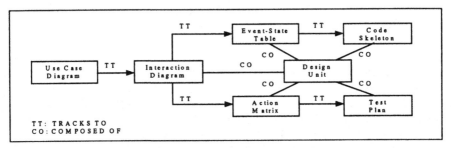

Figure 1. Overview of Carlson's Software Design Methodology

3. High-Level Design

To demonstrate the application of the design unit concept, we must first introduce an example design specification produced by our methodology. We begin with descriptions of a *Withdraw Money* use case and a *Deposit Money* use case drawn from an automatic teller machine application. The analysis of the *Withdraw Money* and the *Deposit Money* use cases results in the interaction diagrams shown in Figures 2 and 3, respectively.

3.1 Use Case Description

Withdraw Money **Use Case**: The use case *Withdraw Money* is initiated when a customer inserts a cash card. This event is recognized by the interface object *System Panel* and passed to the control object *System Controller*. The *System Controller* reads its card number and requests the password.

When the customer enters the password, this event is recognized by the interface object *System Panel* and passed to the control object *System Controller*. The *System Controller* verifies the card number and password by sending a message to the service object *Bank*. If approved, the *System Controller* requests the amount of cash. If not, the *System Controller* requests the password again.

When the customer enters the amount, this amount is recognized by the interface object *System Panel* and passed to the control object *System Controller*. The *System Controller* checks the account balance with the customer *Account*. If the balance is smaller than the amount requested, the transaction fails. If not, the *System Controller* calculates the balance by sending a message to the service object *Account*. Then the system returns money and prints a receipt.

Deposit Money **Use Case**: The use case *Deposit Money* is initiated when a customer inserts a cash card. This event is recognized by the interface object *System Panel* and passed to the control object *System Controller*. The *System Controller* reads its card number and requests the password.

When the customer enters the password, this event is recognized by the interface object *System Panel* and passed to the control object *System Controller*. The *System Controller* verifies the card number and password by sending a message to the service object *Bank*. If approved, the *System Controller* requests the amount of the money to be deposited. If not, the *System Controller* requests the password again.

When the customer enters the deposit, the amount is recognized by the interface object *System Panel* and passed to the control object *System Controller*. The *System Controller* accumulates the amount to the current balance by sending a message to the service object *Account*. Then the *System Controller* requests the envelope that includes the deposited money. When the customer deposits the envelope, the system prints a receipt and ejects the card.

3.2. Interaction Diagrams

At this point in the software development methodology, the designer produces an interaction diagram for each use case. The interaction diagram represents an interaction of objects through message passing between the objects in time sequence. The notation used to depict an interaction diagram comes from [3] and utilizes several extensions to the notation found in UML. The interaction diagrams for the *Withdraw Money* and *Deposit Money* use cases are shown in Figures 2 and 3, respectively.

The interaction between the system and a customer combines four separate dialogues, *Insert Card*, *Enter Pin Number*, *Enter Amount,* and *Receipt*, as shown in Figure 2. Each external event starts a particular dialogue with the system that, in some cases, is repeated. After receiving a response from the system, the actor decides whether that dialogue with the system is to be repeated or a different dialogue is to be initiated. The labels at the left side of the interaction diagram indicate that a dialogue may be repeated. For example, label A means that the actor can reinitiate the *Enter Pin Number* dialogue.

An analysis of the *Enter Amount* scenario yields two different use case scenarios, *Transaction Failed* and *Transaction Succeeded*, shown in Figure 2. In the *Enter Amount* scenario, when a customer enters the withdrawal amount, it is verified by the system. If the balance is smaller than the amount requested, the *Transaction Failed* scenario follows. Otherwise, the *Transaction Succeeded* scenario follows. In order to describe multiple use case scenarios we use a graphical notation where numbers are used to relate distinctive in-messages to their corresponding out-messages. For example, in Figure 2 the *System Controller* sends the *Transaction Failed* message to the actor when receiving a *Reject* message while the *System Controller* sends the *Calculation Balance* message to the *Account* object when receiving an *Accept* message.

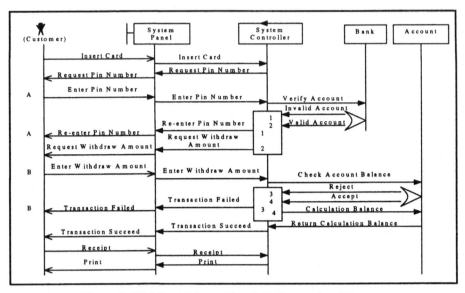

Figure 2. *Withdraw Money* Use Case Interaction Diagram

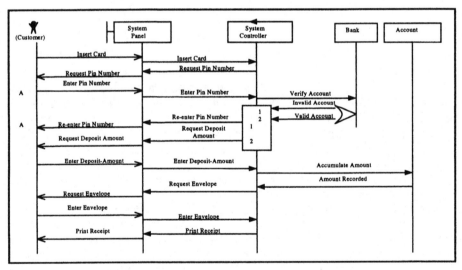

Figure 3. *Deposit Money* Use Case Interaction Diagram

4. Design Units

Each interaction diagram can be partitioned algorithmically into a layered architecture of functional components called design units. Several partitioning strategies are possible, each providing different properties at the boundary points between adjacent design units. These properties can be exploited by our test generation strategies. The goal of these design units is to maximize the ease of generating code, integrating automatic testing techniques, and managing subsequent changes. Each design unit is described below:

Method Unit: Method executed by an object in response to a message.

The simplest choice is to let each method be a design unit. Figure 2 has twenty-eight method units, as listed in the left column of Table 1. Each method represents a distinctive method unit in the interaction diagram such as *Insert Card, Request Pin Number, Enter Pin Number, Verify Account, Invalid Account, Re-enter Pin* Number, *Valid Account, Request Amount, Enter Amount, Check Account Balance, Reject, Accept,* etc. Method units provide a good choice during unit testing.

State Unit: Sequence of methods executed during the interval bounded by consecutive states as defined by an algorithmically defined event-state table.

State units can be algorithmically identified in several ways [3]. To simplify the discussion, we have chosen to focus on a state model for the *System Controller* control object based on the messages received by and sent from it. A state unit can be characterized by a state pair [Si, Sj], where Si is a current state and Sj is a subsequent state. Each state pair can be enhanced at design time by predicate conditions associated with each of these states. Such information is useful when state based testing techniques are applied. A state unit consists of multiple method units. In the interaction diagram shown in Figure 2, nine state units have been algorithmically identified. For example, when receiving the event *Insert Card* in state S0, the state of the control object is changed to state S1 and the action *Request Pin Number* is initiated. In state S1, the event *Enter Pin Number* can occur subject to a possible constraint on state S1 over the number of time it can be attempted. This constraint could form the basis for a possible state S1 test.

Maximal Linear Unit: Sequence of methods executed during the interval bounded by consecutive choices, either actor or object choices.

A maximal linear unit consists of one or more state units. A maximal linear unit is the same as a dialogue unit if no choice nodes exist. The MLUs described below focus on the state units associated with the *System Controller* control object. In Figure 2, a choice node for the *System Controller* control object occurs when it receives either the *Invalid Account* or *Valid Account* message from the *Bank* object and either the *Reject* or *Accept* message from *Account* object. Thus, the maximal linear units for the *Withdraw Money* use case are [*Insert Card, Request Pin Number*], [*Enter Pin Number, Verify Account*], [*Invalid Account, Re-enter Pin Number*], [*Valid Account, Request Amount*], [*Enter Amount, Check Account Balance*], [*Reject, Transaction Failed*], [*Accept, Calculate Balance, Return Current Balance, Transaction Succeed*], and [*Receipt, Print*]. Maximal linear units provide the test engineer with the elements with which to apply straight line testing techniques.

Dialogue Unit: Sequence of methods bounded by input from an actor and the system's response to that actor.

A dialogue unit consists of one or more maximal linear units. In the interaction diagram shown in Figure 2, we can identify all possible paths from the actor and the system's response to the actor. The dialogue units include [*Insert Card, Request Pin Number*], [*Enter Pin Number, Verify Account, Invalid Account, Re-enter Pin Number*], [*Enter Pin Number, Verify Account, Valid Account, Request Amount*], [*Enter Amount, Check Account Balance, Reject, Transaction Failed*], [*Enter Amount, Check Account*

Balance, Accept, Calculate Balance, Return Current Balance, Transaction Succeed],
and [*Receipt, Print*]. Dialogue units are useful for establishing user acceptance test
specifications.

Table 1. Enumeration of Design units – Withdraw Money Use Case

Method Unit	State Unit	MLU	Dialogue Unit		
Insert Card [2]	S0, S1	MLU1	DU1		
Request Pin Number [2]					
Enter Pin Number [2]	S1/S3, S2	MLU2			DU2.2
Verify Account				DU2.1	
Invalid Account	S2, S3	MLU3	DU2		
Re-enter Pin Number [2]					
Valid Account	S2, S4	MLU4			DU2.2
Request Withdraw Amount [2]					
Enter Withdraw Amount [2]	S4/S6, S5	MLU5			DU3.2
Check Account Balance				DU3.1	
Reject	S5, S6	MLU6			
Transaction Failed [2]			DU3		
Accept	S5, S7				
Calculate Balance		MLU7			DU3.2
Return Current Balance	S7, S8				
Transaction Succeed [2]					
Receipt	S8, S0	MLU8	DU4		
Print [2]					

Table 2. Enumeration of Design Units - Deposit Money Use Case

Method Unit	State Unit	MLU	Dialogue Unit		
Insert Card [2]	S0, S11	MLU11	DU11		
Request Pin Number [2]					
Enter Pin Number [2]	S11/S13, S12	MLU12			DU12.2
Verify Account				DU12.1	
Invalid Account	S12, S13	MLU13	DU12		
Re-enter Pin Number [2]					
Valid Account	S12, S14	MLU14			DU12.2
Request Deposit-Amount [2]					
Enter Deposit-Amount [2]	S14, S15				
Accumulate Amount		MLU15	DU13		
Amount Recorded	S15, S16				
Request Envelope [2]					
Enter Envelope [2]	S16, S0	MLU16	DU14		
Print [2]					

Table 1 and 2 summarize the different design units that can be obtained
algorithmically from the interaction diagrams for the *Withdraw Money* and *Deposit
Money* use cases, respectively. Each column represents one of the above design unit
categories. Each event in the interaction diagram is represented by a method unit. The
second column identifies the sequence of methods that define a state pair. For

example, the method units, *Insert Card* and *Request Pin Number*, are associated with the state pair [S0, S1]. Dialogue units DU1, DU2, DU3 and DU4 shown in Table 1 represent a basic interaction between the actor and the system. Dialogue units can be further decomposed. For example, DU2 consists of two subdialogues DU2.1 and DU2.2 while DU3 consists of two subdialogues DU3.1 and DU3.2.

5. Testing

Software testing is a critical element to verify that a correct system is being built. Glen Myer [13] states "Testing is a process of executing a program with the intent of finding an error." It means that testing activity is initiated after completion of the software development process. However, McGregor [10] noted that "There are a number of products of the software development process that should be tested, including: requirement models, analysis and design models, architecture individual components and integrated system code." It means that a good test plan should establish test specification earlier in the software development process. Our approach emphasizes the generation of test specifications in the design stage while traditional software testing concentrates on testing program source code.

5.1 Test Plan Generation

In an action matrix, each row represents a use case scenario and each column represents one of the design units identified for that application. Each scenario includes an ordered collection of design units. Figure 4 shows messages associated with each state unit identified for the *Withdraw Money* and *Deposit Money* use cases in the automatic teller machine application.

Index	State Unit
A1	Insert Card / Request Pin Number
B1	Enter Pin Number / Verify Account
C1	Invalid Account / Re-enter Pin Number
D1	Valid Account / Request Withdrawal Amount
E1	Enter Withdrawal Amount / Check Account Balance
F1	Reject / Transaction Failed
G1	Accept / Calculation Balance
H1	Return Current Balance / Transaction Succeed
I1	Receipt / Print

Index	State Unit
A2	Insert Card / Request Pin Number
B2	Enter Pin Number / Verify Account
C2	Invalid Account / Re-enter Pin Number
D2	Valid Account / Request Deposit Amount
E2	Enter Deposit-Amount / Accumulate Amount
F2	Amount Recorded / Request Envelope
G2	Enter Envelope / Print

Figure 4. State Unit Index Table for Withdraw Money and Deposit Money Use Cases

The action matrix is generated algorithmically from the interaction diagram [8]. The hierarchical action matrix integrates the hierarchy of design units into the action matrix tables. In the hierarchical action matrix, each scenario is represented by a row and design units are represented by a column. The top rows of the hierarchical action matrix contain a hierarchical composition of the design units from state units to dialogue units. Each number i in a cell shown in Figure 5 and 6 indicates that the particular scenario performs the specific state unit, shown in Figure 3 (a) and (b), as the i th step in the scenario. The symbol (+) in the design units is used to denote that the sequence of state units (e.g., (2, 3) in the *Invalid Account* Scenario and (4, 5) in the *Transaction Failed* Scenario) is repeated in DU2.1 and DU3.1. This table is used to select testing techniques, their scope and order of application.

Design Units	DU1	DU2			DU3				DU4
		DU2.2		DU2.2	DU3.2		DU3.2		
		DU2.1 +			DU3.1 +				
	MLU1	MLU2	MLU3	MLU4	MLU5	MLU6	MLU7		MLU8
Use Case Scenarios	A1	B1	C1	D1	E1	F1	G1	H1	I1
Withdraw Succeed Scenario	1	2		3	4		5	6	7
Invalid Account Scenario	1	2	3						
Transaction Failed Scenario	1	2		3	4	5			

Figure 5. Hierarchical Action Matrix for a Withdraw Money Use Case

Design Units	DU11	DU12			DU13		DU14
		DU12.2		DU12.2			
		DU12.1 +					
	MLU11	MLU12	MLU13	MLU14	MLU15		MLU16
Use Case Scenarios	A2	B2	C2	D2	E2	F2	G2
Deposit Succeed Scenario	1	2		3	4	5	6
Invalid Account Scenario	1	2	3				

Figure 6. Hierarchical Action Matrix for a Deposit Money Use Case

Different testing techniques may be appropriate depending on the choice of design units. Each column shown in Figure 5 is equivalent to a state unit shown in Figure 4 (a) and suitable to specific unit testing techniques. Method unit testing depends on the object type, e.g., interface, control, or service object. State based testing techniques can be used with state units. After executing unit testing, integration testing is begun. Integration testing techniques can be used with a use case unit or an ordered list of use case scenarios. Maximal linear units rely on path testing techniques. User acceptance testing can be used with dialogue units or use case units. Based on this choice, the test plan contains a set of design units together with appropriate unit testing technique to be applied to these units.

5.2 Software Test Metrics

Software test metrics are used to evaluate the use case scenarios defined by the action matrix so that a test plan will emerge which improves the productivity of the testing process. The purpose of these metrics is to "optimize" the order in which the scenarios defined by the rows of the hierarchical action matrix are tested. This approach was adapted from Musa's work on Operational Profiles [15, 16]. Musa's approach assumes that the test engineer has sufficient insight to assess the "criticality" of state units and assign weighting factors to the elements of the action matrix [12, 14]. The software test metrics described in this paper focus on the design units based reusability properties of the scenarios.

5.2.1 Most Critical Scenario. The first metric is an adaptation of Musa's 'most critical operational profile' approach [15, 16]. It assumes that the designer can make these judgments and establish weight factors based on the "criticality" of state units.

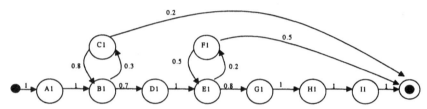

Figure 7. Use Case Dialogue Map for a Withdraw Money Use Case

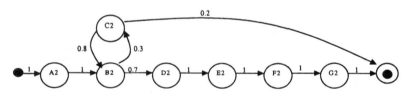

Figure 8. Use Case Dialogue Map for a Deposit Money Use Case

Figures 7 and 8 show use case dialogue maps [8] to apply the calculation of total probability of occurrence in each use case scenario. Figure 7 shows a use case dialogue map for the *Withdraw Money* use case while Figure 8 shows a use case dialogue map for the *Deposit Money* use case. The *Withdraw Money* use case consists of three different scenarios. The direct path of 'Withdraw succeed scenario' consists of the sequence of state units 'A1 -> B1 -> D1> E1 -> G1 -> H1 -> I1' with the amount of weighted values shown in Figure 7. The direct path of 'Invalid account scenario' in the *Withdraw Money* use case consists of the sequence of state units 'A1 -> B1 -> C1' with the amount of weighted values shown in Figure 7. The direct path of 'Transaction failed scenario' consists of the sequence of state units 'A1 -> B1 -> D1 -> E1 -> F1' with the amount of weighted values shown in Figure 7. The direct path of 'Deposit succeed scenario' consists of the sequence of state units 'A2 -> B2 -> D2 -> E2 -> F2 -> G2' with the amount of weighted values shown in Figure 8. The direct path of 'Invalid account scenario' in the *Deposit Money* use case consists of the sequence of state units 'A2 -> B2 -> C2' with the amount of weighted values shown in Figure 8.

For all state units within a particular use case scenario of the *Withdraw Money* and *Deposit Money* use cases, we can calculate total probability of occurrence as follows:

(1) In case of a *Withdraw Money* use case

Withdraw succeed scenario = $1 * 1 * 0.7 * 1 * 0.8 * 1 * 1 * 1 = 0.56$

Invalid account scenario = $1 * 1 * 0.3 * 0.2 = 0.06$

Transaction failed scenario = $1 * 1 * 0.7 * 1 * 0.2 * 0.5 = 0.07$

(2) In case of a *Deposit Money* use case

Deposit succeed scenario = $1 * 1 * 0.7 * 1 * 1 * 1 * 1 = 0.7$

Invalid account scenario = $1 * 1 * 0.3 * 0.2 = 0.06$

For the *Withdraw Money* use case, the metrics produce the following ranking of the three scenarios: variant 'withdraw succeed scenario' (0.56), variant 'invalid account scenario' (0.06), and variant 'transaction failed scenario' (0.07). The three scenario variants would be tested in the order: withdraw succeed scenario, transaction failed scenario, and invalid account scenario.

In case of the *Deposit Money* use case, the metrics produce the following ranking of the two scenarios: variant 'Deposit succeed scenario' (0.7) and variant 'Invalid account scenario' (0.06). The two scenario variants would be tested in the order: 'Deposit succeed scenario' and 'Invalid account scenario'.

Design Units AND Action Units	DU1	DU2			DU3				DU4
		DU2.2		DU2.2	DU3.2		DU3.2		
		DU2.1+			DU3.1+				
	MLU1	MLU2	MLU3	MLU4	MLU5	MLU6	MLU7		MLU8
Use Case Scenarios	A1	B1	C1	D1	E1	F1	G1	H1	I1
Withdraw Succeed Scenario	1	2		3	4		(5)	(6)	(7)
Invalid Account Scenario	1	2	(3)						
Transaction Failed Scenario	1	2		3	4	(5)			

Figure 9. Most Reusable Component (Withdraw Money Use Case)

Design Units AND Action Units	DU11	DU12			DU13		DU14
		DU12.2		DU12.2			
		DU12.1 +					
	MLU11	MLU12	MLU13	MLU14	MLU15		MLU16
Use Case Scenarios	A2	B2	C2	D2	E2	F2	G2
Deposit Succeed Scenario	1	2		(3)	(4)	(5)	(6)
Invalid Account Scenario	1	2	(3)				

Figure 10. Most Reusable Component (Deposit Money Use Case)

5.2.2 Most Reusable Components. Figures 9 and 10 employ three different types of geometric figures: a rounded rectangle, a diamond, and an oval. The oval implies the particular component is used just one time on a single one of the paths. The diamond implies the component is used in two paths. The rounded rectangle implies the component is used in three paths. The reusability weight is defined as the number of paths that use the particular component. The values can indicate whether a particular action unit is reusable or not. Therefore, Figure 11 summarizes the reusability rating of each scenario in the *Withdraw Money* and *Deposit Money* use cases.

The analysis in Figure 11 (a) indicates that the 'Withdraw succeed scenario' has the highest reusability rating ($13 = 3 * 2 + 2 * 2 + 1 * 3$). This indicates that it makes the highest use of state units that it shares with other scenarios. Hence, testing the 'Withdraw succeed scenario' first might have the highest benefit when the other paths are tested later because the highest number of shared state units have already been scenario tested.

Weighted Value \ Scenarios	Withdraw Succeed Scenario	Invalid Account Scenario	Transaction Failed Scenario
▢ 3	2	2	2
◇ 2	2		2
◯ 1	3	1	1
Total Weight	13	7	11

(a)

Weighted Value \ Scenarios	Deposit Succeed Scenario	Invalid Account Scenario
◇ 2	2	2
◯ 1	4	1
Total Weight	8	5

(b)

Figure 11. Evaluation Table for Use Cases (a) Withdraw Money (b) Deposit Money

6. Conclusion

In this paper, we explored the premise that in a mature software testing processes, design can be used to drive software development and testing as coordinated activities. We introduced the concept of design units identified by component analysis of design in order to achieve a consistent and integrated approach to design and testing. The design units form a hierarchical approach to unit testing which integrates user acceptance and scenario testing techniques as well. The software testing metrics described in this paper provide the test engineer to optimize the order in which both the units and scenarios defined by the action matrices are executed. It is to minimize test cases, to maximize the reuse of well-tested existing paths, and to improve the productivity of the testing process through scenario prioritization.

References

1. Beck, K. and Cunningham, W., "A Laboratory for Teaching Object-Oriented Thinking", In OOPLSA '89, pp. 1-6, Addison-Wesley, Reading, MA, 1989.
2. Booch, G., *Object-Oriented Design with Applications*, Benjamin/Cummings, Redwood City, CA, 1991.

3. Byun, K., *A Use Case Based Approach to Algorithmic Event-State Table Generation*, Ph.D. Thesis, Illinois Institute of Technology, 1999.
4. Carlson, C. R., "Object Oriented Modeling and Design", Lecture Notes, Illinois Institute of Technology, 1999.
5. Coleman, D., et al., *Object-Oriented Development: The Fusion Method*, Prentice Hall, Englewood Cliffs, NJ, 1994.
6. Hurlbut, R., *Managing Domain Architecture Evolution through Adaptive Use Case and Business Rule Models*, Ph.D. Thesis, Illinois Institute of Technology, 1998.
7. Jacobson, I., et al., *Object-Oriented Software Engineering: A Use Case Driven Approach*, Addison-Wesley/ACM Press, Reading, MA, 1992.
8. Kim, Y. and Carlson, C. R., "Scenario Based Integration Testing for Object-Oriented Software Development", Proceeding of Eighth Asian Test Symposium (ATS'99), pp. 283-288, November 1999.
9. Martin, J. and Odell, J., *Object-Oriented Analysis and Design,* Prentice Hall, Englewood Cliffs, NJ, 1992.
10. McGregor, J., "Planning of Testing", Journal of Object-Oriented Programming, pp.82-85, February 1997.
11. McGregor, J. and Korson, T., "Integrating Object-Oriented Testing and Development Processes", Technical Report, Software Architectures Inc., 1994.
12. Mealy, G. H., "A Method for Synthesizing Sequential Circuits", Bell System Technical Journal, Vol. 34, 1955.
13. Meyer, G. J., *The Art of Software Testing*, John Wiley & Sons, New York, 1979.
14. Moore, E. F., "Gedanken Experiments on Sequential Machines", In Automata Studies, Princeton University Press, Princeton, NJ, 1956.
15. Musa, J. and Everett, W., "A Software Reliability Engineering Practice", IEEE Computer, Vol. 26, No. 3, pp. 77-79, March 1992.
16. Musa, J., "The Operational Profile in Software Reliability Engineering: An Overview", AT&T Bell Labs, NJ, 1993.
17. Object Management Group, "OMG Unified Modeling Language Specification (draft)", Version 1.3, June 1999.
18. Rumbaugh, J., *Object-Oriented Modeling and Design*, Prentice Hall, Englewood Cliffs, NJ, 1991.
19. Saxena, G., *A Framework for Building and Evaluating Process Maturity Models*, Ph.D. Thesis, Illinois Institute of Technology, Chicago, IL 1999.
20. Shlaer, S. and Mellor, S., *Object Lifecycles: Modeling the World in States*, Prentice Hall, Englewood Cliffs, NJ, 1992.

Retrieving Software Components Using Directed Replaceability Distance

Hironori Washizaki and Yoshiaki Fukazawa

Department of Information and Computer Science, Waseda University
3-4-1 Okubo, Shinjuku-ku, Tokyo 169-8555, Japan
{washi, fukazawa}@fuka.info.waseda.ac.jp

Abstract. In component-based software development, the mechanism by which the software components which best satisfy a user's query are retrieved is indispensable. However, conventional retrieval methods cannot evaluate the total characteristics of a component, because they consider a single aspect of the component or require an additional description. In this paper, we propose a new distance metric, "directed replaceability distance" (DRD), which represents how different two components are in detail from the viewpoint of structure, behavior, and granularity. We have developed a retrieval system which uses DRD as a measure of the difference between a user's query prototype component and the components stored in a repository. In this paper, we outline the concept of DRD and the usefulness of our retrieval system.

1 Introduction

Recently, software component technology, which is based on the development of components in combination, has attracted attention because it is capable of reducing development cost[1]. A software component is a unit of composition with contractually specified interfaces, provides a certain function, and can be independently exchanged. In a narrow sense, the software component is defined as that which is distributed in the form of an object code (binary code) without source codes. According to this definition, the internal structure of the software component is not available to the public. In this paper, "software component" is used according to this definition. Since it is natural to model and implement components in an object-oriented paradigm/language[1], we limit this study to the use of the OO language for the implementation of components.

Researchers have noted that a technique for retrieving and selecting a component which satisfies a requirement specification has not yet been established[2]. Since software can be distributed over the Internet, the reuse of components over the Internet is emerging[2]. Today, a component repository and a retrieval mechanism which appropriately supports the retrieval of components from the repository are necessary to enable such reuse.

The important characteristics of components are the following[3]:

- Structure: the internal participants and how they collaborate

- Behavior: stateless behavior and behavior which relates to the states
- Granularity: the component size and the classification
- Encapsulation: how much design/implementation decisions are hidden
- Nature: main stage used in the development process
- Accessibility to Source Code: the modifiability of the component

We aim to reuse components that are mainly distributed in the form of the object code, and the components used at the implementation stage. Therefore, in designing the retrieval mechanism, it is not necessary to consider the two characteristics "nature" and "accessibility to source code". "Encapsulation" is important because it is directly related to the testability of the component. However, users retrieve a component generally on the basis of its functionality, and it is possible to verify the encapsulation of a component after retrieval. Therefore, "structure", "behavior", and "granularity" can be considered important characteristics of the component in terms of retrieval.

2 Component retrieval

Conventional retrieval approaches for the software component which is in the wide sense can be classified into four groups: automatic extraction approach (text-based approach), specification-based approach, similarity distance-based approach and type-based approach.

The automatic extraction approach is based on the automatic extraction of structural information from components[4]. The user's queries are expressed as keywords corresponding to the names of interfaces, components, and so forth. This approach is effective in the case that all source codes of the components are available. However, in the case that the source codes are not available, as assumed in this paper, the extracted information is insufficient for the retrieval[5].

The semi-formal specification-based approach is based on catalog information of the components[2]. The user's queries are given as keywords which correspond to a specification of the catalog. In addition, the formal specification-based approach, which uses semantic description of the component's behavior, has been proposed[6]. In general, the description uses the first-order predicate logic, so this approach guarantees precise adaptability to the user's query. However, the preparation costs of both approaches become very large because the additional descriptions are necessary.

The similarity distance-based approach is based on the similarity between a user's query and the component stored in the repository. There are two major approaches in the similarity evaluation method: an approach using the class inheritance relation in OO language[7] and an approach using the similarity of element names (names of interfaces, etc.)[5]. The user's queries are given by a prototype of the component which satisfies the user's requirement.

The type-based approach is based on component type and component interface type[8]. The user's queries are given by type information expected to realize the user's requirement. Search results are classified according to adaptability, for example, exact match and generalized match, but more detailed ranking with each match set cannot be obtained.

These conventional approaches consider only a single characteristic of the component when retrieving. Therefore, these approaches cannot evaluate the total semantic adaptability of the component[2]. The retrieval mechanism should be able to consider two or more characteristics simultaneously when retrieving. In addition, not all components circulated over the Internet have additional specification descriptions[5]. Therefore, the retrieval mechanism should not require any additional information other than the components themselves.

3 Directed Replaceability Distance

We propose directed replaceability distance (DRD) as a distance metric to represent semantically the degree of difference between two components. In a situation in which component c_q is used and the system requirements are the same before and after the replacement, when c_q is replaced with another component c_s, the parts where c_q is used must be modified. $DRD(c_q, c_s)$ indicates the necessary adaptation cost in such a situation. At this time, considering the surroundings of c_q, it is assumed that all interfaces of c_q are uniformly used.

First, we define three primitive distances: the structural distance DRD_S, the behavioral distance DRD_B and the granularity distance DRD_G. These primitive distances are normalized between 0 and 1, and correspond to respective characteristics of the component under consideration: the structure, the behavior and the granularity. Then, DRD is defined as a combination of DRD_S, DRD_B, and DRD_G based on the dynamically weighted linear combination model[9]. As a result of using this combination model, the degree of consideration for each of the three characteristics can be changed according to the user's attention by changing assignment of weight values. $DRD(c_q, c_s)$ is defined as follows.

$$DRD(c_q, c_s) ::= w_1 DRD_S(c_q, c_s) + w_2 DRD_B(c_q, c_s) + w_3 DRD_G(c_q, c_s)$$
$$\sum_{i=1}^{3} w_i = 1, \ w_i \geq 0$$

The structural distance DRD_S reflects the difference between components' names and the difference between the components' interface structures (signatures). For example, there are three interfaces, $I_1 \sim I_3$, shown in Fig. 1 and I_1 is assumed to be used. I_2 is different in terms of the argument type compared with I_1. However, considering numeric types, the accuracy of **int** is higher than that of **short**. Therefore, it is expected that the necessary adaptation work for interface replacement of I_1 with I_2 is almost completed with the narrowing type cast for parts where I_1 is used. On the other hand, compared with I_1, I_3 is markedly different in terms of the name and the argument type. Therefore, the adaptation cost when replacing I_1 with I_2 is smaller than that when replacing it with I_3. DRD_S can be calculated from the sets of such interface structural differences which components have before and after replacement.

The behavioral distance DRD_B reflects the difference between the components' interface execution results and the difference between the types of the

structural example	behavioral example
I_1 : void setData(int aData)	I'_1 : { data = aData; }
I_2 : void setData(short aData)	I'_2 : { data = new Integer(aData); }
I_3 : void setBar(String aData)	I'_3 : { }

Fig. 1. Examples of interfaces with different structures/behaviors

components' readable properties, whose value changing can be observed. ActiveX[11] and JavaBeans[12] are the component systems which support the readable/writable property mechanism using the IDL definition or the naming conventions. For example, there are three interfaces, $I'_1 \sim I'_3$, shown in Fig. 1 and I'_1 is assumed to be used. It is also assumed that these three interfaces have a common interface declaration I_1, and **data** is a readable property using the introspection mechanism provided by the target component system. When I'_1 is invoked, the value change of the property whose type is **int** is observed. In the case of I'_2, the type of the changed property is **Integer**. Therefore, I'_1 and I'_2 are considered to be similar in terms of behavior because **int** and **Integer** as types are very similar. However, the invocation of I'_3 does not bring about any changes in the readable properties. Therefore, I'_3 is significantly different in terms of behavior compared with I'_1. DRD_B can be calculated from the sets of interface behavioral differences which components have before and after replacement.

The granularity distance DRD_G reflects the difference between component sizes and the difference between component interface execution times. For example, there are three components, **Bar** (component size: 10kbytes, total interface execution time: 10msec), **Car** (15k,20) and **Dar** (100k,150). **Bar** is assumed to be used. **Bar** and **Car** are similar in terms of component size and the total execution time of interfaces. On the other hand, the values for **Dar** are large compared with those for **Bar**. Therefore, if the resource constraint is severe, the replacement of **Bar** with **Dar** is more difficult than the replacement with **Car**. DRD_G can be calculated from the component granularity difference and the set of interface granularity differences.

In the following, only the structural distance is described precisely. The structural distance is defined as follows, using the word distance dw for the names of components and the element set distance ds for the sets of interface structures.

structure of component C_S,   interface structure I_S
$$C_S ::= \{name : String, interfaces : \{i_1 : I_S, ..., i_n : I_S\}\} \quad c_q, c_s : C_S$$
$$c_q = \{name = n_q, interfaces = is_q\} \quad c_s = \{name = n_s, interfaces = is_s\}$$
$$DRD_S(c_q, c_s) ::= \frac{dw(n_q, n_s) + 2ds(is_q, is_s)}{3}$$

The word distance $dw(w_q, w_s)$ between words w_q and w_s is defined as follows, using the longest common substring w_p. Here, $|W|$ is the length of the word w.

$$dw(w_q, w_s) ::= \frac{|w_s|(|w_q| + |w_s| - 2|w_p|)}{(|w_s| + 1)(|w_q| + |w_s| + 2|w_s||w_p|)} \quad \text{or } 1 \text{ (if } w_p \text{ does not exist)}$$

The element set distance $ds(R_q, R_s)$ between element sets, which are R_q as the one replacement before and R_s as the one replacement after, is defined as follows. Here, $|R|$ is the number of R elements. First, f_1 selects the mapping between R_q and R_s with the minimum total distance $dx(q, s)$ according to the types of q and s for all pairs $< q, s >$. Second, in the case that $|R_q| > |R_s|$, f_2 creates ordered pairs $< q', \text{root} >$ with the root, according to the type of q', for all elements q' in the remainder of R_q after calculating f_1. However, in the case that $|R_q| < |R_s|$, f_3 creates ordered pairs $< \text{root}, s' >$ with the root, according to the type of s', for all elements s' in the remainder of R_s after calculating f_1. Finally, ds summarizes $f_1 \sim f_3$, and divides the total by the largest value between $|R_q|$ and $|R_s|$.

The situation where the number of targets is greater than the number of queries is more desirable than that where the number of targets is less than the number of queries. The definition of ds satisfies this desirability, because $dx(q, \text{root}) > dx(\text{root}, q)$, always. The distance $dx(q, s)$ is $dis(q, s)$ or $dt(q, s)$, according to whether the types of q and s are the interface structure (I_S) or the normal type (t).

$$R_q = \{q_1 : x, ..., q_m : x\}, \quad R_s = \{s_1 : x, ..., s_n : x\}$$
$$f_1(R_q, R_s) ::= \min_{dx(q,s)} \sum_{<q,s> \in [R_q, R_s]} dx(q, s)$$
$$f_2(R_q, R_s) ::= \sum_{q' \in R_q - (R_q \cap R_s)} dx(q', \text{root}) \quad (|R_q| > |R_s|)$$
$$f_3(R_q, R_s) ::= \sum_{s' \in R_s - (R_q \cap R_s)} dx(\text{root}, s') \quad (|R_q| < |R_s|)$$
$$ds(R_q, R_s) ::= \frac{f_1(R_q, R_s) + f_2(R_q, R_s) + f_3(R_q, R_s)}{max(|R_q|, |R_s|)}$$
$$\text{root} = \begin{cases} \{name = null, signature = \{\} \to \ll \text{root} \gg\} & (x = I_S) \\ \ll \text{root} \gg & (x = t) \end{cases}$$

The interface structure I_S is composed of the name of the interface and the functional type of the signature. The interface structural distance $dis(i_q, i_s)$ between interface structures i_q and i_s is defined as follows, using the word distance dw between the names of interfaces and the functional distance df between the signatures of interfaces.

$$I_S ::= \{name : \text{String}, signature : F\} \quad i_q, i_s : I_S$$
$$i_q = \{name = n_q, signature = sig_q\} \quad i_s = \{name = n_s, signature = sig_s\}$$
$$dis(i_q, i_s) ::= \frac{dw(n_q, n_s) + 2df(sig_q, sig_s)}{3}$$

The functional distance $df(f_q, f_s)$ between functional types f_q and f_s is defined as follows, using the element set distance ds for arguments and using the normal type distance dt for the return value.

$$\text{functional type } F ::= \{params : \{t_1 : t, ..., t_n : t\} \to return : t\} \quad f_q, f_s : F$$
$$f_q = \{params = p_q \to return = r_q\} \quad f_s = \{params = p_s \to return = r_s\}$$
$$df(f_q, f_s) ::= \frac{ds(p_s, p_q) + dt(r_q, r_s)}{2}$$

The value type (int, ...), the object type (Object, ...), and the value-wrapper type (Integer, ...) are enumerated as the normal type. Using the object-oriented type system[10], these types form a single Is-a graph which makes $\ll \text{root} \gg$ the top. We use the subclass relation as the subtyping relation of the object type.

Since the value-wrapper types have primitive values as the value types, we use the subset subtyping of those primitive values as the subtyping relation of the value-wrapper type. Fig.2 shows a standard Is-a graph in Java language.

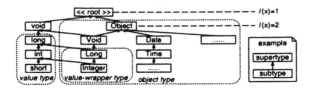

Fig. 2. Standard Is-a hierarchical graph

The subtyping relation is described as *subtype* $<:$ *supertype*. When $s <: q$, the necessary cost for the replacement of q with s seems to be low. However, it is probable that the cost for the replacement of s with q is high. Therefore, $dt(t_q, t_s) < dt(t_s, t_q)$ should be true when $t_s <: t_q$. When the deepest supertype of t_q and t_s is t_p, the normal type distance $dt(t_q, t_s)$ is defined as follows.

$$l(x) ::= (\text{depth of type } x \text{ from } \ll root \gg), \quad l(\ll root \gg) = 1$$
$$dt(t_q, t_s) ::= \int_{1+l(t_s)\frac{2l(t_p)}{l(t_q)+l(t_s)}}^{1+l(t_s)} \frac{1}{x^2} dx = \frac{l(t_s)(l(t_q)+l(t_s)-2l(t_p))}{(l(t_s)+1)(l(t_q)+l(t_s)+2l(t_s)l(t_p))}$$
$$t_s <: t_q \wedge t_q <: t_p \wedge t_s <: t_p \Rightarrow 1 \le l(t_p) < l(t_q) < l(t_s)$$
$$\Rightarrow 0 < \frac{l(t_s)(l(t_q)+l(t_s)-2l(t_p))}{(d(t_s)+1)(l(t_q)+l(t_s)+2l(t_s)l(t_p))} < \frac{l(t_q)(l(t_s)+l(t_q)-2l(t_p))}{(l(t_q)+1)(l(t_s)+l(t_q)+2l(t_q)l(t_p))} < 1$$
$$\Rightarrow 0 < dt(t_q, t_s) < dt(t_s, t_q) < 1$$

4 Component retrieval system: RetrievalJ

When c_q represents a user's query and c_s represents a target component, DRD (c_q, c_s) reflects the degree of adaptability of the target component to the user's query. Therefore, when retrieving components from the repository, if a prototype component which satisfies a user's query, particularly the interface requirements, is given, DRD between the prototype and one of components stored in the repository can be used as the index for search ranking. This mechanism does not require additional information other than the component itself. In the example in Fig. 3(a), the component C_1 is chosen as that which best satisfies a user's query S_q. We have developed a component retrieval system called RetrievalJ, in Java, using the DRD technique. We prepared two types of systems: a stand-alone type and a Web type. JavaBeans is the targeted component system.

We have also prepared the query generator. This generator is a visual tool and can generate **Report** objects which express characteristic information about the component, without the development of a prototype component. By using this tool and giving specifications for a component and its interfaces visually, the user can generate **Report** objects for comparison with the components stored in the repository.

The repository is composed of description files which contain automatically extracted component information. For the description format, we defined CSML (Component Specification Markup Language) as the subset of XML language.

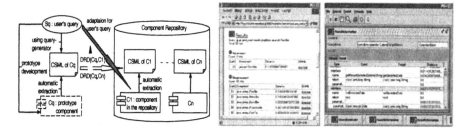

Fig. 3. (a) retrieval using DRD (b) screenshots

RetrievalJ is composed of the five main classes: **RetrievalJ, Analyzer, Report, ComparableElement, Translator. ComparableElement** is the class for comparison of characteristic information. **Translator** converts **Report** objects into **ComparableElement** objects corresponding to types of primitive distances (structure, behavior, granularity).

RetrievalJ accepts the user's query as the component, and outputs the result of the search as a list form and an individual form. In the list form, all components are ranked in order of the small size of each DRD to the user's query (Fig. 3(b)–left side). Moreover, regarding the arbitrary component in the list, primitive distances between the user's query and the target component are displayed in detail (Fig. 3(b)–right side). Then the user can download the arbitrary component from the search results.

Analyzer statically and dynamically analyzes a component. In the static analysis, **Analyzer** collects the name of the component, the size of the component, and structural information on the interfaces by introspecting a Bean-Info object as meta information of the JavaBeans component. In the dynamic analysis, **Analyzer** records the execution time of interfaces, the execution result of interfaces, and information on the value change of readable properties by instantiating the component internally and invoking all of the interfaces of the component using the initial/any value for interface arguments. Because the component does not have any dependence on another by definition, the dynamic analysis is automatically possible.

5 Evaluation

In practice, we have clarified that the structure is the most important among the component characteristics, so we value the structural distance most in the weight assignment. Moreover, because the component system has been currently limited to JavaBeans, the importance of granularity is lowered in relation to the behavior. Therefore, we use the retrieval result as ranked in order of the small size of the $DRD(c_q, c_s) ::= 0.5DRD_S(c_q, c_s) + 0.3DRD_B(c_q, c_s) + 0.2DRD_G(c_q, c_s)$.

As conventional methods, we use Spanoudakis's similarity method ([SC94][7]) and Michail's similarity method ([MN99][5]). Both methods are similar to our method in that their preparation costs are extremely low. In [SC94], the components are ranked high whose positions in the class inheritance hierarchy are closest to the user's query component. In [MN99], the components are ranked high whose similarities of the set of terms to the user's query component are large with respect to term frequency.

We use 250 components provided in [12–18] as evaluation samples. From among all of the samples, we set 12 agreement groups, in which all components are domain-specific, which functionally resembled each other: Calendar(number of components : 5), ProgressBar(3), SMTP(3), POP3(3), Gauge(2), Calculator(2), Clock(3), Finger(2), Stock Information(2), Scroll Bar(2), GUI for SMTP (2), GUI for POP3(2). It is easy to replace a component in the agreement group with another component in the same group. Therefore, when the component is given as the user's query from a certain group, the retrieval performance is high if the components in the same group as the query are ranked high.

5.1 Recall and precision ratios

The recall ratio $R(x)$ and the precision ratio $P(x)$, concerning the order x of the search results, are defined as follows.

$$R(x) = \frac{\text{(number of components in the same group of the query within order } x)}{\text{(number of components in the same group of the query)}}$$
$$P(x) = \frac{\text{(number of components in the same group of the query within order } x)}{x}$$

We used a component Calendar[15] from the Calendar group as the user's query for our method, [SC94] and [MN99]. The results in terms of recall and precision ratios obtained using the three methods are shown in Fig. 4(a). The results of our method for both the recall and precision ratios are always higher than those of [SC94] and [MN99], so the retrieval performance of our method is higher than that of either [SC94] or [MN99].

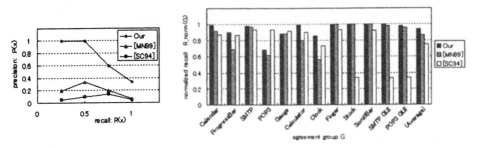

Fig. 4. (a) Recall–Precision   (b) Normalized Recall

This result originates in that components in the Calendar group have interfaces which provide a common function concerning the calendar domain, and those interfaces are similar, particularly with respect to the structure. For example, we discuss the interfaces which provide the acquisition function of the selected day. Table 1 shows the interface structural distances (dis) between the interfaces which are found to be in common using our method, when a component Calendar[15] is given as the user's query. Table 1 also shows the ranks of components in the Calendar group using three methods. Those common interfaces are similar in terms of names and types of return. In our method, because consideration is given to the structural similarity of interfaces, components in the Calendar group are ranked high in comparison with all other components.

[SC94] considers only the class inheritance relation. Even if the functions are the same, if the two components' developers are different, the positions of components in the class inheritance hierarchy are generally different. Therefore, the retrieval performance of [SC94] is the lowest among those of the three methods. [MN99] considers the difference between interfaces, but the consideration is limited to the name; the type of interface is not considered.

Table 1. Comparison of interface structures and result of ranking

component	interface	return	dis	Our	[SC94]	[MN99]
Calendar[15]	getResultSelectedDateAsString	String	–	–	–	–
SSCalendar[17]	getAllSelectedDates	Message	0.067	1	19	4
CalendarBean[14]	getSelectedDate	String	0.011	2	76	14
CalPanel[17]	getDate	int	0.071	5	20	5
CalendarViewer[12]	(none)	(none)	0.187	12	21	63

5.2 Normalized recall

The normalized recall $R_{norm}(G)$ of an agreement group G is set as follows.

$rank(c) ::= $ (rank of component c) $\quad |G| ::= $ (number of components in G)

$N ::= $ (number of total components) $\quad R_{norm}(G) ::= 1 - \frac{\sum_{c \in G} rank(c) - |G|}{|G|(N-|G|)}$

Normalized recalls for all agreement groups obtained using the three methods are shown in Fig. 4(b). A certain component in the same group as target G is used as the user's query. The results of our method indicate an equal and maximum value to the result of [MN99] in three groups, and indicate a value higher than the result of [MN99] in all other groups. With respect to [SC94], the results of our method indicate a higher value in 10 groups. Moreover, the average value of our method (0.9387) exceeds those of [SC94](0.7535) and [MN99](0.8659). Therefore, the retrieval performance of our method is higher than the performances of [SC94] and [MN99], regardless of the domain type of the user's query.

5.3 Changeability of valuing characteristics

We have prepared two components which are the same for all interface structures: Bean1 has been implemented to function as a GUI label, and Bean2 does not function at all. We use the structural distance $(1.0DRD_S)$ and the behavioral distance $(1.0DRD_B)$ as our methods. When the GUI label is given as the user's query, each measurement value of the two components as obtained using our methods, [SC94] and [MN99] is shown in Table 2. [SC94] and [MN99] cannot clarify the difference between Bean1 and Bean2, because these methods do not consider the behavior of the component. In our method, a user can recognize that Bean1 satisfies the query more closely than Bean2 by changing the characteristic to which the user pays attention from the structure to the behavior.

Table 2. Similarity/distance of Bean1,Bean2 (result rank)

retrieval method	Bean1 (rank)	Bean2 (rank)
[SC94]: similarity	0.39346 (2)	0.39346 (2)
[MN99]: similarity	1362.08 (4)	1362.08 (4)
Our: structural distance $1.0DRD_S$	0.03987 (1)	0.03987 (1)
Our: behavioral distance $1.0DRD_B$	0.00096 (1)	0.02175 (84)

6 Conclusion

In this study, we have presented a new distance metric, DRD, and realized a component retrieval system, RetrievalJ. Our approach is excellent with respect to the preparation cost because additional information are not necessary. Moreover, the user can change the degree of consideration for any characteristic according to the user's attention when retrieving. RetrievalJ is available from http://www.fuka.info.waseda.ac.jp/Project/CBSE/. We will verify the possibility of using RetrievalJ together with other retrieval methods.

References

1. J.Hopkins. Component Primer. Communications of the ACM, Vol.43, No.10 (2000)
2. R.Meling, E.Montgomery, P.Ponnusamy, E.Wong, D.Mehandjiska. Storing and Retrieving Software Components: A Component Description Manager. Australian Software Engineering Conference (2000)
3. S.Yacoub, H.Ammar, A.Mili. Characterizing a Software Component. International Workshop on Component-Based Software Engineering (1999)
4. R.Seacord, S.Hissam, K.Wallnau. Agora: A Search Engine for Software Components. IEEE Internet Computing, Vol.2, No.6 (1998)
5. A.Michail and D.Notkin. Assessing Software Libraries by Browsing Similar Classes, Functions and Relationships. International Conference on Software Engineering (1999)
6. J.Penix and P.Alexander. Efficient Specification-Based Component Retrieval. Automated Software Engineering, Vol.6, No.2 (1996)
7. G.Spanoudakis and P.Constantopoulos. Measuring Similarity Between Software Artifacts. International Conference on Software Engineering and Knowledge Engineering (1994)
8. A.Zaremski and J.Wing. Signature Matching: a Tool for Using Software Libraries. ACM Transactions on Software Engineering and Methodology, Vol.4, No.2 (1995)
9. S.Lai and C.Yang. A Software Metric Combination Model for Software Reuse. Asia-Pacific Software Engineering Conference (1998)
10. L.Cardelli. Type Systems. in Handbook of Computer Science and Engineering. Chapter 103, CRC Press (1997)
11. D.Platt. Essence of COM with ActiveX. Prentice Hall (2000)
12. J.Neil. JavaBeans Programming from the Ground Up. McGraw-Hill (1998)
13. E.Harold. JavaBeans: Developing Component Software in Java, IDG Books (1998)
14. internet.com Corp. JARS.COM. http://www.jars.com/
15. IBM Corp. alphaBeans. http://www.alphaworks.ibm.com/alphabeans/
16. Digital Cat, LLC. Digital Cat's Java Resource Center. http://www.javacats.com/
17. Singapore Java Users Group. Showcase. http://www.sjug.org/showcase/
18. K.Yasumatsu. KFC. http://openlab.ring.gr.jp/kyasu/

Generating Application Development Environments for Java Frameworks

Markku Hakala[1], Juha Hautamäki[1], Kai Koskimies[1],
Jukka Paakki[2], Antti Viljamaa[2], Jukka Viljamaa[2]

[1]Software Systems Laboratory, Tampere University of Technology
P.O. Box 553, FIN-33101 Tampere, Finland
{markku.hakala, csjuha, kk}@cs.tut.fi
[2]Department of Computer Science, Universirty of Helsinki
P.O. Box 26, FIN-00014 University of Helsinki, Finland
{antti.viljamaa, jukka.viljamaa, jukka.paakki}@cs.helsinki.fi

An application framework is a collection of classes implementing the shared architecture of a family of applications. A technique is proposed for defining the specialization interface of a framework in such a way that it can be used to automatically produce a task-driven programming environment for guiding the application development process. Using the environment, the application developer can incrementally construct an application that follows the conventions implied by the framework architecture. The environment provides specialization instructions adapting automatically to the application-specific context, and an integrated source code editor which responds to actions that conflict with the given specialization interface. The main characteristics and implementation principles of the tool are explained.

1   Introduction

Product line architecture is a collection of patterns, rules and conventions for creating members of a given family of software products [4, 14, 17]. *Object-oriented frameworks* are a popular means to implement product line architectures [10]. An individual application is developed by *specializing* a framework with application-specific code, e.g., as subclasses of the framework base classes. The specialization interface of a framework defines how the application-specific code should be written and attached to the framework.

Typically, the documentation provided together with a framework describes informally the specialization interface of the framework. Usually this is done simply by giving examples of possible specializations. Unfortunately, such descriptions cannot be used as the basis of building systematic support for the specialization process. An attractive approach to solve this problem is to define the specialization process of a framework as a "cookbook" [8, 18, 22, 23, 25]. Related approaches include also motifs [19] and hooks [9]. The support offered by these approaches ranges from improving the understanding of frameworks to providing algorithmic recipes for separate specialization tasks. Our work continues this line of research, but we focus on issues that we feel are not adequately addressed so far. In particular, these issues include:

1. *Support for incremental, iterative and interactive specialization process.* We strongly believe that the specialization of a framework, or even its single hot spot, should not be regarded as a predefined sequence of steps, far less an atomic, parameterized action. The application developer should be able to execute the specialization tasks in small portions, see their effect in the produced source code, and go back to change something, if needed. This kind of working is inherent to software engineering, and the tool should support it. Therefore, specialization should be guided by a dynamically adjusting list of specialization steps that gradually evolves based on the choices made in the preceding steps. In this way, the application developer has better control and understanding of the process and of the produced system.

2. *Specialized specialization instructions.* The problem with traditional framework documentation is that it has to be written before the specialization takes place. Therefore the documentation has to be given either with artificial examples or in terms of the general, abstract concepts of the framework, not with the concrete concepts of the specialization at hand. In an incremental specialization process the tool can gather application-specific information (e.g., names of classes, methods and fields) and gradually "specialize" the documentation as well. This makes the specialization instructions much easier to follow.

3. *Architecture-sensitive source-code editing.* In our view, the architectural rules that must be followed in the specialization can be seen much like a higher level typing system. In the same sense as the specialization code must conform to the typing rules of the implementation language, it must conform to the architectural rules implied by the framework design. A framework-specific programming environment should therefore enforce not only the static typing rules of the programming language but also the architectural rules of the framework.

4. *Open-ended specialization process.* The specialization process should be open-ended in the sense that it can be resumed even for an already completed application. We feel that this is important for the future maintenance and extension of the application.

In this paper we propose a technique to define the specialization interface of a framework in such a way that it can be used to generate a task-driven application development environment for framework specialization. We demonstrate our tool prototype called *FRED* (*FRamework EDitor*) that has been implemented in Java and currently supports frameworks written in Java. The approach is not however tied to a particular language.

Different techniques to find and define the specialization interfaces for Java frameworks using FRED have been discussed in [12], summarizing our experiences with FRED so far. We have applied FRED to two major frameworks: a public domain graphical editor framework (JHotDraw [15]) and an industrial framework by Nokia intended for creating GUI components for a family of network management systems. This paper focuses on the characteristics of the FRED tool and its implementation principles.

In the next section we will present an overview of the FRED approach. In Section 3 we will discuss the underlying implementation principles of FRED. Related work is discussed in Section 4. Finally, some concluding remarks are presented in Section 5.

The FRED project has been funded by the National Technology Agency of Finland and several companies. FRED is freely available at http://practise.cs.tut.fi/fred.

2 Basic Concepts in FRED

A basic concept for defining the specialization interface in FRED is a *specialization pattern*. A specialization pattern is an abstract structural description of an extension point (a hot spot) of a framework. Specialization pattern is typically of the same granularity as a recipe or hook [9].

In principle, a specialization pattern can be given without referring to a particular framework; for example, most of the GoF design patterns [11] can be presented as specialization patterns. However, we have noted that this is usually less profitable for our purposes: a framework-specific specialization pattern can be often written in a way that provides much stronger support for the specialization process, even though the specialization pattern followed one or more general design patterns. This is due to the fact that the way a design pattern is implemented in a framework affects the exact specialization rules and instructions associated with that pattern. Hence, for the purposes of this paper we can assume that a specialization pattern is given for a particular framework.

A specialization pattern is a specification of a recurring program structure. It can be instantiated in several contexts to get different kinds of concrete structures. A specialization pattern is given in terms of *roles*, to be played by structural elements of a program, such as classes or methods. We call the commitment of a program element to play a particular role a *contract*. Some role is played by exactly one program element, some can be played by several program elements. Thus, a role can have multiple contracts. This is indicated by the *multiplicity* of the role; it defines the minimum and maximum number of contracts that may be created for the role. Combinations are from one to one (1), from zero to one (?), from one to infinity (+), and from zero to infinity (*). E.g., a specialization pattern may define two roles; a base class and a derived class, where the base class role must have a single contract, but the derived class role may have an arbitrary number of contracts. Respectively, a single program element can have multiple contracts and participate in multiple patterns.

A role is always played by a particular kind of a program element. Consequently, we can speak of class roles, method roles, field roles etc. For each kind of role, there is a set of *properties* that can be associated with the role. For instance, for a class role there is a property inheritance specifying the required inheritance relationship of each class associated with that role. Properties like this, specifying requirements for the concrete program elements playing the role are called *constraints*. It is the duty of the tool to keep track of broken constraints and instruct the user to correct the situation. Other properties affect code generation or user instructions; for instance, most role kinds support a property default name for specifying the (default) name of the program element used when the tool generates a default implementation for the element.

When a specialization pattern is framework-specific, certain roles are played by fixed, unique program elements of the framework. We say that such roles are *bound*; otherwise a role is *unbound*. Hence, a bound role is a constant that denotes the same program element in every instantiation of the pattern, while unbound roles are variables that allow a pattern to be applied in different contexts.

Specialization patterns, together with the contracts for the bound roles and the framework itself, constitute a developer's kit delivered for application programmers. We call the process of creating the rest of the contracts *casting*. As each contract acts as a bridge between a role and a suitable program element, casting essentially requires the specializer to produce specialization-specific code for the contracts. The set of contracts for a given software system is called a *cast*. It consists of the contracts defined by bound roles as well as the contracts established by the framework specializer. Together, the contracts convey the architectural correspondence between the source-code and the framework specialization interface. If a pattern defines relationships between roles, these relationships must manifest in the program elements that are contracted to the roles. Thus, the connection between framework and specialization-specific code are made explicit. It is also equally necessary to define mutual relationships between the different parts of the specialization, an important aspect often overlooked.

Casting is the central activity of framework specialization. Each contract is a step required for developing an application as a specialization of a framework. In a sense, casting can be regarded as the instantiation of specialization patterns. The main purpose of FRED is to support the programmer in the casting process. This is achieved by presenting missing and breached contracts as programming tasks that usually ask the user either to provide or correct some piece of code. Based on the relationships encoded in the pattern and the contracts already made, the tool is able to suggest new contracts as the specialization proceeds, leading to an incremental and interactive process which follows no single predetermined path.

Let us illustrate the concept of a specialization pattern with a simple example. Suppose there is a graphical framework which can be extended with new graphical shapes. The framework is designed in such a way that a new shape class must inherit the framework class Shape and override its draw method. In addition, the new class must provide a default constructor, and an instance of the new class must be created and registered for the application in the main method of the application-specific class.

The required specialization pattern is given Table 1. FRED provides a dedicated tool for defining the specialization patterns. However, we use here an equivalent textual representation format to facilitate the presentation. In the example, we have followed the naming convention: if a role is assumed to be played by a unique program element of the framework (it is bound), it has the same name as that element.

In Table 1, the creator of the pattern has specified some properties for the roles. Some properties, when not specified, have a default value provided by the tool. Properties description and task title are exploited in the user interface for a general description of the role and for the task of creating a contract, respectively (see Figure 1). Properties return type, inheritance and overriding are constraints specifying the required return type of a method, the required base class of a class, and the method required to be redefined by a method. Property source gives a default implementation for a method or for a code fragment, while Insertion tag specifies the tag used in the source to mark the location where this code fragment should be inserted. Tags are written inside comments, in the form "#tag". Tags are used only in inserting new code to an existing method.

Note that the definitions of properties may refer to other roles; such references are of the form <#r>, where r is the identification of a role. By convention, if <#r> appears within string-valued property specification (e.g., task title), it is replaced by the name of the program element playing the role. This facility is used for producing adaptable textual specialization instructions. In constraints, references to other roles imply relationships that must be satisfied by the program elements playing the roles. For example, the class playing the role of SpecificShape must inherit the class playing the role of Shape. The role SpecificShape is also associated with a multiplicity symbol "+", meaning that there can be one or more contracts for this role for each contract of Shape. However, as Shape is bound, it has actually only a single contract.

Table 1. Textual representation of a specialization pattern

NewShape		
Bound roles	*Properties*	
Shape : class	description	Base class for all graphical figures.
draw : method	description	The drawing method.
Unbound roles	*Properties*	
ApplicationMain : class	description	The application root class that defines the entry point for the application.
main : method	description	The method that starts the application.
	type	void
	source	Canvas c = new Canvas();
		/* #CanvasInitialization */
		c.run();
args : parameter	type	String[]
	position	1
creation : code	insertion tag	CanvasInitialization
	description	Code creating a prototype instance of <#SpecificShape> by invoking constructor <#SpecificShape.defaultConstructor>.
	task title	Provide creation code for <#SpecificShape>
	source	c.add(new <#SpecificShape>());
SpecificShape+ : class	description	Defines a graphical figure by extending <#Shape>.
	task title	Provide a new concrete subclass for <#Shape>
	inheritance	<#Shape>
	default name	My<#Shape>
defaultConstructor : constructor	task title	Provide a constructor for <#SpecificShape>
draw : method	task title	Override <#Shape.draw> to draw <#SpecificShape>
	overriding	<#Shape.draw>

Nesting of roles in Table 1 specifies a containment relationship between the roles, which is an implicit constraint: if role *r* contains role *s*, the program element playing role *r* must contain the program element playing role *s*. This makes the specialization pattern structurally similar to the program it describes.

During casting, new contracts are created for the roles and associated with program elements. This process is driven by the mutual dependencies of the roles and the actions of the program developer, including the direct editing of the source code. The framework cast consists of contracts which bind roles Shape and draw to their counterparts in the framework. Given this information, FRED is able start by displaying two mandatory tasks for the specializer. These are based on the roles SpecificShape and ApplicationMain, since these roles do not depend on other application-specific roles. The user can carry out the framework specialization by executing these tasks and further tasks implied by their execution. Eventually there will be no mandatory tasks to be done, and the specialization is (at least formally) complete with respect to this extension point.

Roughly speaking, FRED generates a task for any contract that can be created at that point, given the contracts made so far. For example, it is not possible to create a contract for draw unless there is already a contract for SpecificShape, because draw depends on SpecificShape. A task prompting the creation of a contract is mandatory if the lower bound of the multiplicity of the corresponding role is 1, and there are no previous contracts for the role; otherwise the task is optional. FRED generates a task prompt also for an existing contract that has been broken (e.g., by editing actions). We will discuss the process of creating contracts in more detail in Section 3.

The organization of the graphical user interface is essential for the usability of this kind of tool, and the current form is the result of rather long evolution. We have found it important that the user can see the entire cast in one glance, and that a task is shown in its context, rather than as an item in a flat task list. For these reasons the central part of the user interface shows the current cast structured according to the containment relationship of the associated roles. Since this relationship corresponds to the containment relationship of the program elements playing the roles, the given view looks very much like a conventional structural tree-view of a program. The tasks are shown with respect to this view: for each contract selected from the cast view, a separate task pane shows those tasks that produce or correct contracts under the selected contract, according to the containment relationship of the corresponding roles. For example, if a contract has been created for SpecificShape, and this contract is selected, the task pane displays a (mandatory) task for creating a contract for the draw role.

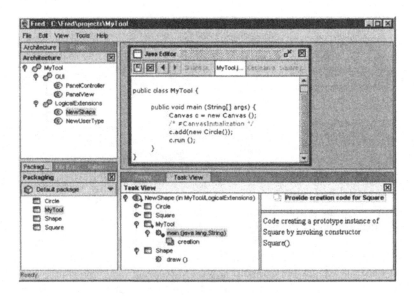

Fig. 1. User interface of FRED

The user interface of FRED is shown in Figure 1. It contains a number of views to manage Java projects and the casting process. In the figure, the application developer has opened the Architecture View, which shows the project in terms of subsystems and instantiated specialization patterns. The Task View shows the existing contracts in the left pane. Tasks related to a selected contract are shown in the right pane of the Task View. A small red circle in the left pane indicates that there are mandatory tasks related to that contract, a white circle indicates an optional task. The lower part of the right pane shows the instructions associated with the role (that is, given by property description).

Figure 1 shows the FRED user interface in a situation where the application developer has already carried out the necessary tasks related to a new subclass Circle. In addition, the developer has done an optional task for creating yet another sublass named Square, and the resulting mandatory task for providing its draw method. The remaining mandatory task is indicated by a red circle. This task is selected in the figure, and the user is about to let the tool generate the creation code at the appropriate position.

To carry out the specialization the developer needs to complete all the rest of the mandatory tasks, and the mandatory tasks resulting from the completion of these tasks. However, this process need not be a linear one. A mechanism is provided to undo contracts, providing the means to backtrack the instantiation process and reconsider the decisions made.

Although the example is very simple, it demonstrates our main objectives. The specialization of the framework is an interactive, open-ended process where the application developer gets fine-grained guidance on the necessary specialization tasks and their implications in the source code. The specialization instructions are adapted to the application context (see the task title and instructions in Figure 1). The source editor is tightly integrated with the casting process: for example, if the user accidently changes the base class of Circle by editing, the tool generates a new task prompting the user to correct the base class. Therefore, much like a compiler is able to check language-specific typing, FRED enforces architecture-specific typing rules. If the user then re-edits the source and fixes the base class, the task automatically disappears.

3 Implementation

To understand how the tool fulfils its responsibilities we have to investigate the specialization patterns and their interpretation little deeper. A specialization pattern, as presented in previous chapters, is given as a collection of roles, each defined by its properties. The approach permits quite arbitrary properties and kinds of roles, and indeed we consider the independence of exact semantics (provided by these primitives) as one of the principal strengths of our approach. The current FRED implementation offers one alternative set of primitives tailored for Java. Changing the set of primitives it is possible to turn FRED into a development environment for a different language, a different paradigm or even a different field of engineering.

The properties supported by the current FRED implementation can be roughly categorized into constraints and templates. A constraint attaches a requirement on a role or a relationship between two roles. The constraints must be satisfied by the program elements playing a role, and can be statically verified by FRED. A template in turn is used for generating text, mostly code, instructions or documentation. Templates support a form of macro expansion that makes it possible to generate context-specific text.

Properties can refer to other roles of the pattern. Whenever the definition of role *r* refers to role *s* (at least once) or role *r* is enclosed in role *s*, we say there is *dependency* from *r* to *s*, or that the role *r* depends on *s* or has a dependency to *s*. From a pattern specification it is possible to construct a directed graph, whose nodes and edges correspond to roles and dependencies, respectively. In addition, each node of the graph carries the multiplicity of the associated role. The resulted graph describes declaratively the process of casting, and is interpreted by the tool to maintain a list of tasks. Actually, the bound roles and dependencies to them can be omitted from this graph, as being constant bound roles do not change the course of the casting process. Likewise, the dependencies that can be deduced from other dependencies can be discarded from the graph, i.e., a dependency from *r* to *s* can be removed if there is directed path from *r* to *s* in the graph.

A graph based on the specialization pattern NewShape, from Chapter 2, is presented in Figure 2. In this diagram, the boxes denote roles. The label of a node is made up of the role name and a multiplicity symbol. A dependency is presented by an arc, or nesting in case the role is nested in the original specification. In addition to denoting an edge, nesting works as a name scope, as in the original pattern specification. Different kinds of visual decorations are used on the nodes to denote their kind. A class role is presented with a thick border and a method role with a thinner one. A parameter role is circular and a code snippet is denoted with bent corner. Bound roles are absent from the diagram. Nesting, decorations and omitted nodes are all just means of compacting the graph and carry no specific semantics in the discussion to follow.

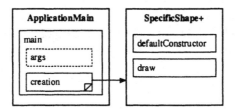

Fig. 2. A diagram of the NewShape specialization pattern

The pattern graph is the basis of casting. The process starts by selecting a pattern and creating a cast for it. Initially, the cast consists of contracts for bound roles. For each unbound role, a number of contracts must be eventually established in the cast. The state of the cast at any point during the casting can be presented as a graph of contracts. The edges of also this graph are called dependencies, and are implied by the dependencies of the pattern. To be more precise, if a role *r* depends on role *s*, each contract of role *r* depends on some unique contract of role *s*, determined unambiguously during the casting. In the cast graph, we need to include only contracts established by the specializer and can thus ignore the contracts for bound roles and the related dependencies. Likewise, as with pattern graphs we can omit redundant dependencies.

Figure 3 presents a diagram of an example cast graph (on the left), and its relation to some specialization-specific source code (on the right). The diagram presents some point in the middle of casting of NewShape pattern. We use a notation similar to presenting pattern graphs. In the diagram, the boxes denote contracts, and the arcs and nesting denote the dependencies. The label of a node refers to the role associated with the contract. A colon is used before the label to mark that the node doesn't represent a role but a contract of the role. Similar to pattern graphs, we use border decorations on the nodes, depending on the kind of the role the contract stands for. It is easy to read from the figure which parts of code play which roles in the pattern. The figure also shows that the dependencies between roles (e.g. from creation role to SpecificShape role) have implied dependencies between contracts. This is also evident in the nesting of contracts.

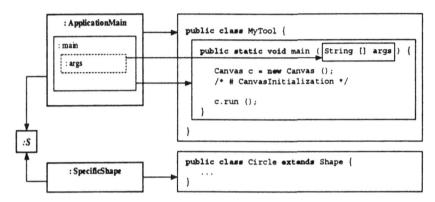

Fig. 3. An example of cast that relates specialization code to the roles of the pattern

The function of the development tool can be defined in terms of the pattern graph and the cast graph. The exact process of casting can be reduced to nondestructive graph transformations on the cast graph, based on the pattern graph. In fact, the pattern graph can be seen as a relatively restricted, but compact way of specifying a graph grammar. This representation can be derived systematically to a more conventional presentation of a graph grammar [6], a set of transformation rules. We shall now describe the process of casting more accurately.

A graph grammar can be defined with a start graph and a set of graph transformation rules. The start graph of a grammar produced from a pattern graph contains a single node, start role S, that besides acting as a starting point of graph transformations carries no special meaning. The transformation rules in turn, are generated by the algorithm in Figure 4.

For each role r in the pattern graph:
    $R :=$ A graph that contains r and all roles and dependencies on every directed path that
           goes from r to a sink of the pattern graph.
    If R contains only r then add start role S to R
    $L := R - r$ and all dependencies from r.
    Add transformation rule $L ::= R$ to the grammar.
End

Fig. 4. An algorithm that generates the transformation rules from a pattern specification

This results in a simple grammar, consisting of a single non-destructive transformation rule for each role of the original pattern. The rules are expressed in terms of roles and are responsible in generating a network of contracts, the cast. Moreover, due to the regularity of the generated rules, an application of any of the rules results in a single new contract and its dependencies.

In Figure 5 we see a graph grammar that has been produced from the pattern graph presented in Figure 2. As there were seven roles in the pattern graph, there are seven numbered rules. The full name of the associated role, along with the multiplicity symbol is placed above each rule.

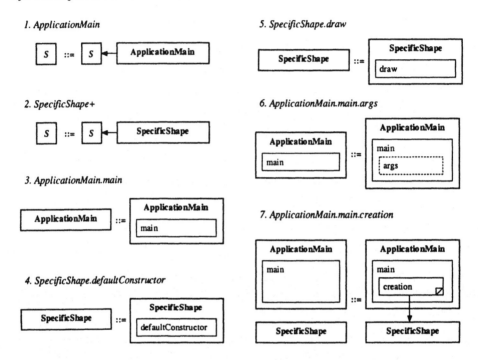

Fig. 5. The graph grammar of NewShape, derived from its pattern graph

Casting starts by creating a cast with a special start contract, a contract of start role *S*. It's only purpose is to start the casting process and is not bound to any program element. The transformation rules, whose left hand sides contain only *S*, are first applicable. In general, the left hand side of the transformation rule is matched against the current cast, and the rule is applicable for each found match, i.e., for each suitable sub-graph of the cast. Then, the matched sub-graph is substituted with the right hand side of the rule, resulting in a new contract and a set of dependencies in the cast graph. The multiplicity of a role constrains the number of times the rule can be applied for each different sub-graph. E.g., the rule 2 above is matched always, rule 5 is matched only once for each contract of SpecificShape, and rule 7 matched for each pair of contracts of main and SpecificShape.

Whenever a transformation rule is applicable for some match, the tool applies the rule to produce a new contract for that match. This contract is *incomplete* as it is not bound to any program element at that time. An incomplete contract corresponds to a task in the user interface, shown to the developer as a request to provide a new program element to complete the contract. The task is either mandatory or optional, depending on the multiplicity and number of contracts already created for the same match. Once the contract is completed by a suitable program element, it is added to the cast making new transformation rules applicable.

As an example, look at Figure 3. At that point the user has already created a class for SpecificShape, as well as the main class with the main method. At this point, the user may apply rule 2 to create a new SpecificShape, or rules 4 or 5 to continue with the existing SpecificShape – the Circle, or with rule 7 to add the intialization code within the main method. These choices are presented as programming tasks, from which only the task for rule 2 is optional. Figure 6 presents the situation after application of transformation rule 7. A new contract has been added to the cast and made available for matching.

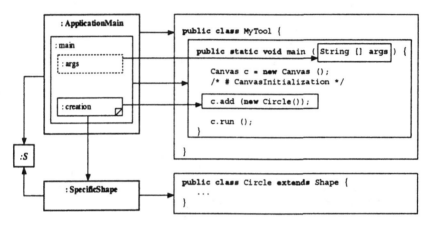

Fig. 6. Result of an application of a grammatical rule to the cast graph of Figure 3

Code generation, adaptive specialization instructions, constraints and other properties are evaluated in the context of a single contract, always linked to a graph of contracts in a way determined by the piecemeal application of grammatical rules. This means that whenever a property refers to role r, this reference can be unambiguously substituted by a contract of r obtained by following the dependencies in the cast graph. Furthermore, this can be substituted by a reference to the associated program element. E.g., in the case of the contract of for the role creation in Figure 6, all references to SpecificShape can be substituted with references to the class Circle. Thus, the constraints can be evaluated separately for each contract and it is possible to provide contract-specific instructions and default implementation, like the line of code in this case.

Most contracts are not automatically determined based on the source code, but instead explicitly established by the developer by carrying out tasks. As a side effect, some code can be generated, but a contract can also be established for an existing piece of code, thus allowing a single program element to play several roles. Once a contract is established for a piece of code, the environment can use this binding for ensuring that the code corresponds to the constraints of the role. For this purpose, FRED uses incremental parsing techniques to constantly maintain an abstract syntax tree of the source code and can thus provide immediate response for any inappropriate changes to the code.

4 Related Work

To tackle the complexities related to framework development and adaptation we need means to document, specify, and organize them. The key question in framework documentation is how to produce adequate information dealing with a specific specialization problem and how to present this information to the application developer. A number of solutions have been suggested, including *framework cookbooks* [18, 25], *smartbooks* [23], and *patterns* [16].

As shown in this paper, an application framework's usage cannot be adequately expressed as a static and linear step-by-step task list, because a choice made during the specialization process may change the rest of the list completely. That is why cookbooks [18, 25], although a step to the right direction, are not enough. Our model can be seen as an extension of the notion of framework cookbooks.

Another advanced version of cookbooks is the SmartBooks method [23]. It extends traditional framework documentation with instantiation rules describing the necessary tasks to be executed in order to specialize the framework. Using these rules, a tool can be used to generate a sequence of tasks that guide the application developer through the framework specialization process [22]. This reminds our model, but whereas they provide a rule-based, feature-driven, and functionality-oriented system, our approach is pattern-based, architecture-driven and more implementation-oriented.

Froehlich, Hoover, Liu and Sorenson suggest semiformal template on describing specialization points of frameworks [9] in the form of *hooks*. A hook presents a recipe in a form of a semiformal, imperative algorithm. This algorithm is intended to be read, interpreted and carried out by the framework specializer.

Fontoura, Pree, and Rumpe present a UML extension *UML-F* to explicitly describe framework variation points [8]. They use a UML *tagged value* (a name-value-pair that can be attached to a modeling element to extend its properties) to identify and document the hot spots such that each of the variation point types has its own tag.

Framework adaptation is considered to be a very straightforward process in [8]. UML-F descriptions are viewed as a structured cookbook, which can be executed with a wizard-like framework instantiation tool. This vision resembles closely that of ours, but we see the framework specialization problem to be more complex. The proposed implementation technique is based on adapting standard UML case tools, which does not directly support FRED-like interactivity in framework specialization.

The specification of an architectural unit of a software system as a pattern with roles bound to actual program elements is not a new idea. One of the earliest works in this direction is Holland's thesis [13] where he proposed the notion of a contract. Like UML's collaborations, and unlike our patterns, Holland's contracts aimed to describe run-time collaboration. After the introduction of design patterns [11], various formalizations have been given to design patterns resembling our pattern concept (for example, [7, 20, 21, 26]), often in the context of specifying the hot spots of frameworks. Our contribution is a pragmatic, static interpretation of the pattern concept and the infrastructure built to support its piecemeal application in realistic software development. In fact, our patterns can be seen as small pattern languages [2] for writing software.

In [5] Eden, Hirshfeld, and Lundqvist present LePUS, a symbolic logic language for the specification of recurring motifs (structural solution aspect of patterns) in object-oriented architectures. They have implemented a PROLOG based prototype tool and show how the tool can utilize LePUS formulas to locate pattern instances, to verify source code structures' compliance with patterns, and even to apply patterns to generate new code.

In [1] Alencar, Cowan, and Lucena propose another logic-based formalization of patterns to describe *Abstract Data Views* (a generalization of the MVC concept). Their model resembles ours in that they identify the possibility to have (sub)tasks as a way to define functions needed to implement a pattern. They also define parameterized *product texts* corresponding to our code snippets.

We recognize the need for a rigor formal basis for pattern tools, especially for code validation. We emphasize support for adaptive documentation and automatic code generation instead of code validation.

5   Conclusions

We have presented a new tool-supported approach to architecture-oriented programming based on Java frameworks. We anticipate that application development is increasingly founded on existing platforms like OO frameworks. This development paradigm differs essentially from conventional software development: the central problem is to build software according to the rules and mechanisms of the framework. So far there is relatively little systematic tool support for this kind of software development. FRED represents a possible approach to produce adequate environments for framework-centric programming. A framework can be regarded, in a broad sense, as an application-oriented language, and FRED is a counterpart of a language-specific programming environment. Our experiences with real frameworks confirm our belief that the fairly pragmatic approach of FRED matches well with the practical needs. Our future work includes integration of FRED with contemporary IDEs and building FRED-based support for standard architectures like Enterprise Java Beans.

References

1. Alencar P., Cowan C., Lucena C., A Formal Approach to Architectural Design Patterns. In Proc. *3rd International Symposium of Formal Methods Europe*, 1996, 576-594.
2. Alexander C., *The Timeless Way of Building*, Oxford University Press, New York, 1979.
3. Boris Bokowski, CoffeeStrainer - Statically-Checked Constraints on the Definition and Use of Types in Java, Proceedings of *ESEC/FSE '99*, Springer-Verlag.
4. Bosch J., *Design & Use of Software Architectures — Adopting and Evolving a Product-Line Approach*. Addison-Wesley, 2000.
5. Eden A., Hirshfeld Y., Lundqvist K., LePUS — Symbolic Logic Modeling of Object Oriented Architectures: A Case Study. *NOSA '99 Second Nordic Workshop on Software Architecture*, University of Karlskrona/Ronneby, Ronneby, Sweden, 1999.
6. Ehrig H., Taentzer G., Computing by Graph Transformation: A Survey and Annotated Bibliography, Bulletin of the EATCS, 59, June 1996, 182-226.
7. Florijn G., Meijers M., van Winsen P., Tool Support for Object-Oriented Patterns. In: Proc. *ECOOP '97 (LNCS 1241)*, 1997, 472-496.
8. Fontoura M., Pree W., Rumpe B., UML-F: A Modeling Language for Object-Oriented Frameworks. In: Proc. *ECOOP '00 (LNCS 1850)*, 2000, 63-83.

9. Froehlich G., Hoover H., Liu L., Sorenson P., Hooking into Object-Oriented Application Frameworks. In: Proc. *ICSE '97*, Boston, Mass., 1997, 491-501.
10. Fayad M., Schmidt D., Johnson R., (eds.), *Building Application Frameworks — Object-Oriented Foundations of Framework Design*. Wiley 1999.
11. Gamma E., Helm R., Johnson R., Vlissides J., *Design Patterns — Elements of Object-Oriented Software Architecture*. Addison-Wesley, 1995.
12. Hakala M., Hautamäki J., Koskimies K., Paakki J., Viljamaa A., Viljamaa J.: Annotating Reusable Software Architectures with Specialization Patterns. In: Proc. *WICSA '01*, Springer 2001, to appear.
13. Holland I., The Design and Representation of Object-Oriented Components. Ph.D. thesis, Northeastern University, 1993.
14. Jacobson I., Griss M., Jonsson P., *Software Reuse — Architecture, Process and Organization for Business Success*. Addison-Wesley, 1997.
15. JHotDraw 5.1 source code and documentation. http:// members.pingnet.ch/gamma/JHD-5.1.zip, 2001.
16. Johnson R.: Documenting Frameworks Using Patterns. In: Proc. *OOPSLA '92*, Vancouver, Canada, October 1992, 63-76.
17. Jazayeri M., Ran A., van der Linden F., *Software Architecture for Product Families*. Addison-Wesley, 2000.
18. Krasner G., Pope S., A Cookbook for Using the Model-View-Controller User Interface Paradigm in Smalltalk-80. *Object-Oriented Programming*, 1988.
19. Lajoire R., Keller R., Design and Reuse in Object Oriented Frameworks: Patterns, Contracts and Motis in Concert. In: *Object Oriented Technology for Database and Software Systems*, Alagar V., Missaoui R. (eds.), World Scientific Publishing, Singapore, 1995, 295-312.
20. Meijler T., Demeyer S., Engel R., Making Design Patterns Explicit in FACE — A Framework Adaptive Composition Environment. In: Proc. *ESEC '97 (LNCS 1301)*, 94-111.
21. Mikkonen T., Formalizing Design Patterns. In: Proc. *20th International Conference on Software Engineering (ICSE '98)*, IEEE Press, 1998, 115-124.
22. Ortigosa A., Campo M., Salomon R., Towards Agent-Oriented Assistance for Framework Instantiation. In Proc. *OOPSLA '00, Minneapolis, Minnesota USA, ACM SIGPLAN Notices*, 35, 10, 2000, 253-263.
23. Ortigosa A., Campo M., SmartBooks: A Step Beyond Active-Cookbooks to Aid in Framework Instantiation. *Technology of Object-Oriented Languages and Systems* 25, June 1999, IEEE Press. ISBN 0-7695-0275-X
24. Pasetti A., Pree W., Two Novel Concepts for Systematic Product Line Development. In: Donohoe P. (ed.), *Software Product Lines: Experience and Research Directions (First Software Product Lines Conference, Denver, Colorado)*, Kluwer Academic Publishers, 2000.
25. Pree W., *Design Patterns for Object-Oriented Software Development*. Addison-Wesley, 1995.
26. Riehle R., Framework Design — A Role Modeling Approach. Ph.D. thesis, ETH Zürich, Institute of Computer Systems, February 2000.

Author Index

Lecture Notes in Computer Science

For information about Vols. 1–2069
please contact your bookseller or Springer-Verlag